THE WORLD OF BARBARA PYM

£1.00

CW00829092

The World
of Barbara Pym

Janice Rossen

MACMILLAN
PRESS

First published 1987

Published by
THE MACMILLAN PRESS LTD
Houndmills, Basingstoke, Hampshire RG21 2XS
and London
Companies and representatives
throughout the world

Printed in Hong Kong

British Library Cataloguing in Publication Data
Rossen, Janice
The world of Barbara Pym.
1. Pym, Barbara—Criticism and
interpretation
I. Title
823'.914   PR6066.Y58Z/
ISBN 0-333-42372-0

For Dr William Rossen
(of the learned kind)

Contents

Acknowledgements

This is a book about England – or, more precisely, about a small corner of it as perceived and recreated in Barbara Pym's novels. I am grateful to the many people who have welcomed me into that world and who have made it intelligible to me.

Thanks are due to the Bodleian Library, Oxford, and to the Huntington Library, San Marino, where most of the work was completed. I would particularly like to thank Colin Harris, Serena Surman and others in Bodleian Room 132 for their help regarding the manuscripts. I am especially grateful to the Bodleian and to Hilary Pym and Hazel Holt for allowing me to quote from the collection of Pym's private papers. Robert Smith kindly gave permission to quote from his letters to Barbara Pym. I am also grateful to Helen Gleadow for permission to quote from Rupert Gleadow's letters. Thanks are due to the Estate of Barbara Pym, Macmillan London Ltd and E. P. Dutton Inc for giving me permission to quote from *An Unsuitable Attachment*, *Quartet in Autumn*, *The Sweet Dove Died*, *A Few Green Leaves* and *A Very Private Eye: An Autobiography in Diaries and Letters*; to the Estate of Barbara Pym, Jonathan Cape Ltd and E. P. Dutton Inc for permission to quote from *Some Tame Gazelle*, *Excellent Women*, *Jane and Prudence*, *Less than Angels*, *A Glass of Blessings* and *No Fond Return of Love* and to Faber & Faber Ltd for permission to quote from Philip Larkin's volume *The Whitsun Weddings*. I am also grateful to *Journal of Modern Literature* for allowing me to reprint the essay on Pym at Oxford. Conversations with the following people have proven invaluable: Hilary Pym, Hazel Holt, Robert Smith, Tim Rogers, Joy Vines and Philip Larkin. My thanks to each of them.

For the writing of the book I am especially indebted to Brian Curnew, who advised me on the Anglican Church chapter, and to Terence Martin, who advised me on the Oxford chapter. Stanley Porter, John Augustine and Elizabeth Pomeroy have been faithful supporters throughout. I am most grateful to my husband, William Rossen, to whom I am indebted for much Education and Learning, as well as infinite cups of tea and much laughter.

List of Abbreviations

Page numbers are noted in brackets within the text. I quote from Dutton editions of Pym's novels throughout, using the following abbreviations:

STG *Some Tame Gazelle* (1950; rpt 1983)
EW *Excellent Women* (1952; rpt 1978)
JP *Jane and Prudence* (1953; rpt 1981)
LTA *Less than Angels* (1955; rpt 1980)
GB *A Glass of Blessings* (1958; rpt 1980)
NFR *No Fond Return of Love* (1961; rpt 1982)
QA *Quartet in Autumn* (1977; rpt 1978)
SDD *The Sweet Dove Died* (1978; rpt 1979)
FGL *A Few Green Leaves* (1980)
UA *An Unsuitable Attachment* (1982)
VPE *A Very Private Eye: An Autobiography in Diaries and Letters* (1984)

References to Pym's private papers are cited according to manuscript and folio number, also within brackets in the text. The papers are lodged in the Bodleian Library, Oxford.

Introduction

Midway through *Less than Angels*, an anthropology student named Digby has retired to his room to write a seminar paper. The narrator continues:

> Such things are of an ephemeral nature so it is perhaps unnecessary to record its title. It consisted of a mass of information culled from books, illuminated by what Digby considered a rather startling interpretation of his own. It is the ambition of all who read a paper of whatever kind to have it recorded that 'a lively discussion followed', and Digby worked with this end in view. (*LTA*, 161)

With a similar ambition in the present author's mind, this study examines some of the elements in Pym's fiction which have their roots in the background of her personal life. Pym was a detached and ironic stylist, and it comes as something of a surprise to discover how autobiographical her novels are – in fact, much about Barbara Pym seems surprising if only because of her relative obscurity in literary circles until as recently as 1977, when her work achieved a modest renaissance. Her reputation as a novelist has continued to grow since then, as her friend Robert Smith assured her it would in 1965, when he urged her to continue writing despite the lack of success she encountered at the time in placing her work: 'And do, do keep on writing. One day the BP cult will broaden out. If only I taught Eng. Lit. I would introduce you as a Special Subject' (MS PYM 160, fol. 97).[1]

In describing the aim and contents of this study of her novels, I would first like to give a brief biographical framework to enable the reader better to place in context the analysis of her work which follows. I shall first note Pym's novels and the order in which they were written and published, and then key events and people.

Pym's publishing history is a bit confusing, as several of her novels were published long after they were written. Her novels fall into three distinct periods, with some subtler distinctions: early (c. 1929–49), middle (1950–63) and late (1964–80). Her early fiction ranges from juvenilia in the novel *Young Men in Fancy Dress*, written when she was sixteen years old, through some twelve novels in

1

varying stages of completion. Of these early works, the novel *Crampton Hodnet* has been published posthumously in 1985, and *Some Tame Gazelle*, which Pym began in 1934, was revised extensively and eventually published in 1950.

The middle period extends from 1950 to 1963, when she published the following novels with Cape: *Some Tame Gazelle* (1950), *Excellent Women* (1952), *Jane and Prudence* (1953), *Less than Angels* (1955), *A Glass of Blessings* (1958) and *No Fond Return of Love* (1961). In 1963 she sent Cape the manuscript of *An Unsuitable Attachment*, which the firm refused. (I count this novel with the middle group, as it was written in this sequence, though it was actually published posthumously by Macmillan in 1982.)

The late period of her fiction extends from 1963, with the refusal of *An Unsuitable Attachment* by Cape and by numerous other presses, until 1980, when the author died. During the ostensibly 'silent years' of 1963–77, Pym did keep on writing, though nothing was accepted for publication during this time. She completed *The Sweet Dove Died* and *Quartet in Autumn*, which were refused for publication, and an 'academic novel' about a provincial university, which she never sent out. Following the 'rediscovery' of her fiction in 1977, Macmillan (and Dutton in the US) published *Quartet in Autumn* (1977), *The Sweet Dove Died* (1978) and *A Few Green Leaves* (1980). This last novel was begun after 1977 and was published posthumously. Pym also wrote more than twenty short stories, most of which are unpublished at present, though some of which will be published posthumously.

In the chapters which follow, I allude to some of these unpublished works, which are now lodged in the Bodleian Library, Oxford, along with letters, diaries and early drafts of published fiction.[2]

Pym's books are easily documented; important people and events in her life are not so simply categorised. Details can be found in *A Very Private Eye: An Autobiography in Diaries and Letters*, in which volume her literary executor has edited some of Pym's personal writings for publication and given them biographical context. I give only a bare sketch here. Pym was born in 1913, attended Huyton College (a girls' boarding school) in Liverpool, and read English at St Hilda's College, Oxford from 1931–4. Her undergraduate years are indelibly marked by her relationships with three men: Rupert Gleadow, who was her first real beau, Henry Harvey, who became 'the Great Love of Barbara's Life', and J. Robert Liddell, a fellow writer who became a life-long friend.[3] After going down from Oxford, Henry Harvey went to Finland to teach English, and later married a Finnish woman. Pym continued to correspond with Liddell, also a friend of the Harveys', and sent him some early drafts of novels. Also of immense importance to Pym was her sister Hilary, four years younger, who attended Oxford after Barbara left. She read classical archaeology at Lady Margaret Hall, and worked for many years at the BBC. In *Some Tame Gazelle*, Pym's Oxford *roman-à-clef*, Hilary Pym appears as Belinda Bede's sister Harriet, Henry Harvey appears as the Archdeacon, Henry Hoccleve, and Robert Liddell as the librarian, Dr Nicholas Parnell.

After going down from Oxford, Pym lived for most of the time with her parents until the Second World War broke out. She moved to Brighton in 1941 and met Gordon Glover, with whom she had a brief and painful love affair which ended abruptly (at his initiative). In order to recover from the effects of this disappointment, Pym enlisted in the Women's Royal Navy Service (popularly known as the Wrens, or WRNS) and was sent to Italy from 1944–5. When she returned to England after her service term, Pym set up house with her sister Hilary and found a job as an editorial assistant with the International African Institute in London. She worked there from 1946 until her retirement in 1974, when she and Hilary moved to Finstock, a small village near Oxford.

Some especially important people to Pym during this time were Robert Smith and Philip Larkin, both of whom became close friends and corresponded with her for several years. Smith was a lecturer in history who taught in various universities in Africa. (He has since retired.) Philip Larkin was an eminent British poet and University librarian at Hull. Richard Roberts made perhaps the deepest mark on her affections during this period. Pym met Roberts when she was in her fifties and he was a few years younger, and it proved at first an exhilarating, later an anguishing experience, when he drifted off. Pym saw this relationship as the inspiration for her novel *The Sweet Dove Died*.

This brief sketch does scant justice to a balanced perspective of Pym's life, but should serve to place some significant people and events as they relate to her novels. The most important occasion was the 'rediscovery' of her fiction in 1977, which had far-reaching implications both for her personally and for her literary reputation. In January of 1977, the London *Times Literary Supplement* held a mock survey among several literati to inquire whom they held to be the most 'overrated' and 'underrated' authors. Barbara Pym was the only living writer to be mentioned twice (as 'underrated', naturally), and was cited by Philip Larkin and Lord David Cecil, both of whom assured her that they had not conferred beforehand. Following this notice, publishers again began to inquire about her work, and her novels began to be published again, to her great delight. Since that time, her reputation has continued to grow on both sides of the Atlantic.

In view of the recent nature of this 'rediscovery' of Pym's fiction, its context, scope and uniqueness are still in the early stages of evaluation (or 're-evaluation'). This study offers an extended analysis of her novels, thus laying a groundwork for more detailed studies of her work. Fine distinctions remain to be made and further revelations to be brought forward. Thus the book takes a sweeping view of Pym's work, sets forth what I perceive to be her fundamental ideas and perspective, and also brings a biographical approach to bear on her novels where it illuminates them further. My aim throughout has been to show the close relationship between her life and her work, and the way in which a sometimes dull or anguished life could be made to yield telling, bittersweet, yet delightful novels by the author's transformation of her own experience into fiction.

The following chapters address in turn several of Pym's abiding interests – even passions: English Literature, Oxford University, Spinsterhood, the Anglican Church and Anthropology. I have tried to show not only their personal significance to her, but the way in which they shaped her writing, and what elements in them she appropriated for her fiction. Chapter 1 defines Pym work in the context of the Victorian and contemporary British novel, suggests probable influences on her fiction, and gives special attention to her liberal use of quotations from other sources. Chapter 2 is biographical in approach, dealing with Pym's years as an undergraduate at Oxford, and showing the use she made of her time at the University in her subsequent fiction. Chapter 3 addresses the subject of spinsterhood and what Pym referred to in her diaries as 'the uncertainties of loving'. It draws from letters and diaries, touches on some biographical aspects of relationships she portrayed in her fiction, and refers to some early, unpublished work. Chapter 4 discusses her use of the Anglican Church in its role as a preserver of British culture and discusses Pym's affinities with Trollope. Chaper 5 focuses on anthropology as both subject matter and method of approach.

Chapter 6 examines Pym's conception of the artist, and in particular the way in which the anthropological techniques she borrowed – notably 'field work' – are applied by her heroines who either write fiction or narrate their own stories. Chapter 7 focuses on her last three novels, primarily *A Few Green Leaves*, and the themes of loneliness, mortality, ageing and rejection which dominate these works. Its main thesis holds that her final novel offers a retrospective view of her fiction by incorporating most of her major themes and by returning to an earlier prose style. Most importantly, the novel serves as an *apologia*, by reaffirming through its heroine's choice the author's personal choice to devote her life to writing fiction.

Since all of these themes intersect each other in her fiction, they overlap within each chapter as well. Each subject shades into the next, emphasising the 'miniaturist' aspect of Pym's work. She writes on a small scale, illuminating a narrow but significant range of life. Above all, Pym's novels are English – in subject, literary influence and style. If this study has a single thesis, it would be that Barbara Pym wrote out of her own life and experience, and that in consequence a provincial, British view colours the whole of her work. Other critics have paved the way for a favourable reception of Pym's fiction by writing warm appreciations, and I have taken the liberty of offering a more critical view. In the end, I think that such a perspective will not diminish one's appreciation of her work, though it points to some of her limitations. I hope it will lead to a deeper understanding of the nature of her achievement as a writer. At the least, such contentions should provide ample matter for future scholarly debate. Echoing Digby's desire in *Less than Angels* for vigorous discussion to follow the presentation of his work, I also have written 'with this end in view'.

1
A Style of One's Own

' "These humble people remind me of Gray's *Elegy*", [the Arch-deacon] said affectedly with his head on one side', describing to Agatha and Belinda his clerical rounds of visiting at the workhouse in *Some Tame Gazelle* (*STG*, 65). Characters in Pym's novels are often reminded of people, sentiments and situations in other literary works; indeed, in the conversation which follows this pronounce-ment, the Archdeacon's wife, Agatha, is 'reminded of *Piers Plowman*, Belinda of the poetry of Crabbe, which she could not remember very exactly, but she felt she had to be reminded of something out of self-defence ...' (*STG*, 65). In her first novel especially, as well as in her subsequent fiction, Pym is an intensely literary author; she always seems conscious of the weight of glory which precedes her. Literary tradition provides a counterpart for her own fiction, as she weaves numerous quotations from other works into her own text. This stems initially from her education at Oxford University. And the Victorian and contemporary novels she read after going down from Oxford influenced her style, as in some instances she consciously copied them. In this chapter I shall discuss the key influences on Pym's writing, the way in which she incorporates fragments of other texts into her own fiction, and finally the way in which she forged her own literary style. Paying ironic deference to the works of the past, she creates a place for her own fiction.

In terms of literary context and affinities, Pym has most often been compared by her readers to Jane Austen. Though she does not exactly resemble Austen, as many have suggested, there is an echo of the minor Victorian women writers about her work. Her choice of subject matter also links her nineteenth-century writers.[1] Her fiction recalls the provincial worlds of Austen and Trollope, where clergymen come to tea and where spinsterhood seems a mildly shocking state of affairs. She creates a twentieth-century society with roots in Victorian times, where traditional stereotypes receive a slightly comic twist. In excluding distinctly experimental modes of writing fiction, she also abandons or neglects political satire. Thus spinster figures such as Gissing's 'Odd women' are replaced by 'distressed gentlewomen' of such refinement and taste that they are acknowledged by the other characters to ' "need *good* clothes, the elderly ones" ' (*JP*, 125).

Pym admired the work of Charlotte M. Yonge, whose fiction is patently sentimental. A minor Victorian writer, Yonge conceived of her mission in writing novels as that of exalting the Church. Her plots typically have to do with large Victorian families and with the finer shades of moral dilemmas. The ideal most often exalted is that of filial obedience to parents. In *The Heir of Redclyffe*, one of her most well-known novels, the hero is falsely accused of a shady monetary transaction, much in the manner of Trollope's *Last Chronicle of Barset*. Perhaps most distinctive in Yonge's fiction is the large number of deathbed scenes, in which the Christian believer is seen to depart this world in grace and peace, often leaving behind a grieving yet understanding spouse. One of Pym's characters remarks on the number of attractive widows to be found in Yonge's novels.

Jane Austen provided an example and model for Pym's writing, as appears in one of the beginning sketches for a novel, where Pym pencilled in a note to herself to check Austen's novels, and study their conclusions: 'Read some of Miss Austen's last chapters and find out how she manages all the loose ends' (MS PYM 96, fol. 7). In light of her admiration for Austen, it comes as something of a surprise to learn how deeply Pym resisted – even resented – having her own work compared with Austen's, however favourable the comparison seemed. Her friend Robert Smith catches some of this ambivalence in his essay on her fiction (the first, in fact, to be published on Pym's novels). In placing her work in literary context, he writes: 'when an assessment of Miss Pym is to be embarked upon a greater name is usually invoked (sometimes apologetically, but apparently irresistibly) – that of Jane Austen. Can Miss Pym be claimed as the Jane Austen of our times?'[2]

Why should it seem annoying for a modern woman novelist to be compared to Austen? It might be construed as the highest of praise – something to be modestly disclaimed in public, yet none the less a source of exultation in private. Yet the comparison seemed to irritate and disturb Pym. She alludes to the issue in her radio talk, 'Finding a Voice', in relation to both Austen and Trollope, simply in terms of how much these two authors might have influenced her. Alleging that critics 'sometimes tentatively mention these great names' in connection with her own work, she goes on to discount the comparison as little short of heresy: 'But what novelist of today would *dare* to *claim* that she was influenced by such masters of our craft?' (MS PYM 96, fol. 8). A modern author might '*try*' to write in a similar vein, but Pym implies that such an attempt would be essentially futile: 'that is as far as any "influence" could go'.

Pym seems not only sincerely unhappy to hear her name linked with that of Austen, but horrified. This reaction has been seconded by her sister, Hilary Pym, who assured me during one conversation that Barbara would 'never' have wanted to be so compared. This ambivalence sheds some light, I think, on Pym's larger use of the English literary tradition in her novels. Part of her reaction stems from the fact that her own work could only seem to diminish and pale in significance when compared to that of Austen. It might have seemed like an impossibly high standard to attain – and, in addition, galling to think that the reader might only approach Pym's fiction in an attempt to find an echo of Austen, and not to discern Pym's unique style. Readers are right to be sceptical of an exact equation of the two authors' work. Still, most intriguing of all is Pym's response to such claims, made in good faith by others eager to gain readers on her behalf: the literary air which permeates her fiction suggests deference to the masters of the past – the Bond of our Greater English Poets contains a hint of the fact that they are 'greater' than contemporary artists. This is reinforced by British tradition, illustrated in Jane Cleveland's passing remark in *Jane and Prudence*: ' "English literature stopped at Wordsworth when I was up at Oxford" ', she says, adding that ' "somehow one doesn't remember things so well that one has read since" ' (*JP*, 147). Pym, on the other hand, certainly seems to have remembered much of what she read, both Victorian and contemporary literature, and liked several twentieth-century novels.

Pym lists her favourite authors in her radio talk, 'Finding a Voice'. Interestingly, she seems to have been more attracted to contemporary writers than to Victorian novelists. She alludes tentatively to classics by 'masters' of the craft, Austen and Trollope, but speaks most warmly of John Betjeman, Stevie Smith, Aldous Huxley, Ivy Compton-Burnett and Anthony Powell. In addition, she mentions elsewhere having read E. F. Benson and Denton Welch. Huxley's *Crome Yellow*, which Pym first read at the age of sixteen, inspired her to begin her own novel immediately. Her diaries mention her having read novels by Virginia Woolf, with the added notation that she herself has written much in the same style.

Victoria Glendinning sums up Pym's interest in this broad range of fiction with this judgement: 'She was an extraordinarily accomplished literary mimic.'[3] Whether or not Pym consciously copied the styles of all of these authors, it is revealing to look at the kind of novels to which she was attracted, and which by implication show affinities with her own writing. Pym seems to have been drawn mainly to social satire, or to provincial comedies of manners. Many of the authors she lists share in common a sprightly tone – a Noel Coward archness – or a malicious, childlike irony reminiscent of Daisy Ashford's *The Young Visitors*, which Pym also read. At their best, these authors are clever; at their worst, they can seem facile. Pym admired the work of E. F. Benson, and his *Lucia* novels became a favourite of Pym and her circle.[4] Yet Pym's work shows more depth and warmth than Benson's, which often finds its humour in publicly humiliating one character or another. Whereas Pym's heroines may be eccentric, Benson's can be malicious.

A slightly different strain of influence is suggested by Pym's fondness for the novels of Elizabeth Bowen; *To the North* was her personal favourite among Bowen's novels. In Pym's fiction, her heroines seem drawn to Bowen's work as well; Ianthe of *An Unsuitable Attachment* idly conceives of herself as a Bowen heroine, and Leonora of *The Sweet Dove Died* reads a Bowen novel during an evening at home. Moreover, Pym's favourite heroines from her own novels, Prudence and Wilmet, show affinities with Bowen's elegant, poised heroines.

Pym was probably most profoundly influenced by the work of Ivy Compton-Burnett, whom she confesses to having imitated, at one point almost to the exclusion of her own style: 'Of course I couldn't help being influenced by her dialogue, that precise, formal conversation . . .' Pym says, and adds that 'a friend and I took to writing to each other entirely in that style' (MS PYM 95, fol. 8). Her close friend from Oxford days, critic and novelist Robert Liddell, admired Compton-Burnett's style and shared his enthusiasm with Pym. He later published the first book on Compton-Burnett's work in 1955. His comments on her use of 'stage-directions' for the performance of her dialogue are revealing in terms of Pym's work as well, as this is the aspect of her fiction in which Compton-Burnett's influence can be most readily detected. In his book on her novels, Liddell lists roughly 250 adverbs, phrases, variations in tone and adjectives used to describe the way in which dialogue in Compton-Burnett's novels is delivered, concluding 'the author can thus give a very great precision to her effects of dialogue'.[5]

Pym's dialogue, especially in her first novel, *Some Tame Gazelle*, is often similarly stylised. To second Liddell's list of examples, Pym's characters speak 'vaguely', 'frivolously', 'irrelevantly' or 'in an irritable tone'. And to repeat his observation about Compton-Burnett's novels, Pym's dialogue similarly achieves an echo of the precision of her mentor's: that, in Liddell's words, 'of incomparable brilliance, bright, glittering, too clever (so they say) for some readers'.[6] As the aside suggests, Compton-Burnett pushes her dialogue to extremes, while Pym borrows one trick of her style and sets it in a more traditional, realistic mode. Her distinctive method includes not only what her characters say, but what they think as well. She turns from one to the other in rapid succession, giving unspoken thoughts almost the same sparkle as dialogue, and pointing up the irony between what the characters feel or perceive and how they are constrained to modify it out of politeness.

Dialogue for both novelists is often heavily stylised and formal. Liddell points out further that Compton-Burnett's work can suffer from the strain of unreality: 'Too often characters will express thought with the precision of philosophers and will answer one anothers' thoughts rather than one anothers' words.'[7] Characters speak in a Compton-Burnett novel in order to reveal or express themselves, while Pym submerges this impulse in part into her characters' private thoughts, which occasionally have the effect of soliloquies. Highly articulate characters such as Jane in *Jane and Prudence* or Dulcie in *No Fond Return of Love* often speak thoughts aloud to an uncomprehending audience. A significant difference between the two authors lies in their choice of subject matter; Compton-Burnett deals mainly with tyrannical relationships within the family structure, whereas Pym most often presents single people in her fiction. Pym's spinsters stand more in danger of being lonely than of being victimised or of becoming villainnesses themselves, as they might be in Compton-Burnett's dark, gothic world.

In her *Compton-Burnett Compendium*, Violet Powell makes a telling statement regarding the change in the author's literary style following the death of her brother in the First World War, after which: 'She pruned her style remorselessly, banishing from her work, at the same time, many aspects of everyday life, which she preferred to ignore or to consider irrelevant for her creative purposes.'[8] This captures a major distinction between Compton-

Burnett's and Pym's work; whereas the former makes do almost without setting, depending almost entirely on conversation for the substance of her fiction, Pym makes 'aspects of everyday life' central to her work.

   If not a direct influence on Pym's writing, Margaret Drabble was important to her as a contemporary novelist; at the least, she caused Pym a pang of self-doubt. 'She gives one almost *too* much', Pym wrote in her diaries after reading *The Ice Age* and *Realms of Gold*, and then went on to conclude, 'but I give too little . . .' (*VPE*, 329). In terms of subject matter, Drabble offers undoubtedly more exotic settings, characters and events. Her narrative is vibrant, on occasion wild, full of passion and sex and existential musings. Does Pym, by contrast, give 'too little'? In comparison with Drabble, she endows her own heroines with a much less adventurous spirit. Drabble seems willing to take the world – with its dangers and passions – as her subject, while Pym approaches it from an oblique slant. One may, I think, admire both authors for their different achievements.

   Despite the marked influence of these twentieth-century novels on Pym's style, what links Pym most directly with the tradition of realism, which many of these authors follow, is her agreement with the basic tenet that art is an imitation of life. As she notes enthusiastically in a journal entry during the Second World War: 'Today I wrote [?] a note telling him what the milk situation was, and it occurred to me, why should not a masterpiece consist of such notes, for after all it is *Life*!' (MS PYM 84, fol. 5–6).

   One can easily point to authors who influenced Pym, but it is more difficult to determine how these writers affected her style. Such influence was not limited to leisure reading alone, as an education at Oxford provided a grounding in literary history. In her undergraduate days at the University, she might often be found sitting in the Bodleian composing a long epic poem in heroic couplets on the subject of 'Sandra' and 'Lorenzo', her fictional names for herself and Henry Harvey, whom she longed to attract. In addition to creating her own fictions in imitation of the style of earlier writers, she developed a propensity to use phrases from poetry as private jokes among her friends. They created their own clichés by drawing from hymns, metaphysical poetry, the epic tradition – anything to hand. The education she received at St Hilda's undoubtedly shaped Pym intellectually, and to some degree this interest was furthered and reinforced by her continued correspondence with her Oxford friends, who applauded her allusive technique for its pedagogical value. Having read the Greater English Poets at Oxford University, Pym was now educating her readers in turn.

Part of the style which Pym created for her novels stems from her concept and use of literary tradition in her fiction. This is especially evident in the first novel that she wrote after going down from Oxford. Looking back on her first published novel, *Some Tame Gazelle*, from a much later perspective, she apologised for her propensity to quote extensively from poetry. In a letter written in the late 1970s to critic Helen Philips, she gives some biographical information about how the novel came to be composed, adding: 'And of course the almost excessive number of obscure quotations shows that the author must have been a young woman just down from reading English at Oxford!' (MS PYM 98, fol. 123).

Part of the delight to be found in parading one's knowledge in this way comes from sheer snobbery – as well as the fun of setting such solemn works in incongruous settings. Pym indulges in this playfulness, but also takes it one step further by satirising such references as pretentious. In *Some Tame Gazelle* she parodies the Oxford University pride in learning, as her characters indulge in exactly this fault. Characters are constantly being 'reminded' of the poetry of someone or other, and at one point the Archdeacon engineers the opportunity for a display of his own knowledge, at a village poetry recital. He insists that one of the children reciting a poem give a rendition of a particularly obscure one, so that he can offer a short disquisition on the linguistic derivation 'of the rare word *dingle*' (*STG*, 42). The ploy succeeds entirely; neighbouring clergyman Father Plowman (of the failed BA) is furious.

Still more interesting is Pym's use of literary quotations later in her work, as her style becomes more mature. She integrates it into her own novels in such a way as outwardly to pay deference to the Great Tradition of the past and yet subtly to undercut it and assert her own individuality. Her sense of the nobility of this past continues in some form long after Oxford, as it contains almost magical properties. Pym records one such episode of communing with the past in her diary, writing: 'Visit to Jane Austen's house with Bob. I put my hand down on Jane's desk and bring it up covered with dust. Oh that some of her genius might rub off on me!' (*VPE*, 250). Later she included a small tag from a Philip Larkin poem in *A Quartet in Autumn*, writing to him that she hoped it would 'bring [her] luck'.[9] The little tags thus become a kind of game, where the proper phrase can serve as a talisman to bring good fortune. In the same way, Pym describes having made several references to other authors in her first attempt at novel writing, *Young Men in Fancy Dress*: 'in this early novel all the "best" or at least the most fashionable names are dropped, from Swinburne and Rupert Brooke to D. H. Lawrence and Beverley Nichols' (MS PYM 96, fol. 5).

At the same time, her treatment of literary tradition in her novels is largely ironical. She exalts it too highly and overpraises it too consistently to make her admiration seem altogether genuine. Thus it serves as a point of comparison for her own work, alternately reinforcing it so as to lend a learned and authoritative cast to her fiction, and also to provide something she can parody. In addition to embracing and using literature from the past, she employs two weapons against it: negating her novels against it, and culling from it in an apparently random and eclectic way. She defines by contrast what she and her characters are 'not', by comparison with other authors and their fiction, thus seeming to apologise for her own difference but actually asserting her own individuality. Her style becomes all the more important to define and to polish, as the subject matter she deals with is generally not compelling enough on its own to carry the reader's interest. And part of the effort to establish her own style means that she must assert herself against the overwhelming claims of established authors. She achieves part of her distance from other works by creating a tangle of quotations, culling from a variety of sources and so seeming to suggest that the main purpose of literature is that of an adornment to life. Thus one quotation is as good as another – a line from a hymn, from a Shakespeare sonnet, from a television advertisement – her particular canon includes all of these and does not differentiate between them.

Definition by negation is suggested in several places in Pym's novels, most notably by her narrators Mildred Lathbury and Wilmet Forsyth. Mildred protests in *Excellent Women* that she is 'not at all like Jane Eyre', nor should the reader expect a similar kind of story (*EW*, 7). At first glance, Mildred is certainly not like Jane Eyre in her writing style. The two women do share something crucial, however, in that they narrate their own stories. They are artists, keen observers of people around them, and they order and gain perspective on their lives by giving confessional accounts of them. Brontë commands more power and grandeur than Pym, but Pym deflects possible criticism by drawing attention to the comparison herself and by mocking it with such exaggerated deference.

Wilmet, the narrator of *A Glass of Blessings*, apologises for herself in much the same manner, protesting that she is unable properly to describe the slightly mad woman who donates blood at the same time that Wilmet does. After making a dramatic scene, the woman mutters to herself, which shocks rather than intrigues Wilmet: 'It seemed like a "stream of consciousness" novel, but I was relieved when she stopped talking for I had been afraid that she might address me. Virginia Woolf might have brought something away from the experience, I thought; perhaps writers always do this, from situations that merely shock and embarrass ordinary people' (*GB*, 78). While not viewing herself as a writer, Wilmet shows the unmistakable marks of a novelist in Pym's tradition of observation: while waiting in the queue, she 'studies' the people around her.

In addition to the fact that she is 'not' like Brontë or Woolf, Pym is also not like Jane Austen. Although she never states this directly, her heroines are often conscious of the shade of Austen's fiction, and eager to disassociate themselves from it. Prudence Bates in *Jane and Prudence* despises her name, as it links her with spinsterly Miss Bates in *Emma*. Prudence would probably reject the name of an Austen heroine with equal firmness; striving as she does for sophistication and elegance, she might prefer to be named after James's Isabel Archer, if she were to be burdened with a literary namesake. Emma Howick in *A Few Green Leaves* also shares the uncomfortable burden of an Austen name, and resents it – although, in fairness, it must be added that Emma was the heroine of whom Austen wrote that no one but the author herself could be expected to like her. Ianthe in *An Unsuitable Attachment* regards Austen's heroines as excessively good; in fact, they are too far above her to be emulated: 'one did not openly identify oneself with Jane Austen's heroines', she feels, though she does conceive of herself as a heroine in a Bowen novel (*UA*, 26). This penchant for Austen typifies Ianthe's singularly old-fashioned nature. And her liking for Emmeline Summers, heroine of Bowen's *To the North*, hints at her susceptibility to passion, though her tragic destiny is not like Emmeline's.

Austen represents the revered, established writer that Pym is not (or is not to herself). To Pym's characters within the novels, Austen receives mixed reviews, in an ambivalence which suggests that Pym seeks to be evaluated as a novelist on her own terms. Thus while

Pym constantly evokes the ghosts of the past, she defines herself as someone different in the process.

As for the use of literary tags in her fiction, the widely different texts represent a wild assembling of favourite jokes and snatches of poetry used in various contexts. The result is a literary pastiche, almost a mixing of genres. For Pym's characters, quotations can embody a particular kind of communication. Poetry is a way of speaking ironically or elliptically. In their reserved social manner, the characters often cannot say for themselves that they are lonely or melancholy, but it is permissible to quote poetry indicative of their mood. Thus Mildred in *Excellent Women* thinks of the phrase from a Christina Rosetti poem about self-sacrifice and being forgotten ('Better by far you should forget and smile') in order to express her own feelings of being unattached (*EW*, 40).

Poetry can also provide a starting point for further creativity and flights of fancy for many characters, often being forcibly pulled into incongruous contexts. The most obvious is that of literal application: ' " Why didst thou promise such a beauteous day / And make me travel forth without my cloak?" ' Aylwin Forbes inquires in *No Fond Return*, when the weather turns unexpectedly cold (*NFR*, 222). For Jane in *Jane and Prudence*, literature is not a dead letter, but a constant well-spring of creativity. She makes several witty remarks of her own, using the same technique of literalising. Upon hearing that ladies' man Fabian Driver is to have heart for his ration from the butcher, Jane enlarges on the theme: ' "A casserole of hearts", murmured Jane in confusion, thinking of the grave and the infidelities. Did he eat his victims, then?' (*JP*, 33). She sees life in terms of possibilities for fiction, with her penchant for suggesting titles for novels out of the 'richness' of village life (*JP*, 21). Ironically, literary criticism has the opposite effect on her. At one point in the novel, Jane is literally put to sleep by her contact with it; reading the Sunday book reviews, she discovers the mention of a character who emerges ' "triumphantly in the round", and somehow this had set her nodding' (*JP*, 60).

Several characters in Pym's novels quote poetry fluently, even some who seem extremely unlikely to have read or remembered it. Geoffrey Manifold unexpectedly throws a line from Coventry Patmore at Prudence in *Jane and Prudence*, to cite one example. Just as often, however, the characters pull the appropriate book off the shelves and read from it, as Rocky does with Matthew Arnold's poems in *Excellent Women*, or as the Archdeacon does in *Some Tame*

Gazelle, in his zeal to read aloud from Wordsworth. Literature becomes an organic part of life, and is even seen to emerge from it, as in many of Jane's frivolous remarks in *Jane and Prudence*. And Pym seldom stretches the reader's credulity too far; when Prudence in the same novel reports that she and Fabian have discussed Donne and Coventry Patmore over drinks together, the narrator adds that Prudence has been doing most of the talking on this subject.

Through these numerous examples, Pym suggests different ways in which literature can be used to enhance life. Poetry is a strongly-felt presence, a corpus of rich treasures to be mined on any occasion. Pym incorporates it in her fiction self-consciously, identifying many of the quotes, yet occasionally with an ironic twist. The novelist displays her learning, and that of her characters, yet at the same time she punctures an excessive reverence for the canon by her nonchalance in what she chooses and the way in which she treats it. Many and various genres illuminate life; the Great Poets do not have a corner on the market. When Ianthe in *An Unsuitable Attachment* hears a snatch of a television advertisement: 'Something something something means / *Lots* and *lots* of chocolate beans', she immediately reflects: 'What the "something" was she didn't catch – perhaps Life itself?' (*UA*, 113). Moreover, Pym's characters are often revealed to have rather lower tastes than their erudite conversation suggests. Mildred of *Excellent Women* confesses that she has always meant to read great works such as *The Brothers Karamazov*, but it has never been the right time to begin. In *Some Tame Gazelle*, the Archdeacon exacts a minor revenge on his clerical guests for the inconvenience they cause by supplying sober bedside books on theology or grammar: 'The Bishop [the Archdeacon's current guest] would naturally want thrillers – the clergy always did, he found – but he was keeping his own supply locked up in his study' (*STG*, 162).

Pym's profuse literary borrowing avoids pretentiousness. The subtle twists and turns, the parodying of other texts while incorporating them in her own, shows a sense of what literary tradition can offer; at the same time it is kept from overrunning her own text.

In closing, I would like to add a few notes on Pym's characteristic style. Primarily, she trivialises life, as when Mildred diminishes all of life into 'birth, marriage, death, the successful jumble sale, the garden fête spoilt by bad weather' such that all of these events are equally weighted (*EW*, 6). Pym consistently diminishes grand passions, in an echo of George Herbert, for whom she has an obvious affection. She focuses in her novels on details, on the 'little things in life' which loom as important.

Curiously, although Pym's realism is emphasised by her constant description of minute details, there is almost no sensuality in her books. Things attain a surface substance, but never a tactile sense. This can be seen in the fact that her characters are often concerned with the aesthetic side of eating, or the preparation and arrangement of food. Leonora's elaborate preparations for dinners with James in *Sweet Dove Died* are a case in point. But one never senses how such a meal might taste, or how it would feel to eat it. There may be brandy on the mantlepiece, as in Mildred's flat in *Excellent Women*, but the reader would never know how it felt as it went down. Culinary preferences are revealing and significant, and on occasion can provide the starting point for philosophical observations, as when Sybil in *A Glass of Blessings* generalises about her fondness for gooseberries: ' "Perhaps they are more a woman's fruit", said Sybil, "like rhubarb. Women are prepared to take trouble with sour and difficult things, whereas men would hardly think it worth while" ' (*GB*, 14).

Still, such scrupulous detail can at times be puzzling because of its disconnection. Physical objects in Pym's fictional world can lack solidity and substance, and often seem ready to crumble at any moment. The woodworm which devours Rocky's desk and chairs in *Excellent Women*, or the rot which Piers and Wilmet imagine destroying items in the furniture depository they see in *A Glass of Blessings*, suggest an element of instability and disintegration in the physical world.

Pym's novels can be best seen as mosaics, composed of little bits of episodes or events pieced together, often with little or no transition between them. Her books are a novelistic version of heroic couplets in poetry; neatly dovetailed and self-contained, the small pieces each link together into a coherent whole. This kind of organisation mirrors her subject matter. She characterised her fictional world in this way, in a talk to a group of fellow writers: '. . .I do feel that the everyday happenings of life are in their way as interesting as the more exciting things.' She goes on to acknowledge that some have criticised her work for this tendency, and concludes: 'I like detail in other people's novels and try to provide it in my own' (MS PYM 95, fol. 84).

Pym's style suits her subject matter; minute questions may well be

addressed in small measures. In depicting emotion which is
reserved or withheld, Pym chooses a style which is similarly
detached in which to present her characters' experience. In *Excellent
Women*, for instance, Mildred presents her life in a series of small
vignettes, arranged in short chapters. She views her life and lives it
in days, rather than dashes and spurts of time; it is an orderly life,
described in an orderly narrative. Though she protests that if she
were to compose a novel it would be done in stream-of-
consciousness mode, she ultimately chooses a different perspective
for her narrative.

In addition, Pym's novelistic style reflects her concern with ritual.
She assumes repetition, and moreover a repetition which presup-
poses meaning. Her heroines often find obscure 'significance' in
small occurrences. Events repeat themselves; one's life 'followed a
kind of pattern', as Jane reflects in *Jane and Prudence* – although Pym
remarks with some asperity about her difficulties as a writer: 'Some
things [in life] do not happen at all, but in a novel they must be made
to happen' (*JP*, 218; MS PYM 98, fol. 64). She confesses that plots are
not her strong point, but I think that this is true only in a certain
sense. Her tightly woven cast of characters provides a case in point:
Pym creates the proper world for a detective novel, lacking only a
mystery plot or a crime which requires to be solved. Though she
employs relatively little suspense on a dramatic scale, unexpected
events occur frequently. Within her interlocking novels, characters
appear, reappear and regroup in odd places and strange combinations, within the same book or in later ones. Pym's novels are
primarily about society, or a group of characters, more than about a
single heroine or family. Even the novels narrated in the first person
show this perspective, as centre stage is shared equally among a
group of characters.

Further, since one of Pym's primary subjects is solitude, many of
the characters are shown alone, and may not have much connection
with each other or meet often. *A Quartet in Autumn* is the most
striking example of this. The relationship between the four fellow
office-workers consists largely of tenuous connections or sketchy
possibilities. Thus it is somehow fitting that Marcia should leave her
house to Norman after her death, though the extravagant gesture
does not at all reflect an intimate relationship between them.

This mosaic-like way of proceeding tends further to dissipate any
tension or mounting plot line – all events seem equally weighted,
each with its place in an orderly scheme.[10] The novels' surface is

pleasant, evenly paced and decorous, showing more affinities with a quartet than with a symphony orchestra. Within this small world, characters group and regroup in various combinations. In depicting human relations, Pym is modest and fastidious, preferring understatement to dramatic intensity. She specialises in, and makes a virtue out of, the funny things seen and overheard; at the same time half ashamed of her limited scope, yet firm in asserting its significance, however narrowly defined that scope might seem. The small absurdities, poignancies and peculiarities, lovingly yet mockingly detailed, are her primary province.

In an age where to be considered charming confers dubious honour, it seems self-defeating to praise Pym's novels for having precisely this quality. Still, I think that her work is appealing or charming in the same manner as Austen's fiction, which is not necessarily to demand that their novels be considered as equal or as similar in method or intent. Pym's novels evidence a fineness of sensibility, a spare elegance and a fanciful wit which place her among British social satirists – and not exclusively among those who are women writers.

To sum up her method and approach, Pym used a culinary metaphor in a diary entry written during the 1950s, when she was composing a stream of novels: 'To make *my* (literary) soup I don't need cream and eggs and rare shell fish, but just this old cod's head, the discarded outer leaves of a cabbage, water and seasoning' (MS PYM 56, fol. 3). Thus she took pride in using bits of seemingly unpromising material. Pym created her own distinctive style, borrowing techniques from other authors as well as actual lines from their works. She succeeded in the aim she defined early in her writing career. In the dedication to her first novel, *Young Men in Fancy Dress*, written at the age of sixteen, she proclaims: 'To H.D.M.G. Who kindly informed me that I had the makings of a style of my own' (MS PYM 1, fol. i).

2

Love in the Great Libraries

'"All this reading"', says Miss Lord, musing on the usefulness of Dulcie's English literature degree in *No Fond Return of Love*, '"But what does it lead to, Miss Mainwaring?"' (*NFR*, 34). Miss Lord's question has its roots in Pym's own education at Oxford, during the years when she began to integrate feminist, academic and romantic problems in her writing. Her fiction is often concerned with women in exactly Dulcie Mainwaring's position: educated, upper middle class, mildly scholarly; indexers, proofreaders, people 'on the dustier fringes of the academic world' (*NFR*, 13). Her Oxford diaries similarly evidence her concerns about the place of women in the academic world. What education leads to for Pym's heroines is generally a subservient role to men in the academic system. And what characteristically accompanies that helping relationship is romantic entanglement; the 'rapture and misery and boredom' of Prudence's love for Dr Grampian in *Jane and Prudence*, for instance – or Dulcie and Viola's passion for Dr Forbes in *No Fond Return of Love*. The peculiar combination of infatuation and study that Oxford represents thus continues long after the characters leave the University. For Prudence, and in many ways for Pym as well, Oxford is a series of admiring young men coming down the drive. Lectures are for meeting handsome scholars. And the Bodleian is for love as well as for books.

Oxford is the setting in which Pym begins to substitute love and work for each other – a crush on 'Gabriel' takes the place of studies in the library, as her diaries show, while Anglo-Saxon becomes a 'cure' for love's melancholy. What begins for her personally at Oxford with this crude sort of exchange is projected with subtlety into the novels, where her middle-aged heroines continue to compensate in a similar manner, substituting romance for scholarship and scholarship for romance, often unconsciously, and with no more perspective or firmness of purpose than they had as undergraduates. As a result, both romance and scholarship become frustrating and unfulfilling outlets, and the characters stagnate in a fruitless cycle of unsatisfactory love affairs and chronically unfinished books.

21

Of Pym's ten published novels and several unpublished works, all show traces of Oxford, but four especially carry on the theme of the relation between love and work stemming from the University: *Some Tame Gazelle, Crampton Hodnet, Jane and Prudence* and *No Fond Return of Love*. Oxford is satirised as it appears in the heroines' later life, where romance and academics continue to be peculiarly interrelated. Their Oxford training results in an earnest intellectual curiosity, which is then used in the service of romantic attraction; they 'research' the lives of their contemporaries. *Who's Who* and *Crockford's Clerical Dictionary*, which are eagerly consulted, are finally more interesting than the dustier tomes.

The supreme comedy of the anxious and quasi-romantic relationship between male employer and female employee typically lies in the fact that the women exacerbate their own dependence on the men by uncritically applying much of the knowledge and many of the skills they acquired in their education. Misused, it becomes an inhibiting rather than a liberating force. From their wide knowledge of literature they construct patterns which are either unrealistic or destructive to live out. Prudence Bates, for example, reads a steady stream of novels about unhappy love affairs and duplicates their pattern in her life. Similarly, Jane Cleveland sanctions her matchmaking by comparing herself to Emma Woodhouse. The irony, of course, is that Jane does not learn from her fictional counterpart's grave mistakes, nor does Prudence benefit from her other favourites, Donne, with his keen perception of love's illusions, or Coventry Patmore, with his exaltation of married love.

Conversely, the heroines use their inventive, creative powers to wrest life into art; to imagine that men are something more than they are, and to puff them up into assuming the role of hero–lover. For these characters, to imagine a romance is almost headier than to have one. Thus, 'all this reading', of which Miss Lord is suspicious in *No Fond Return*, can and does lead in Pym's work to morbid fantasies, and a wide knowledge of English literature becomes potentially dangerous, especially if it is not tempered with judgement. What is perilous for Pym's heroines, however, becomes for the author a means of detachment, a mode of perspective which allows her at once to mock and to transcend illusions by undercutting them with the irony of her novels. As an artist and social satirist, she uses her education and experience to create a wryly feminist perspective on life for academic women. Pym uses material gleaned from her time at Oxford to creative purpose, while her heroines simply duplicate patterns they learned there.

Much of the treatment of romance in Pym's fiction reflects her years at Oxford in the early 1930s, as a comparison with her letters and journals from that time reveals. The bittersweet nature of love is inseparable from the magic of Oxford. Attending a reunion at her college, Prudence, in *Jane and Prudence*, recalls her time as an undergraduate at the University, 'when love, even if sometimes unrequited or otherwise unsatisfactory, tended to be so under romantic circumstances, or in the idyllic surroundings of ancient stone walls, rivers, gardens, and even the reading-rooms of the great libraries' (*JP*, 13). Love in the great libraries extends from Oxford throughout Pym's work in a connection between romance and scholarship, from 'helping a man in his work' to plotting how to catch him with one's best detective skills.

Pym's enthusiasm both for Oxford and for the limitless possibilities it seems to promise is evident from the start. During vacation in her first year she wrote:

> Oh the perfect wife of an Oxford Moderator – that seems to be my true vocation . . . A new term in a new year – golden opportunities (and how) – to get a moderator - a peers [*sic*] heir – a worthy theological student – or events change entirely! But Oxford really is intoxicating. (MS PYM 101, fol. 5)

This sense of adventure epitomised Oxford for Pym, consisting largely of the challenge presented by an inexhaustible supply of interesting men. It does so in fiction for her character Prudence as well. The long parade of lovers coming up the drive in Prudence's imagination is based on Pym's suitors – although the author might in reality have been found surreptitiously following them and then engaging in a bit of research: 'I traced him up Iffley Road', she recorded in her journal, 'so it should be quite easy to find his name' (MS PYM 101, fol. 7). Rupert and Miles and Jockie and Henry represented Oxford for Pym.[1] And what she did with them on punts on the river, in the Bodleian reading-room, eating 'large teas' and 'necking' on leopard-skin couches was part of her education. The inquisitive, infatuated Pym is prominent in the early diaries, where she created a persona, 'Sandra', to embody this side of her personality. The Oxford diaries officially comprise 'the Adventures of Sandra'. Thus before Pym attempted an Oxford novel she cast herself as a character in the grand drama.

Pym's initial expectations of Oxford were shaped by several factors. She came to be there largely through the foresight, planning and sacrifice of her parents, who sent Barbara and her younger sister, Hilary, to boarding school and then up to the University. Though women had attended the University for some fifty years, Oxford only began to grant degrees to women in 1920, and Pym entered St Hilda's to read English literature in 1931.[2] It might be expected that she would encounter particular problems and constraints in entering what had been traditionally and almost exclusively male territory for centuries. The awkward earnestness of making women's colleges actual members of the University and not simply girls' boarding schools – which they seemed to be in the sceptical eyes of the public and the larger academic community – haunted many a don and college head. There were anxious consultations about chaperoning men and women undergraduates, and grave concern about attendant moral issues. In her history, *Women at Oxford*, Vera Brittain describes one typical and hilarious incidence of earnestness on the part of authorities horrified by frivolity: 'The ineradicable addiction of women undergraduates to coffee and cakes at ll a.m. was one of the first subjects which the Proctors referred to the women principals, owing to the supposed waste of time and money involved.'[3] Pym did not enter Oxford primarily as a serious scholar, though naturally this was important to her as well. At the same time she was not particularly used to mixing with the debutante world of the aristocracy, her background being distinctly upper middle class and provincial; thus the sheer number of available men at the University must have seemed 'intoxicating'.

Pym did not go to Oxford simply as a lark, of course, but the immediate excitement of being there was largely outside the pleasures of intellectual pursuits. Her diaries from that time seldom refer to studies: there is an occasional notation about her tutor being pleased with an essay, about a lecture on Beowulf by Professor Tolkien, or about a siege of melancholy and a 'strong pull of Anglo-Saxon' as a cure (MS PYM 101, fol. 1). Oxford generally appears in terms of men, and Pym's posturing as the boy-crazy adolescent is wonderfully artless. She described one lecture, for instance, in terms of the number of handsome males present: 'Incidentally there were 30 men at the lecture and only one decent looking one among them – a dark lad whom I should like to know' (MS PYM 101, fol. 8).

If these examples make Pym appear silly and flighty, it must be remembered that they are the kind of entries many college women might write in diaries, which serve as confidants. As a character remarks in Elizabeth Bowen's *The Death of the Heart*, on the composition of an adolescent girl's diary: ' "To write is always to rave a little ..." '[4] Pym does rave. Yet there is method in her madness. Her early writing reveals an inventiveness, detachment and slightly fantastic turn of mind which characterise her later work.

Besides the purely personal dimensions of Pym's education, there is a larger social one as well. It was exciting but also possibly difficult to be a woman in what was, at the time, so distinctly a masculine world. John Betjeman provides an independent example of some of the pressures for women at Oxford in his delightful satire, *The Oxford University Chest*.[5] In a long chapter on under-graduate life, Betjeman devotes a scant three pages to 'under-graduettes' and describes them entirely in relation to university men; too serious about the Oxford experience, women study exces-sively and raise the examination standards for the rest of the stu-dents. They are cast either as 'embryo schoolmistresses' who carry 'hundreds of books in the little wicker baskets in front of the handle-bars of their bicycles',[6] or, more rarely, pretty and thus capable of inspiring 'gratefulness' rather than fear and envy in their male colleagues. Both characterisations are ridiculous, but together they suggest a subtle pressure which categorises women into one role or the other. If there was a question of choosing from two available models, Pym chose to adopt that of 'Sandra', the glamorous flirt. This image carried its own difficulties, as when, in one diary entry, she recorded an instance where some male friends 'teased me a lot about my appalling reputation: Poor Sandra!' (MS PYM 101, fol. 66).

The University did not only present a chance to choose blithely between feminine roles, to be 'Sandra' rather than a schoolmistress. Pym was engaged almost from the beginning in understanding the ramifications of her choice, by analysing herself and her experience. In addressing the topic of romantic love, the diaries reveal a curious mixture of detachment and artistic embroidering. Further, Pym shows herself well aware of her rhetorical and emotional strategy: she created art out of life to the point where artistic creation replaced passion, which in turn provided material for the author. She wrote during vacation:

This evening it occurred to me that perhaps I don't really love Gabriel [one of her fictional names for Henry Harvey] anymore. How satisfactory if I could really think that – but how empty my life would be without a consuming passion. They are delightful when they aren't too intense – my love for Gabriel has been by no means all honey – in fact no honey at all – except the amusement of seeing him and speculating as to what he was like before I knew him. (MS PYM 102, fol. 27)

Thus the lack of 'honey' is relatively unimportant, as love is secondary to the imaginative process. Fulfilment lies in creating a character out of a man by 'speculating' about him, or giving him a new name and identity. The young author may well be trying to convince herself of the truth of this assertion, and thus may be overstating the case; none the less, the idea of love as painful but amusing is an important theme in Pym's novels, and this passage reveals an early tendency in this direction.

In her correspondence with Rupert Gleadow, a similar detachment is revealed, and a studied self-consciousness on both sides in discussing their relationship. Gleadow, a wealthy, charming and self-confident young man, was in his last year at Oxford while Pym was in her first. [7] He was pronounced by Pym to be 'brilliant – in all sorts of ways' (*VPE*, 15). In a scene which might have occurred in one of her novels, Gleadow became the first person to quote Marvell's 'To His Coy Mistress' to her, surely not a disinterested choice of poem. The two wrote each other a flurry of letters during the time that they were up at Oxford and into the next year until she met Henry Harvey. Only Gleadow's letters survive of their correspondence, but they reveal much about Pym's thoughts as well as his by capturing the spirit of their conversations together. His letters illustrate their intense seriousness and their drive to cast their personal feelings into an analytical mould. Gleadow wrote:

You poured scorn on it when I tried to say that I thought my feelings for you could only be explained on a hypothesis of love, or the beginnings of it: but I'm not so sure now that I was wrong: anyway I wasn't being silly: what I meant, and still do mean, is that I have never felt for *anyone*, not excluding my relations, or Joyce, or Miles, or anyone, such feelings as I have felt for you – and still do feel. In other words, I think that if it had happened a century ago, or even less, we should both have been quite admittedly in love. Only we both happen to be hard-headed moderns. I hope you don't dislike the suggestion. I'm not saying it merely to justify a remark made in Bagley Woods, but because I really have come to think something of the sort. (MS PYM 149, fol. 82)

Later he credited her with keen self-control: 'Perhaps I should have said your emotions never run away with you: your sympathies do not come flowing out of a soft heart: you remember we came to the conclusion than [*sic*] we are both rather hard-headed (or hearted?)?' (MS PYM 149, fol. 109–10). This points to a curious combination in Pym's character of exultation and wildness – 'Sandra', romance, following men in the streets – and detachment – long analytical discussions about love.

A final result of these conflicting tensions during her undergraduate years was the constant pull they caused between love and work. Pym nurtured a reputation for herself for utter romantic abandon to the extent of her inability to concentrate on anything else. She often alluded to her intense love-life at Oxford affecting her studies, a claim which was not entirely unfounded, if evidence is to be believed. She certainly did not fail, academically, carrying off a second 'with', as she wrote with studied nonchalance, 'comparative ease too' (*VPE*, 44).

Still, she seems to have been distracted often from the task at hand. Gleadow finally became incredulous: 'I've often wondered', he wrote to her, 'how much time you did waste in the Bodleian last term day-dreaming: you always used to let on that it was an awful lot . . .' (MS PYM 149, fol. 97). Though the actual object of her deliberations in the library must remain pure conjecture, she did record spending several hours in the Duke Humphrey reading-room gazing at 'Gabriel', consulting the reference books near his seat, and timing her exit so as to meet him casually on the stairs. Thus the library becomes primarily a setting for love rather than studies. And, conversely, work can be an antidote for disappointment in love; after reading *Anatomy of Melancholy*, she concluded: 'Perhaps I'm suffering from the spleen too – in that case I may be completely cured by taking a course of our English poets – which all points to drowning my sorrows in work' (*VPE*, 25). But mostly it is an exhilarating, fatalistic distraction: 'Love! Love! LOVE! Do the dons know how it affects our work – I wonder?' (MS PYM 101, fol. 71).

Pym's exuberance continued in some form throughout her time at Oxford, marked by occasional challenges of reform: 'HERE BEGIN YEARS OF DISCRETION', she wrote grandly, on the occasion of her twenty-first birthday (MS PYM 102. fol. 86). Still, the pains of unrequited love did begin to weigh heavily as time went on. As extracts from her diaries included in *A Very Private Eye* suggest, roughly the last half of her time at the University was dominated by her passion for Henry Harvey, the 'Gabriel' of the earlier Bodleian quotes. Her agonising and intense relationship with him provided the nucleus for her first novel, *Some Tame Gazelle*, which creates a marvellous fiction out of her devotion and his nonchalance. Turning to the other extreme from 'Sandra', the persona who flirts with an apparently endless stream of dazzling suitors, she creates Belinda Bede, a character who exhibits loyalty to the utmost, having faithfully adored the now married Henry Hoccleve for thirty years.

Some Tame Gazelle retells and continues the story recounted in Pym's Oxford diaries, this time in fictional form. As a *roman-à-clef*, it is based on Pym's circle of friends at Oxford, and was written in order to amuse them. The author called it 'my novel of real people' (*VPE*, 45). Circulating in instalments, it served, perhaps, as a substitute for the by-gone days at the University; the group might now be scattered, but in spirit it would always inhabit the timeless world of a small village. Most importantly, the novel was composed specifically ' "for Henry" ' – to allow Pym to express her love and devotion to him (MS PYM 103, fol. 5).

As if to please him by reforming her 'Sandra' persona in fiction, she presents her other counterpart Belinda as initially like Sandra, but deliberately altered in later life. She is viewed here, in the first version of the novel, through the eyes of the librarian Mr Mold, who recalls their undergraduate days at Oxford together:

> Mr Mold remembered Belinda as a tall girl, inclined to be fat, smart in an untidy sort of way, with a perpetual grin on her face and something of a roving eye . . . She seemed much quieter too, although the failure of schemes to trap the elegant Mr Hoccleve did not seem to have embittered her in any way. It was bad luck on her after trying so hard, reflected Mr Mold rather cynically. (MS PYM 2/2, fol. 327)

As a self-portrait, this is a withering snub. It reduces the significance of Belinda's time at Oxford entirely to her 'schemes' to trap Henry and her failure to catch him. The view from Henry's perspective further reinforces her self-criticism and efforts to subdue her youthful enthusiasm. As always, he judges her critically: 'And how Belinda had improved with the years. Her youthful madness had toned down into a charming absent-mindedness. I expect she still loves me as much as ever, he reflected. . .' (MS PYM 2/2, fol. 341–2).

These examples illustrate Pym's attempt to recast the anguish of unrequited love she experienced at Oxford; and further, to apologise for her demonstrative character by abasing herself. Certainly the most prominent aspect of Belinda's character, as stressed by both men, is her abiding love for Henry Hoccleve. And dedication to Henry Harvey, the original of the fictional character, appears to have comprised much of Pym's experience while she was there. She laments over her obsession with him in a journal entry written just following her last year at the University: 'I wish my diary were as interesting and instructive as Anthony a Woods' [*sic*] It must be dull reading with nothing but the falseness of Henry in it' (MS PYM 103, fol. 63). Though the diaries betray anguish at her rejection, the novel diminishes the pain of disappointment by offering perspective through comedy. In her fiction, Pym exaggerates the adolescent crush to a ridiculous extent. And if the diaries are, at times, dull reading, the novel sparkles with wit and vivacity.

In addition to satirising undergraduate love, the novel also mocks scholarship, another major element of University life. The library itself plays an important symbolic role in *Some Tame Gazelle*. Although it is not specifically linked with romantic love, as is often the case in Pym's other novels, its function is similarly displaced or slightly skewed. As representative of one of the world's 'great libraries', Dr Parnell expects that the institution will be used for scholarly pursuits. Yet his overriding concern is for the physical comfort of the scholars, as his monograph on the importance of central heating attests.

Since all of the characters are quite conscious of their Oxford ties, education remains supremely important to them. Consumed by the need to vaunt themselves, the graduates strive to outdo each other in their displays of erudition. Those who decline to enter the competition are appropriately servile: as Belinda declares devoutly, ' "I do so admire people who do obscure research . . . I'm sure I wish I could" ' (*STG*, 68), which, of course, is a wonderful irony at the expense of the 'obscure' researchers. Only Harriet, Belinda's sister, seems determined not to enter the competition for intellectual superiority, but that is because she fights her battle on a different front: preferring men to books, she wants possession of the curate. But, as is usually the case in Pym's novels, Oxford – or the Oxford spirit as it appears here – unites both romance and scholarship inseparably. Thus, in such an intensely literary society, making intelligent use of one's education can provide a distinct advantage in love as well as in scholarship. Interestingly, it is the blue-stocking contingent, the 'schoolmistress' types, to refer back to Betjeman's distinction, who succeed in love. Agatha Hoccleve and Olivia Berridge both get husbands, Olivia stealing the curate, Donne, from under Harriet's nose, and Agatha neatly bagging Henry from Belinda. Education can therefore embolden women to obtain the men they want – both Olivia and Agatha propose to their suitors – or it can console the rejected ones, serving as compensation for the loss of a lover. Belinda will always have the dear Earl of Rochester's poems.

Crampton Hodnet, written while Pym was still in her twenties, is set almost exclusively in Oxford, where she creates a society that combines academics and townspeople. The novel links libraries and love, research, inquisitiveness and romantic attraction for both groups. Mr Latimer, the curate, reflects with dismay on the general fascination in the Anglican circle of clergymen and spinsters with the topic of love: 'It was amazing how, even with the restraining presence of Miss Doggett, they always seemed to be talking about *love* . . .' (MS PYM 10, fol. 89).[8]

As is fitting for such a closely-knit academic society, the first declaration of love between Francis Cleveland and Barbara Bird, the don and his student, occurs at the British Museum, where they have gone for the day to research his book. ('Everyone knew that libraries had an unnatural atmosphere which made people behave oddly', says the narrator (MS PYM 10, fol. 44).) And a representative of the elder community is not far behind; the exchange is overheard by the village gossip, Edward Killigrew, who appears complete with crêpe-soled shoes which enable him to creep close to them unheard. Oddly, his glee in catching them out in a compromising situation is much greater than the lovers' joy in realising that their love for each other is returned. Killigrew pads away ecstatically, first to order a special, celebratory tea ('something called a "Beano" which he decided would fit the occasion very well' (MS PYM 10, fol. 135)), and then to consider how best to retail his juicy bit of information.

For the hidden onlooker, it is naturally more enjoyable to tell the story later than it is to see the scene enacted. Yet the same is true for the lovers, who are more eager to recount, imagine or reflect on their affair than to live it out. At one crucial point in the novel, Barbara literally abandons Francis for the sake of an audience. Pym described the episode in a letter to Henry Harvey as 'Mr Cleveland's elopement and its unfortunate end' (*VPE*, 100). When they stop for the night in Dover en route to Paris, Barbara runs out of their hotel and takes refuge with a girlfriend, Sarah, who lives nearby. Part of her reluctance to stay with Francis is her timidity; physical passion frightens and slightly disgusts her. Still, once she has left him, her view of their relationship changes entirely.

Francis is secretly relieved at her departure, while Barbara ironically takes advantage of her position to paint a glamorous picture of herself as *femme fatale*. She recounts the story of their flight from Oxford, creating a passionate affair and noble renunciation scene out of what had been merely an awkward relationship. She glories in Sarah's comparative inexperience: 'For, when all is said and done, there are few more pleasant occupations than describing a love affair to a sympathetic friend, who is not likely to interrupt with similar experiences of her own' (MS PYM 10, fol. 264). Relationships in Pym's novels are always better in imagination than in actuality. Most importantly, the creation of the story for a rapt audience becomes the pinnacle of the experience and thus replaces the lack of real passion. Love affairs become a means for self-aggrandisement rather than a satisfying end in themselves. Barbara's 'pleasant occupation' of telling her story anticipates Prudence's full-blown, consuming 'occupation' of love affairs in *Jane and Prudence*.

For Francis and his wife, after the aborted elopement the same dreary routine sets in again, to their mixed relief and chagrin. In contrast to Barbara, who inflates the episode by constructing a colourful narrative of it, they seek to diminish the affair by refusing to discuss it at all. His wife feels that she ought to make an angry scene, but finally desists, concluding that: 'Talking very seldom did any good' (MS PYM 10, fol. 293). Hence the relationship between Francis and Barbara is made into two different and equally false entities by the way in which it is reported.

Contrary to the relatively free atmosphere of Pym's diaries where 'Sandra' gleefully acquires an 'appalling reputation', the Oxford of

Crampton Hodnet is stiff and contorted. The romantic lovers are reticent; Francis finally becomes disgusted with Barbara because of her timorousness. After Barbara leaves him in Dover, he admits that he had tired of the affair earlier, when she resisted kissing him. Although he is not an excessively passionate man, as his relief at her departure from Dover suggests, he none the less decides that, in effect, sex is what he really wants and thus Barbara is dispensable: 'Because, when one came to think of it, almost anyone could give understanding.' He goes on to conclude: 'Indeed, Sympathy and Understanding were a great stand-by for plain-looking women who could never hope to be more to a man than dear sisters' (MS PYM 10, fol. 243). Francis turns out to want only that *'one thing'* which Miss Doggett, who appears in this novel and in *Jane and Prudence*, alleges that men want (*JP*, 70).

Part of the unconvincing nature of this early effort lies in its straining for comic effect within such a rigid moral framework and the author's apparent inability to suggest the possibility of strong emotion. Barbara and Francis will clearly never achieve much intensity; Barbara is too pristine and immature and Francis too world-weary to be passionate about anything. Further, *Crampton Hodnet* simply (and not surprisingly) lacks the subtlety of Pym's later works. When Jane asks Prudence if she is 'Fabian's mistress?', the reader sits up expectantly not because of the revelation to come, but because of the relationship between the two friends, while Barbara clearly has nothing of interest to tell, and only succeeds in impressing Sarah.[9]

Pym presents four academic generations in *Jane and Prudence*, which together suggest a wide spectrum of possibilities for Oxford-educated women.[10] None of the available choices is wholly satisfactory. As the college reunion at the opening of the novel indicates, there are two basic kinds of fulfilment recognised: marriage (and children) or 'less obvious ways, [such as] novels or social work or a brilliant career in the Civil Service' (*JP*, p. 10). And, as Jane Cleveland points out about the present gathering of graduates, ' "none of us has really fulfilled her early promise" ' (*JP*, 11).

Miss Birkinshaw, their former tutor, will probably not complete her 'great work on the seventeenth-century metaphysical poets', and Jane's book on John Cleveland will doubtless suffer the same fate (*JP*, 11). Though neither of the women has been intellectually idle, having served as tutors at Oxford, it is none the less a disappointment to them individually and to the college as a whole that they have not contributed to scholarship. Jane's college contemporary, Barbara Bird, has published seventeen novels – a substantial body of work.[11] But it is impossible to judge their value from the narrator's guarded revelations: ' "Much incident and little wit" ', the critics have reportedly judged Bird's latest book, although, with her own erratic publishing history, Pym is perhaps entitled to some irony at the critics' expense (*JP*, 117).[12]

As for the next academic generation, Jane's former student Prudence, now twenty-nine, simply continues the endless cycle of romances she had begun at the University: ' "And Prudence has her love affairs", thought Jane quickly, for they were surely as much an occupation as anything else' (*JP*, 10). Prudence's college contempor-ary, Elinor Hutchinson, embraces the role of 'comfortable spinster', with 'her week-end golf, concerts and theatres with women friends, in the best seats and with a good supper afterwards' (*JP*, 200). This version of spinsterhood as defined by Elinor emphasises both her independence and the high value she places on herself by obtaining the 'best' life has to offer. For Prudence, men prove indispensable in affirming her self-worth. She might enjoy very similar evenings at dinner and the theatre to Elinor's, but demands male companion-ship to make them complete. Later in the novel, when she goes on holiday to Spain with Elinor, she abandons her friend in order to go off with Geoffrey Manifold, when he appears unexpectedly.

In addition to sustaining a series of attachments, Prudence is employed in a minor academic capacity, serving Arthur Grampian as Elinor serves the mysterious 'J.B.', who cannot get off to the Middle East without her. Elinor is comic in her self-importance and apparent indispensability; yet Prudence is still more ridiculous in her role of assistant to Dr Grampian. Her duties at the office consist of minor tasks: proofreading, marking in French accents, on one occasion fixing Dr Grampian a cup of Nescafe, and on another of proving to her employer (though he is mistaken about the source of her tears in this particular instance) that he has still not lost his old 'power' over women. Dr Grampian himself is comic despite his apparent productivity – one is always haunted by the suspicion that Geoffrey Manifold, his other assistant, actually composes as well as edits the mysterious scholarly manuscripts that comprise the work of the office. Even authorship, in this case, proves a dubious distinction: Dr Grampian writes, according to Miss Birkinshaw, 'the kind of books that nobody could be expected to read' (*JP*, 11).

Thus work offers only partial fulfilment, while the pursuit of love is difficult to sustain and its pleasures are transient. Prudence will eventually be forced to assume the role of comfortable spinster – 'one couldn't go on having romantic love affairs indefinitely', in Elinor's judgement (*JP*, 200). At one end of the romantic spectrum, Elinor represents life beyond men, though one which boasts some compensations. Jane's daughter Flora, on the other hand, is at the beginning of the cycle. She appears in the novel as an earlier version of Prudence, who shows an instinctive affinity with the first-year undergraduate and her world. While Jane 'relives' her own Oxford days through her daughter, reminiscing about the past in terms of the academic work, walks on Shotover Hill and church services, Prudence inquires about Flora in her own succinct and immediately relevant terms, asking ' "Has she fallen in love?" ' (*JP*, 82). When Flora appears later in the novel with her boyfriend Paul, Prudence compares herself directly to the younger woman: 'Prudence regarded the young couple with something like envy. To be eighteen again and starting out on a long series of love affairs of varying degrees of intensity seemed to her entirely enviable' (*JP*, 158–9).

The real irony of Prudence's choice is that she is not a passionate woman at all. True to her name, she is 'prudent' in her pleasures and loves. It is the trappings of romance that she craves – the dinners, bouquets of roses, extravagant compliments and love-letters adorned with suitable literary quotations. In one marvellous dinner scene with a suitor, Fabian, she looks into his eyes and thinks, 'The chicken will have that wonderful sauce with it' (*JP*, 102). The aesthetic arrangement of the evening does more than enhance an affair of the heart; it replaces passion altogether.

Prudence is not an entirely one-sided caricature consisting only of egotism; but she is incapable of loving the person at hand, tending to displace her passion to remote objects. Prudence weeps for suffering in the abstract: for Philip, an Oxford beau suddenly remembered, now dead for years, or Madge, a woman in hospital whom she has never met, but hears about in a casual conversation. Prudence is a curious combination of fanatical self-sufficiency and vulnerability. In a notebook entry about Prudence written while she was composing the novel, Pym described her from this perspective: 'Fabian finds underneath Prue's [*sic*] promising veneer a sensitive vulnerable creature wanting love, marriage, perhaps even children – the things women did want' (MS PYM 41, fol. 14). Still, the overruling passion of Prudence's life is her continuing cycle of romances.

Thus the Oxford women – Jane, Prudence, Barbara, Elinor – can do a variety of things, but somehow it is all vaguely dissatisfying or second best. Their education can advance yet also hinder them, by encouraging a perpetual undergraduate life. Elinor marvels at Prudence and her 'emotional upsets', but then adds: ' " Still, you were just the same at Oxford, I remember" ' (*JP*, 200).

To return to a point made earlier, the reading that the heroines do and their training in English literature does affect their perspective profoundly. Though not all of them are scholars or novelists, they view their lives in terms of art. Jane sees her role as vicar's wife in comparison to a Trollope novel and her matchmaking in light of Austen's *Emma*. The comedy of this contrast is that Prudence is actually and literally 'Miss Bates' – and as likely as Austen's spinster of the same name to remain single, though not as an enforced choice. Jane transforms life into art, as well: she enthuses that her move to a new village makes her and Nicholas ' "like people coming into the cinema in the middle of a film . . ." ' (*JP*, 19). For her part, Prudence appropriates a verse of Marvell to sanction her cheerful fatalism about the new affair she embarks upon with Geoffrey Manifold – 'Conjunction of the Mind, Opposition of the Stars' lends grandness to the fact that sooner or later she will tire of him as she has of his predecessors.

Further, the role of artistic imagination is crucial to sustaining Prudence's 'occupation'. Jane reflects on the necessity of literally creating lovers:

> But of course, she remembered, that was why women were so wonderful; it was their love and imagination that transformed these unremarkable beings. For most men, when one came to think of it, were undistinguished to look at, if not positively ugly. Fabian was an exception, and perhaps love affairs with handsome men tended to be less stable because so much less sympathy and imagination were needed on the woman's part? (*JP*, 217)

Arch and heavily satirical as this conclusion is, it none the less points to the fact that Prudence is an illusionist who transforms men into actors in her personal drama. This exchange is the reverse of substituting books for reality, because she creates art out of life, or heroes out of mortals. And it is Jane who is conscious of this illusion-making, never Prudence herself.

Prudence's fertile imagination works both to form new loves and to bury past ones. She first responds to Fabian's rejection, for instance, by making an elegant epistle from it – she writes him a letter which is 'a little masterpiece in its way' – and then by staging a drama for solo performer. She arranges herself consciously as a solitary figure when she dines alone in a restaurant, casting others around her as a fascinated audience which asks, ' "Who is that interesting-looking young woman, with the traces of tears on her cheeks, eating smoked salmon?" ' (*JP*, 198). This playing at grief is as narcissistic as her earlier passion for Fabian was – all is arranged for effect.

Prudence becomes so skilled at creating new fictions from old patterns that she can live in them almost entirely, substituting fantasy for reality. She and Geoffrey Manifold, for instance, together imagine the plot of a French film – an unhappy love story, appropriately enough – with such accuracy that they do not need to see it at the cinema. Similarly, Pym, with masterful conciseness, need not describe the inevitable downfall of Geoffrey Manifold and the subsequent rise of Edward Lyall in Prudence's romantic panoply. Prudence ends the novel with a full hand: intense devotion from Geoffrey, marked interest from Edward and a dinner invitation from Arthur Grampian. Yet the apparent richness of Prudence's life is sterile; a way of perpetually substituting fantasy for reality, 'unsatisfactory' love affairs for a suitable marriage, and shallow romance for meaningful or creative work.

In *No Fond Return of Love*, the two heroines are also literary women, Dulcie having been educated at Oxford and Viola (less fortunate in everything, it seems) at the University of London. Like Jane and Prudence, they represent the possible negative effect of education, the affairs that fade and books that are never written. Viola attempts original work, boasting of ' "a couple of articles " ' and a novel, but these are obviously doomed (*NFR*, 41). Dulcie goes to the other extreme, deliberately caricaturing herself as one who helps others but does not, or cannot, think for herself. She claims kinship with the other minor academic types at the conference where the two women meet, asking glibly, ' "Do we all correct proofs, make bibliographies and indexes, and do all the rather humdrum thankless tasks for people more brilliant than ourselves?"' (*NFR*, 13).

The most telling connection in the novel with Pym's experiences at Oxford is the truth that love so drastically affects one's work. (Do the dons realise? Do the employers realise?) For both women, as for Prudence, love is closely tied to their work, if only because all three are infatuated with their employers. Viola's professional relationship with Aylwin Forbes, the scholar whom she has assisted in the past, is haunted by her passion for him. Love and work appear inseparable when Viola's expertise becomes a comic bargaining point for Aylwin's love. Desperate for his attention, she offers to compile the index for his recently completed book, in the same spirit in which Dulcie later urges Aylwin to choose a wife who can 'help him' in his work.

Academics ultimately frustrate Viola both in not yielding satisfying work – she can never complete her own projects – and in not giving her the man she wants. In the end, her intense need for love prevails at the cost of work altogether. She turns out to be, in Dulcie's scornful view, merely a 'rather dull woman, wanting only to be loved', the proof of this being that Viola marries Bill Sedge, a polyester knitwear salesman (*NFR*, 168). The fact that he is an Austrian (foreigner, Not English), a salesman (bourgeois), and in the business of polyester clothing at that (synthetic material), makes him appear symbolically an *ersatz* husband. Aylwin Forbes, with his intellectual prowess and advanced degree (he is a doctor 'of the learned variety', as he says) is regarded by both women as the superior man. Even so, Bill Sedge's chivalry gives him an edge over his more scholarly rival. Viola emphasises to Dulcie that he treats her 'like a woman' – possibly even like a person – while Aylwin regards Dulcie primarily as a useful academic assistant, even when he has made up his mind to marry her.

The most bizarre and striking echo of Pym's Oxford education to appear in the novel is the passion for contemporary 'research'. Hazel Holt has pointed out in her introduction to *A Very Private Eye* that Pym's penchant for this kind of sleuthing continued throughout her life.

Pym parodies in her character Dulcie the scholarly penchant for collecting and organising facts by making a detective game of her inquisitiveness about Aylwin. Dulcie suffers from a full-scale adolescent crush, and employs the following method of approach:

'. . . this was really the kind of research Dulcie enjoyed most of all, investigation – some might have said prying – into the lives of other people, the kind of work that involved poring over reference books, and street and telephone directories' (*NFR*, 44). Dulcie does a thorough job of 'researching' Aylwin's life, visiting his mother's hotel in Tavistock, his brother's church, his wife's childhood house, even his father's grave. Her intense curiosity completely obsesses her, finally shocking even Viola, who is no less infatuated with Aylwin than Dulcie is. This boundless interest in others reflects a close and bizarre relation between love and work; as Dulcie confesses about her motivation, research provides a kind of substitute for what she lacks: ' "I love finding out about people", said Dulcie. "I suppose it's a sort of compensation for the dreariness of everyday life" ' (*NFR*, 18).

Eccentric and 'difficult' as both heroines are, each is rewarded with a man, and Pym concludes the novel with a happy ending of staggering and unreal proportions, where Aylwin's egotism swells to enormous size. He bursts with pride at his insight that he loves and wants to marry Dulcie. In the taxi on the way to her house to propose to her, he reflects on his decision with self-satisfaction:

> Yet here he was being true to type after all. For what might seem to the rest of the world an eminently 'suitable' marriage to a woman no longer very young, who could help him with his work, now seemed to him the most unsuitable that could be imagined, simply because it had never occurred to him that he could love such a person. It was all most delightfully incongruous. Just the sort of thing Aylwin Forbes would do. (*NFR*, 253)

His sudden reversal is terrifically comic – he is utterly fatuous and condescending to his intended fiancée. Again, echoing the relationship between fictional prototypes and life present in *Jane and Prudence*, Aylwin models himself on a character in Austen's novel *Mansfield Park*. He plans to plead his suit to Dulcie in light of Edmund's suitable and apparently – though not actually – sudden love for Fanny. Similarly, his namesake novel, *Aylwin*, a gothic, spiritualist Victorian book, exalts the theme of a pure and beautiful woman 'helping' the earnest hero to become his noblest self. And Dulcie will eagerly embrace him on both counts, sanctioned as he is by literary precedents.

Education is shown to be useful in *No Fond Return* precisely because it fulfils traditional values for women. Aylwin's proposal vindicates Dulcie to Miss Lord, who despairs of Dulcie catching a husband because she 'reads too much'. Dulcie's education proves undeniably useful in capturing Aylwin. The ability to index and proofread and to track him down through consulting maps and reference books finally earns her the ideal marriage. If she had not gone to Tavistock on her search for his childhood surroundings, she would not have encountered Aylwin, then lectured him about a '"*sensible* marriage"', and perhaps not have appeared as a suitable candidate herself (*NFR*, 223). Still, the uneasy balance between the two lovers suggests a dry feminist complaint. It occurs to Aylwin that he might love as well as use Dulcie, not use as well as love. The usefulness – and the man – have definite priority, and the wife is in many ways indistinguishable from an exceptionally efficient employee. Romances in Pym's novels are hard won.

Barbara Pym came full circle. She retired in 1974 from her job at the International African Institute in London, where she had worked as assistant editor of an anthropological journal since 1946. She then went to live with her sister, Hilary Walton, in Finstock, a small village near Oxford.[13] At last Pym was honoured at the University itself, the place from which it was sweetest to be praised. Her later notebooks record great excitement about attending a prize dinner at University College. Perhaps most gratifying was the fact that her novels began to be published again after a sixteen-year hiatus. At this time she also wrote a short story which was based on a college dinner she attended with a friend. It reveals as much as anything else the centrality of Oxford in Pym's vision.

The story is rather halting and stark; novels were always her forte. But it is important because it contains an essential Pym theme: a near miss fraught with possible significance, but lapsing ultimately into the realm of the imagination. The plot is simple: the heroine, an older and Oxford-educated woman, attends a sumptuous college dinner as a guest of her long-time friend George. In characteristic fashion, Pym describes the food in detail – her private papers contain a beautifully printed menu which lists all the courses as they appear in the story. During dinner she notices Gervase across the room, an old flame whom she has not seen since undergraduate days. When they meet later, he turns out to have forgotten her completely. She is similarly mistaken about Gervase; when she inquires after his wife, he asserts, startled, that he has never married. After a few moments of stumbling conversation in the courtyard, they part, completely sundered: 'Standing by an ornamental pool, they suddenly had nothing more to say to each other.' [14] Once to have meant so much to him – or once to have had him mean so much to her? – and now nothing.

And that is in a sense what Oxford – or life – is, for Pym. One is forgotten, youth and passion fade: '"Oh, those days of wine and roses! They are *not* long"', as her character Jane Cleveland says (*JP*, 7).

Pym drew on Oxford heavily in her writing, and though it does not often appear as an actual setting in her novels, its centrality and importance is immense. In the sense that she wrote intensely about Oxford feelings, relationships and attitudes, she did write the Oxford novel she longed to write, after her emotions had duly 'simmered down' to a wry, piercing detachment (MS PYM 101, fol. 85). That is, if one can ever entirely simmer down about Oxford: '"Ah, we flung roses riotously!"' glows Jane (*JP*, 159), and to the last it will be a perplexing, haunting, yet utterly intoxicating place and myth.

3

Spinsterhood

Perhaps more than any other British novelist, Barbara Pym takes spinsters as her great subject. Popular opinion might protest that the author chose an unpromising topic for her fiction, and she was aware that this objection would be raised. In 1972 she wrote in her diary: 'The position of the unmarried woman – unless, of course, she is somebody's mistress, is of no interest whatsoever to the readers of modern fiction.' Still, with characteristic resourcefulness, she added immediately: 'The beginning of a novel?' (*VPE*, 269). This choice of subject – the single woman's difficulties – shows a distinct connection with the nineteenth-century novel. The primary subject of the novel of manners, or of all comedy, is marriage, and in order to achieve this resolution, authors such as Austen, Trollope, Brontë and Eliot marry off their heroines at the end of their respective novels. This general procession *en masse* to the altar emphasises the bleakness or peculiarity of alternative singleness. Those women characters who do not achieve this blessed state of union, such as Eliot's Maggie Tulliver, often find the only possible escape in meeting with a tragic death.

Pym's heroines, on the other hand, may well continue single at the close of the novel – and moreover count themselves fortunate to do so. If one recasts Austen's *Emma* so that Emma continued to live with her father yet did not marry Mr Knightley, or revises *Jane Eyre* so that Jane never returned to Thornfield to marry Mr Rochester, the result would approximate a central aspect of a typical plot in Pym's novels. More accurately, she explores what might have happened if, for instance, no such character as Mr Knightley existed, and Emma had married Frank Churchill or Mr Elton by default instead. In this modern age, romance is at a discount: 'I am not at all like Jane Eyre', writes Mildred Lathbury in *Excellent Women*, about the fortunate Victorian governess 'who must have given hope to so many plain women' (*EW*, 7). Instead, Pym echoes Trollope's figure of spinster – heroine Lily Dale, who invokes for herself a new title to show her willed renunciation of marriage: 'Lily Dale, Old Maid', she writes in her diary in *The Last Chronicle of Barset*.

41

Pym preserves the Victorian moral frame of the woman as a useful, domestic servant to her family; yet in her twentieth-century settings, this ideal acquires an ironic twist. Spinsters no longer remain in the family, as they must in Austen's fictional world, or in the Victorian world depicted in Ivy Compton-Burnett's modern novels. Thus Pym's heroines inherit some qualities from their Victorian sisters, in their domesticity and earnestness, yet they often remain single and isolated.

Despite its possible drawbacks in keeping the reader's interest, the subject of spinsterhood provides new territory for exploration, and Pym examines the single state with reference to this Victorian background. In his essay on the figure of the spinster in Pym's fiction, Robert Graham praises Pym's 'far-reaching portrayal of a figure all but ignored by researchers in sociology, psychology and gerontology' and sees the central focus in her early novels as 'an evaluation of marriage and singleness as inherently positive or negative states'.[1] The advantages of singleness do constitute a major subject for her. In Pym's first novel, *Some Tame Gazelle*, sisters Belinda and Harriet Bede share a home together as '[spinsters] in the middle fifties' and continue to do so in defiance of several offers of matrimony (*STG*, 7). Subsequent novels reinforce the importance of the spinster figure remaining single either by choice or by necessity. Mildred Lathbury in *Excellent Women*, Prudence in *Jane and Prudence*, Catherine in *Less than Angels*, Leonora in *The Sweet Dove Died* and Letty in *Quartet in Autumn* – each remains unmarried at the end of the novel.

Yet despite the fact that they are deprived of husbands, the heroines are not to be pitied by the reader, as they are either sufficiently elegant or independent to disdain a need for a husband, or at the least, resigned to doing without one. A further interesting development occurs in the spinsters' ongoing relationships with men. They may not marry, but they none the less continue to deal with men, who assume various roles as clergymen, lovers or fellow-workers. The narrowness of the spinster's life by no means limits her to contact only with other women. And in these continuing relationships with men, women are often called upon to adopt subservient roles. Still, if they must outwardly humour the difficult men who look to them for admiration, they may also secretly enjoy their own superiority as women. And life remains full of compensatory pleasures: 'reading, domestic life, and cats' marked Pym's own avocational interests as she described them, and the same pleasures sustain many of her heroines.[2] Pym's spinsters manage to create pleasant lives for themselves, between church work, chatting with the neighbours and putting up plum jam.

But one feels a disturbing undercurrent in all of this; and the source of the tension lies in the spinsters' cheerful acceptance of their lot. Each adopts an implicit vow of self-denial. For some reason not immediately apparent, Pym's heroines tend to limit the scope of their lives wilfully. Many of the author's titles reflect this diminishing or minimising – 'some' tame gazelle, a 'few' green leaves, 'less' than angels; finally, a flat negative, in 'no' fond return of love. Moreover, the title of her best novel slants the reader's perception in an odd way: 'excellent' women implies a counterpart of 'mediocre' men. Her delineation of the male character is problematic all through her fiction, even if the 'excellence' of women referred to in the title is perceived as mildly sardonic. The spinsters this phrase refers to may be excessively good; the narrator, Mildred, reflects at one point that self-consciously virtuous people are never really very nice. More to the point, Pym's spinsters are fatally attracted to men: for them, 'love' is always a verb, never a noun; further, it is an active verb, not a passive one, as they are so seldom loved in return. ' "Something to love" ' forms a refrain in all of Pym's fiction, and the necessity to give 'to' someone haunts most of her women characters (*STG*, 17).

As for the men in her fictional world, Graham points out that they tend to be inferior to the women, and he further concludes that this suggests a possible corollary to the real world of twentieth-century England. Studies 'indicate', he writes, that 'single men are inferior in education, occupation, and income to their female counterparts . . .'[3] The married men in Pym's novels, one might add, fare hardly better on the social scale than do the single men. To narrow the field still further to a specific case, misfortune and frustration haunted Pym's personal experience in love. Thus, if she wrote directly out of her own life, it would seem little wonder that nearly all of her male characters appear feeble, vain and egotistical, albeit charming. The author expressed astonishment when readers of her novels complained that she did not seem to like men: 'That really isn't my attitude at all', she protested. 'To quote a joke phrase, some of my best friends are – have been – men!' (MS PYM 95, fol. 32). But as for romance as opposed to friendship, the reverse was often true; not all of her relationships were so pleasant and fruitful. And if she attempted to right a score by satirising men in her novels, no one would blame her, though the novels suffer at times from an incomplete portrayal of masculinity.

Yet her fiction extends beyond a simple exercise in revenge. Pym not only writes a survival manual for spinsters (hot-water bottles, milky drinks before bed and a perspective of tolerant amusement); but she creates a picture of single women in love. Her women characters hide, struggle with and indulge in infatuations as they would in forbidden sweets. The continuing tension which lies between men and women occurs largely within the woman herself. She feels herself to be ridiculous in her vulnerability, yet she remains drawn to men, and often cannot restrain herself from pursuing her lover and declaring herself. Mildred in *Excellent Women* formulates a generalisation from the Wrens' love for Rocky, when he had been much admired in Italy; concluding that 'perhaps they had been wise enough not to tell their love' (*EW*, 172). Pym's heroines often find themselves in this predicament.

Conversely, male characters form a strong bastion of indifference to women, which they carry to the point of closing ranks against them in the inversion of homosexuality. The novels restage this conflict in various settings. Taken to an extreme, devotion from women can result in an overprotectiveness which emasculates men, as in Leonora's relations with James in *The Sweet Dove Died*. Even in its more genial manifestations, the woman still remains a supplicant for the man's love. Harriet attempts to tame curates by feeding them jellies and cakes in *Some Tame Gazelle*, and women characters in other novels attempt to hold men with 'uxorilocal' domestic arrangements, where they provide shelter for their men as well as meals, devotion and cups of tea. Given this overwhelming need to care for and give to men, the central dilemma for the spinster becomes a question of how to prevent herself from giving too much, and thus overpowering, scaring and ultimately 'sending away' the man on whom she dotes.[4]

Thus Pym provides a feminist view of relations between the sexes, showing the frustration women feel in romantic attraction. Her spinsters could be content – if only they did not keep falling in love and having their emotions troubled in the process. Not all of her heroines suffer from unrequited love to the same degree, of course. Prudence of *Jane and Prudence*, for instance, has achieved the distanced perspective which many of Pym's heroines strive for. She arranges a series of love affairs with such superb artistry that she ends by experiencing them in entirely aesthetic and narcissistic terms.

Still, most of Pym's heroines do experience the full weight of their disappointments, or sense them being deliberately held at bay. In consequence, they seek to avoid being stirred into emotion and betrayed into further regret. Wilmet formulates this fear when she writes in *A Glass of Blessings*: 'April was balmy and delicious, and cruel in the way the poet did mean, mingling memory and desire. The memory was of other springs, the desire unformulated, unrecognised almost, pushed away because there seemed to be no place for it in the life I had chosen for myself' (*GB*, 148). The *Waste Land* motif of April's 'cruelty' reverberates throughout Pym's fiction, capturing a fine edge of poignancy. Spinsterhood in any of its various aspects cannot be divorced from the influence of men, or from the fascination they continue to exert over women; feeble as they appear to be, men are none the less allied to a vitalising force while at the same time remaining tantalisingly out of reach.

Much of Pym's work is Austen's *Persuasion* writ modern; yet while her twentieth-century Anne Elliotts remain worthy and constant, no Captain Wentworths appear in order to reward them. Because of the relative lack of admirable men, spinsterhood may represent a welcome alternative to marriage, but it does not preclude or prevent the inevitable state of infatuation. The interplay between these two forces of singleness and infatuation becomes dynamic and fascinating, in far more than sociological terms. Pym depicts not only the way in which the spinster outwardly arranges her life, but how she perceives her situation and how she battles the disruptive elements which threaten her dearly-bought serenity. In this way, Pym explores the private emotional ramifications of singleness as well as the social ones. Spinsterhood remains inseparable from loving, whose uncertainties pose a constant threat.

The most abiding characteristic of all of her heroines' experience – especially of spinsters – is that of solitude. This comprises a surprisingly large share of her books, given the fact that they are comedies of manners. Her heroines often seem to be found preparing meals or doing the washing up. Pym devotes much of her narrative to describing what individual characters see, think and feel when they are by themselves and, further, to the fact that they are intensely conscious of themselves being alone. Solitude comprises a world of its own, providing opportunity for private reflection and, more importantly, the vantage-point from which the heroines can observe themselves. This state borders on narcissism, especially when the observers also watch those around them so keenly. In both her novels and diaries, Pym often portrays a woman sitting alone at a table in a restaurant, a setting in which the woman remains alone yet sees herself as a performer with a projected audience around her.

Thus when narrator Mildred Lathbury declares that if she writes a novel it will comprise 'an hour in the life of a woman at the sink', she describes one aspect of *Excellent Women* aptly (*EW*, 161). This vision characterises that of the typical spinster and 'excellent woman'. During the course of the novel, the reader sees Mildred prepare numerous pots of tea and coffee, wash up in both her own kitchen and in Helena's, prepare cod on one occasion and baked beans on another. In the latter two examples, she does this, significantly, for herself. The preparation of the meal is not, as far as Mildred knows, especially going to lead to a dramatic encounter, though Rocky enters unexpectedly on one occasion; rather, it will probably remain solitary from beginning to end. Yet she chooses to describe life in the kitchen because it provides a corollary to her present state of mind.

One thinks of other examples of this kind – Letty and Marcia in *Quartet in Autumn* preparing solitary meals for themselves, Catherine Oliphant in *Less than Angels* making herself tea after an emotional shock, Prudence in *Jane and Prudence* giving herself, on Jane's advice, a *'good breakfast'* on the morning she learns of Fabian's engagement to another woman, and so on (*JP*, 194). This captures an important aspect of spinsterhood: single people necessarily eat alone, and solitude in this setting can be made to seem comic or pathetic. In an extreme example of this corollary, Marcia starves herself into a state of malnutrition in *Quartet in Autumn*, in the same way that she goes mad through spiritual starvation, through rejecting contact with other people. Meals are by definition (or at least by strong Victorian tradition) a social time, and the absence of fellow diners stresses the aloneness of the single woman. But more importantly, the question of self-image is tied directly to what the characters eat when they are alone. Ianthe in *An Unsuitable Attachment* and Prudence in *Jane and Prudence* show that they place a high value on themselves because they make solitary meals an occasion. The fact that Prudence's dinner salad contains a little garlic, and that the cheese to follow was 'nicely ripe' conveys Prudence's high self-esteem (*JP*, 47).[5]

Besides comprising a natural realm for women, the kitchen also provides a convenient setting in which to show characters thinking while their hands are occupied. Such menial work can induce an hypnotic state which in turn reveals much in unguarded moments. It captures the essence of the characters themselves and of what spinsterhood is. For example, when Dulcie in *No Fond Return of Love* stands in the kitchen sorting plums, she seems most preoccupied with the question of excess garden produce; she contemplates putting some jam up and taking fruit to the neighbours. Yet she also uses the occasion to divert herself. She thinks about the plums in order deliberately to distract herself from pining for Aylwin. By combining these two strains of thought, Pym captures the essence of infatuation: obsession with the object of devotion interspersed with mundane tasks of everyday life, whose dullness becomes transformed by the absorbing object of love.

One of the most common aspects of infatuation as Pym represents it is the devotion evidenced by women and the corresponding indifference shown by men. The dynamics of the relationship are such that men can awaken this devotion simply by existing. Because of their indifference to women, they offer an unattainable romantic goal. The 'something to love' which Pym's heroines seek is best illustrated by Mildred's imaginative transformation of Everard Bone in *Excellent Women*, when she envisions him as a clergyman. In this role, he would be properly forbidding, and thus could be loved 'secretly with no hope of encouragement, which can be very enjoyable for the young or inexperienced' (*EW*, 92).

Pym's heroines struggle between infatuation – imagining or even anticipating and expecting a union with the beloved – and substitution or displacement – focusing on other things in order to distract themselves from thinking of the man they love. Pym's private diaries evidence this sort of anguished, controlled will to divert herself. Infatuation seems a necessary affliction, and leads to all kinds of responses, from distraction away from the man in question to denial of expectations altogether. Still more revealing in this light is an unpublished short story, which carries the tenet of self-denial to an extreme. It depicts a bitter heroine named Barbara, who complains to her sister Hilary that everyone has deserted her, particularly her male friends. She concludes: ' "I expect nothing . . . then I am not disappointed when I receive nothing" ' (MS PYM 94,

fol. 238). Pym enlarges on this bald statement of resignation later, in
her efforts to forget Gordon Glover after her brief and (for Pym)
disastrous affair with him during the Second World War. She wrote
in the diary kept just after their separation that she tried to bring
herself through her depression by '[making] things to look forward
to, however small' (*VPE*, 114). This dimming of hope in romantic
love is sharply reined in to focus on other, compensatory pleasures,
the small occasions which can provide meaning.

Through subsequent disillusioning experiences, Pym became a
self-appointed specialist in the subject of unrequited love. As
reviewers of *A Very Private Eye* have pointed out, she was not bereft
of admirers. For Pym, as for her fictional character Leonora in *The
Sweet Dove Died*, 'one had had one's chances', and the reader, like
Leonora's friend Meg, ought to be well aware of this (*SDD*, 166). Yet
the vision of love reflected in her novels is none the less wistful and
bittersweet. It appears from her private writings that she struggled
constantly with unrequited love and its attendant frustration and
uncertainty, adopting various remedies and poses, from nonchalance to denial to pursuit. Later in her life she seems to have reverted
to her early conclusion of willed indifference; she responds to the
rebuff she receives from Richard Roberts by an admonishment to
herself to remain unattached. She wrote to her friend Robert Smith
about the relationship in terms of admonition: she will 'be more
cautious in future – not allowing [herself] to get fond of anybody'
(*VPE*, 243). A similar passage in her diary elaborates on this view
and also speculates on the universality of this experience: 'Perhaps
to be loved is the most cosy thing in life and yet many people,
women I suppose I mean, know only the uncertainties of loving,
which are only sometimes cosy when one accepts one's situation
(rarely, perhaps). Wouldn't unrequited love be a good subject for a
novel?' (MS PYM 45 fol. 18).

Unrequited love represents a classic, universal subject for a novel,
and served Pym well for ten – one is tempted to ask, is there any
other subject ever? Yet the observation remains relevant because
Pym's particular slant on unrequited love comprises part of her
unique achievement as a writer. She incorporates reverberations of
Austen and Brontë in her novels, and transforms Austen's classic
happy endings and Brontë's Victorian melancholy into a contemporary light-hearted irony. Cosiness holds a high value in her view,
and the need to perceive life in these terms is evident in spinsters in
her fiction. Cosiness, or security, offers the best possible defence

against the crushing and repeated blows encountered in relationships with men. As Belinda reflects in *Some Tame Gazelle*, all change is of itself an evil, and she experiences overwhelming joy and relief when Harriet refuses Mr Mold's proposal and does not leave their house together.

It is possible to love with only minimal uncertainty, under special circumstances. The idyllic provincial world offered by *Some Tame Gazelle* captures this fine balance perfectly, in Belinda Bede's thirty-year crush on Archdeacon Henry Hoccleve. The heroine defines this as beneficial for precisely the reason that it is cosy and stable:

> Belinda, having loved the Archdeacon when she was twenty and not having found anyone to replace him since, had naturally got into the habit of loving him, though with the years her passion had mellowed into a comfortable feeling, more like the cosiness of a winter evening by the fire than the uncertain rapture of a spring morning. (*STG*, 15)

In this variation on the theme of man's indifference, Belinda has learned to 'accept' her situation of unrequited love for Henry to the point of making a virtue out of her renunciation and self-denial. Further, it is not simply a situation of 'accepting' passively, but of actively creating a myth of unrequited love, as in the above quotation. Belinda chooses to indulge in fantasy instead of to face reality.

This 'acceptance of one's situation' depicted in fiction becomes significant when compared to her response to the situation imposed on her in her life. In dealing with her rejection by the original of Henry Hoccleve, Pym created a separate persona for her rejected-in-love self much as she had done at Oxford in the figure of 'Sandra': in this case she creates the 'spinster'.

Not only did she create the fictional Belinda Bede in her first novel, which she sent to her two friends Henry Harvey and Robert Liddell while composing it, but she identified herself with the spinster figure directly by posing in her letters to them as a sort of brilliant Stevie Smith eccentric: 'And Miss Pym is looking out of the window – and you will be asking now who is this Miss Pym, and I will tell you that she is a spinster lady who was thought to have been disappointed in love, and so now you know who is this Miss Pym' and so on, she writes to Robert Liddell, Henry Harvey and Henry's wife Elsie (surely an important change in Pym's audience) in 1938,

· four years after going down from Oxford (*VPE*, 67). This burlesque does not express a particularly daring or unexpected mode of defence – the combination of petulance, archness and brittleness seems forced and artificial rather than clever. But what strikes one forcibly none the less is the fact that she first employed this defence while she was still so young. At twenty-two, Pym began to write *Some Tame Gazelle*, with its exaggerated self-denigration, and the letter I have just quoted finds her at twenty-six still unmarried and thinking of herself as a confirmed spinster.

Once formulated, the motif persisted in defining Pym's view of herself, often revealing a bitter edge. The anxiety to find a husband, which she felt intermittently after leaving Oxford and while living at home with her parents for the next few years, modulated eventually into an overwhelming feeling of chagrin. Her singleness humiliated her. This was especially true after the ending of her relationship with Gordon Glover. One diary entry from this period stages a dramatic tableau to illustrate this theme: 'It almost makes me glad to be unattached – the calm faced woman in the restaurant wearing good tweeds, not unattractive but her left hand is ringless. Spinster' (MS PYM 108, fol. 58). Pym exaggerates, perhaps, but does not entirely jest here. The tension of being single bothered her in part because she could have chosen to marry, and thus it seemed something purposely to decide. She recorded one conversation about such expectations with a friend who was also single during their time in the Wrens: 'We talked about our lives as we walked. Of course we're both pretty splendid. We both want the same kind of things. And fancy people not getting married and having children when they are able to' (MS PYM 109, fol. 83). The two women are surprised at themselves for not doing the expected thing – marrying and having children – because they do want it, at least on some level. They do not (in this discussion, at any rate) blame the men they know for failing to come up to standard, but instead regard themselves as making a deliberate choice. Similarly, many of Pym's single heroines have opportunities to marry and choose not to.

Thus the uncertainties of loving Henry Harvey which Pym experienced in her relationship with him at Oxford seem to have evolved into the spinster figure as portrayed in her letters to him and in her first novel. The way in which she continues to explore this subject in her subsequent fiction is still more interesting. The early unpublished novels which follow the first version of *Some Tame Gazelle* devise several alternative ways of responding to disappointments in love. These range from the obvious revenge fantasy, where the indifferent male becomes a broken, contrite man, to the comforting resolution of a happy marriage. These early efforts tend to seem forced and unreal, though they show the author beginning to formulate themes she will use later with greater authority and perspective.

A brief survey of some of Pym's early works will illustrate this point. One of the important issues for a spinster is that of attractiveness – Pym was self-conscious about her appearance and felt that the way she looked lessened her chances of attracting a man. Similarly, the outwardly 'plain-looking woman' appears in the short stories as a woman likely to be passed over by a handsome man in favour of a prettier girl, and as a result she is relegated to the role of 'dear sister' (MS PYM 94, fol. 255). Significantly, Pym cast herself in this role in her letters to Henry Harvey's wife, Elsie, in a pose obviously intended to be ironic and magnanimous. Still, the 'dear sister' figure often hides a Cinderella in disguise – a single woman who ultimately triumphs in love. In one representative short story which portrays this progression, the hero finds that he has deceived himself as to the value of his bride. She is beautiful but, problematically, foreign. After marrying abroad, he returns to England with his wife only to see the 'plain' English heroine he has previously rejected marry another man. Hilda, the heroine, is now 'very unlike the dim, mousy creature who had been jilted' by the hero earlier (MS PYM 94, fol. 141). She makes her husband an excellent wife, while the chagrined former suitor sinks into a dramatic decline and pleads feebly for the heroine's friendship.[6]

Pym strikes a still sharper note of revenge in an Ibsen-like short story where the hero, Henry, returns to England with his foreign wife, named Elsie. A spinster called Barbara subsequently discloses that her supposed 'ward' of nineteen is actually her illegitimate daughter by Henry. This variation is more stark than the majority of the other stories and shows the strong influence of Ivy Compton-Burnett, both in style and subject matter. It can be seen as a stylistic experiment as much as a pervasive subject in Pym's thought. Yet it still reveals the fascination that the idea of unrequited love for Henry held for her, and the recurring theme in her work of the indifference and weakness of men. The stories often provide a setting in which the spurned woman can tell her grief to the world. In this case, the character 'Barbara' may reveal her guilty secret – with the ultimate result that she gains 'Henry' in the end. Elsie conveniently dies, and the two former lovers will now 'comfort' each other in their old age.[7]

In a novel set in Finland, Pym experiments with several possible approaches for women who are cursed with loving a recalcitrant male. The hero, Gervase, is beset by three women: Vikki, a Finnish vamp, Ingeborg, a Swedish girl to whom he eventually becomes engaged, and Flora, the English girl whom he has virtually promised to marry before the novel opens. Flora follows him to Finland in order to discover exactly how their relationship stands. She berates Gervase for his indecision – it is significant that she tells him he is a cad to his face – and suffers from his rejection, but finally ends by marrying a handsome Finnish count. As for the foreign women, Vikki fails to catch the hero with her seductive wiles, while Ingeborg attracts and wins Gervase almost entirely by virtue of her passivity.

Like other heroines in Pym's early fiction who have been wronged, Flora allows her indignation full expression in this novel. Further, she receives support in her grief. The surrounding community – mostly British expatriate – is outraged on her behalf. And the handsome male Finns welcome her to weep (literally) on their bosoms. Thus the heroine is supported by society in her attempt to claim her rights or to justify herself. This social acceptance provides almost as much comfort as does her final triumph in securing a husband – and this victory is sweet. The count, her fiancé, is not only handsome but rich, while in making Ingeborg his wife, Gervase also becomes saddled with his fiancée's complaining mother. Thus the happy ending of marriage presents one possibility for wronged heroines. Another example of this occurs in the unpublished novel *Civil to Strangers*, where the married heroine, a plain woman, is improbably vamped by two handsome men, by dint of which courting her husband begins to appreciate her. As a virtuous housewife, Cassandra never complains to her husband of his neglect or of his continual efforts to snub her intellectually. Yet the admiration of the other two men provides the catalyst for her to point out his callousness (as well as to arouse his jealousy).

In contrast to this hackneyed, predictable scenario for a rejected woman, Mildred in the later novel *Excellent Women* suffers a much more private and thus more intense grief. She receives support in her singleness from her community as well, but the church pities her for the wrong reason, because she is officially regarded as the 'rejected one' for the vicar's hand. She is actually in love with Rocky

Napier, who is not only married and thus forbidden, but who continually wounds her by his deceptive charm and actual indifference to her. Mildred cannot tell anyone her real sorrow, and the fact that it remains hidden intensifies her grief. She may receive some consolation from being pitied, but she remains fundamentally misunderstood.

Another prominent feature of Pym's early writing about romance is the predicament of the spinster as she is type-cast in society. Various responses on the part of single women surface; the heroine in *The Lumber Room*, Beatrice Wyatt, is a don at Oxford and thus manages a successful and distinguished career – though there is a curious twist here. The novel opens with Beatrice going up to Oxford on the train from the country village where she lives with her mother and unmarried sister. Arriving at her digs and unpacking, she smokes a careless cigarette, in a scene which recreates the undergraduate life in a perpetual extension. Beatrice's development is arrested rather than broadened. This impression is strengthened when she enjoys a pleasant love affair with a young undergraduate, though she is continually conscious of its inevitable ending. The affair is saturated with bittersweet nostalgia, as Beatrice attempts to end the affair in self-defence before it ends on its own. In a variation of the Cinderella theme, she is blessed in being courted by this younger man; and although he eventually leaves, she ends with – surprisingly – Henry, her former beau, who is now conveniently a widower.

A few spinsters in Pym's fiction declare themselves to be above marriage altogether. In one conversation among English church-women in the Finnish novel, a Miss Liversidge affirms that she has not married because men are not good enough: ' "We intelligent women have a very high standard" ', she says (MS PYM 7, fol. 190). She goes so far as to call on the other single women present to support her in her assertion. The most interesting aspect of the exchange is the conclusion she reaches; rejecting another woman's suggestion that her way of stating the matter is 'kinder', she continues ' "I deplore this attitude to spinsters, as if they were objects deserving of pity" ' (MS PYM 7, fol. 190).

From early on in her writing, Pym was interested in romance, the universal topic, but she was perhaps equally fascinated by the vision of life without romance, especially for women. In keeping with this, solitude forms a palpable presence in her novels. It defines what remains if one does not marry – and it often results in a constant battle to avoid the stirring of memory and desire which love and April bring. In another early short novel written in the late 1940s, Pym illustrates this dilemma in a story which prefigures *Excellent Women*. The heroine of 'Something to Remember', Deborah, resembles Mildred in many ways. She narrates her story and suffers from many of Mildred's fears and anxieties. The short novel begins with a chapter entitled 'A Table too Near the Band', which describes the painful exaltation which Deborah experiences when she becomes stirred by the music in a restaurant at tea, and then emerges outdoors into a fresh spring evening. It is desolate to feel so much. She deliberately tries to distract herself by deciding to return home, adjuring herself: 'Still, there is a comfort in small homely tasks, especially when your spirit has been disturbed by music and the spring air. For the exhilaration does not last for ever' (MS PYM 11, fol. 21). It appears at the end of the novel that the heroine has previously been jilted (by a thoughtless curate), an outcome which is felt by Deborah's confidante to be a pity since Deborah would have been '"so *suitable*"' as a clergyman's wife (MS PYM 11, fol. 69).[8]

Does one infer from this that the heroine's life is ruined because she was rejected by a man? Pym equivocates here. Behind the sardonic edge – Deborah's life is forever doomed to melancholy – hovers a feeling that the heroine is fortunate to be well out of it. Aside from the personal aspect of renunciation, the social implications of the novel in some ways suggest a rewriting of *Jane Eyre*, since the heroine must earn her own living. Her situation is not far removed from that portrayed in Gissing's novel *The Odd Women*, in which Victorian women are left unprovided for and are forced to find employment in a social system which offers nothing for them except matrimony. Deborah seems Victorian in her situation; when the novel opens, she is about to take a new position as companion and secretary to a wealthy woman. She is apprehensive about what her life will be like, half hoping she will discover a Mr Rochester in her new employer. But when she assumes her duties at the Otways', she finds no strange mystery in the house (the closest exception being an astonishing number of stuffed birds); on the contrary, she delights in the elegance of the surroundings, the excellence of the maid service and the fineness of the food. It is spinster heaven.

Pym studies the economics of single living in many settings; spinsterhood necessitates managing and making do with limited resources. One aspect of this is the problem of acquiring 'good things', which looms large for 'distressed gentlewomen' because aristocratic privilege is an integral part of their heritage. These women form a subset in Pym's fictional world as a distinct social group – Mildred Lathbury in *Excellent Women* works in an agency to aid them – and Pym also creates a few particular examples. Harriet speaks of Edith Liversidge in *Some Tame Gazelle* as a ' "decayed gentlewoman" ', a description which shocks Belinda, because Edith is so active: she 'was tough and wiry, dug vigorously in her garden and kept goats' (*STG*, 15). Conversely, Edith's relative Connie Aspinall, who lives with her, requires constant care. Before moving in with Edith, Connie had been a lady's companion to a family in Belgrave Square – ' "so *very* kind" ' they have always been to her, she sighs – and she becomes a parody of the spinster in a Victorian novel whose sole talent is the ability to play a musical instrument (*STG*, 240). Having acquired the ladylike accomplishment of playing the harp, she has become a useless anachronism except for the occasional village concert. Unlike Austen's Jane Fairfax in *Emma*, who is still more musical, and barely rescued from being more ill-fortuned, Connie has no inner resilience which enables her to live life on her own. Her position has permanently stunted her so that she can only exist through her aristocratic employers and their fabled 'kindness' to her.

In two other variations of the *Jane Eyre* story, Miss Prideaux in *A Glass of Blessings* and Miss Vereker in *A Few Green Leaves* were formerly governesses. These women draw their entire identity from their former posts, like Connie Aspinall, and reminisce ceaselessly about earlier days. They live entirely in the past. ' "Two litres of Chianti *from our own vineyards* was sent up to the schoolroom *every day*" ', boasts Miss Prideaux, to Wilmet's polite scepticism (*GB*, 28). The discrepancy here lies in the fact that having drunk of the wine of the aristocratic life, these women feel lost when they are no longer maintained in this style. Jessie Morrow in *Jane and Prudence* illustrates the darker, more bitter side to this inferior social position. Rebelling against her subservient role as ' "that outmoded thing, a companion" ', she determines to escape from it through an advantageous marriage (*JP*, 29).

Thus, in a brilliant anachronism, Pym transfers the typical Victorian figure of the 'distressed gentlewoman' to the twentieth century. And this background lends an air of fatalism and mock heroism to her characters' difficulties in life. There is nothing else for these women to be. Available positions as dependants in a great household steadily disappear through the century, yet their social position still restricts them when they compete in the marriage market. The case of Jessie Morrow's and Prudence Bates's struggle for the eligible widower in *Jane and Prudence* provides a case in point. Prudence possesses an Oxford education, expensive outfits (silk dresses, elegant 'housecoats' and heavy French scent), and an exquisite flat, all of which prove attractive to Fabian. In competing with Prudence for Fabian, Jessie must succeed by her wits alone. In the course of her campaign, she imitates Prudence by dressing for the part. She alters a jumble sale dress, applies cosmetics and appears at Fabian's house, offering herself in the role of seductive mistress. Fabian has been accepting these sorts of attentions as his due from women all along – only Jessie makes him pay for sexual favours with marriage.

Jessie shows a mixture of ambivalence, guilt and defiance when her engagement to Fabian is announced. While not revealing how she has caught Fabian, she declares that she would be ashamed to be thought sexually inexperienced. She refuses to wear a white wedding dress, adding, ' "There can be something shameful about flaunting one's lack of experience" ' (*JP*, 214). This is supremely funny; while the other characters are consumed with curiosity as to what depth the heroines have, in fact, fallen, the spinsters are protected by convention. They refuse to say. Like her rival Jessie, Prudence replies in equally enigmatic fashion to her friend's tortured inquiry, phrased, appropriately, in Victorian terms: ' "are you Fabian's *mistress*?" ' Jane asks, trying to assess the possible damage to Prudence's honour. Stating that ' "there's no need to ask coy questions about it" ', Prudence retains her advantage by not revealing the answer (*JP*, 123).

Pym's inventiveness lies in this reserve and archness. In a Victorian novel the plot would hinge absolutely on the crucial question of chastity, and the heroine's guilt would necessarily be firmly established or denied. Maggie Tulliver in Eliot's *Mill on the Floss* cannot return late from an excursion with a beau without her reputation being ruined forever. Thus Pym's subtlety parodies the twentieth-century preoccupation with and freedom in sex. If it is taken for granted that every couple sleeps together, Pym can imply the reverse for her heroines and thus leave the reader uncertain.' "I see you are thinking the very worst" ', says Catherine in *Less Than Angels*, to another character who infers (not surprisingly), that she has sexual relations with Tom Mallow, the man who shares her flat (*LTA*, 135). She goes on to generalise: ' "Yes, of course women do think the worst of each other ..." ' (*LTA*, 135). Pym's curious reticence on the subject verges on fastidiousness, and some critics have faulted her for her reserve. But such a complaint fails to take account of her real purpose in approaching love from this angle. Society demands 'pure' women, yet some spinsters feel that their only chance to catch a man lies in skilfully exploiting their sexual power. In order to resist the stigma of the 'fallen woman' yet retain an aura of mystery, they escape into subterfuge. Between seduction and innocence, they try to have it both ways, an achievement only possible in the modern age because of the Victorian seriousness about sex that preceded it.

The figure of the 'distressed gentlewoman' and the problem of employment for women recur in Pym's fiction. Yet spinsterhood in the 1950s for upper-middle-class women entails more a question of emotional than of financial needs. In regard to herself, Pym created a definite persona to embody the rejected spinster – she conceived of herself, as her diaries indicate, as persevering in being 'drearily splendid', with occasional lapses, during the period of intense grieving which followed her rejection by Gordon Glover (*VPE*, 121). The quintessence of this lies in an image that she used in one of her Wren diaries when she was in hot pursuit of a man. Wondering whether she ought to abandon the chase, she considers adopting the alternate role of 'spinster washing stockings in a sitting-room in Bayswater' (MS PYM 84, fol. 1). Pym typically responded to disappointments in love by satirising herself as a spinster, and at the same time by adjuring herself to exercise caution in further attempts to establish relationships. She wrote in her diaries while she was with the Wrens in Italy: ' . . . I keep myself in check as I think it would be disastrous to care too much and even if it were mutual nothing would come of it.' She concludes impatiently with 'I can't be bothered with these fleeting affairs – ' (*VPE*, 169).

Thus one result of Pym's time in the Wrens was to confirm her image of herself as a single woman, still attracted by and attractive to men. This is underscored by one conversation with a man she recorded in her diary: 'The first person in Naples with whom I've had any conversation about sex! . . . He told me I would make a good mistress as I would be able to hold a mans [*sic*] interest by my intelligence!' (MS PYM 110, fol. 8). This shows a curious conflation of the clever Oxford graduate and *femme fatale*.

Another result of her service term was to cause her to focus on and create a fantasy about life with women. At one point in her diaries, she suggests playfully that she should write a novel entitled 'Too Many Women' to capture her life accurately at this time (MS PYM 109, fol. 422). Though the novel never materialised, this theme became central to novels written after her term in the Wrens. These novels explore the single woman's lot, which usually consists of melancholy induced by unrequited love, of compensatory domestic pleasures and of resignation to a life containing (for her tastes) too many women. As if to emphasise the separation between the sexes, Pym's fictional world depicts several women characters who live together or alone rather than with men. Marriage remains an enviable achievement to a spinster such as Rhoda in *Less than Angels*, who lives with her widowed sister Mabel in a suburban London house. Even so, she consoles herself for having missed '"the experience of marriage"' in the abstract by rejecting what she sees of it in particular, concrete terms (*LTA*, 36). She compares herself to Mabel and concludes that the prospect of marriage is unattractive after all: 'she would not have liked to have had [the advantages of such a relationship] with poor Gregory Swan' (*LTA*, 36).

The pairs of women who share homes in Pym's fiction illustrate variations on the need for companionship – and the occasionally irksome problems which can result from such a ménage. Miss Lee and Miss Grundy in *A Few Green Leaves* sustain a symbiotic relationship soured by Miss Lee's bossiness and Miss Grundy's anger. In one example of this, the trivial episode of the barbola mirror provides further fuel for the fire. Short of a prize at their 'Bring and Buy' sale, Miss Lee gives the mirror away, which Miss Grundy resents because it had been a present to both of them. This episode is one in a long line of minor frictions, as Miss Grundy broods: 'Another source of quiet resentment on her part' (*FGL*, 74). When Daphne moves from the village to London to share a house with her long-time friend Heather, the two reproduce all too clearly the bleakness of Miss Grundy's and Miss Lee's relationship. In an earlier novel, Mabel and Rhoda in *Less than Angels* become caught in a similar perpetual cycle of irritation and fussiness, rearranging each other's table settings: 'And they would probably go on doing this all their lives' (*LTA*, 153).

In contrast to this antagonism, women can also unite effectively against the outside world, as when Mildred and Mrs Morris in *Excellent Women* '[laugh] together, a couple of women against the whole race of men' (*EW*, 23–4). Another curious example of affinities between women is the household in *A Glass of Blessings*, where Wilmet lives with her husband Rodney and his mother, Sybil. In an early draft of the novel, initially composed in the third person, the narrator explicitly implies that Wilmet's mother-in-law fills a lack in Wilmet's relationship with her husband; the two women share the same sense of humour and the same view of life: 'The arrangement, which might seem irksome and unpropitious to a married couple, worked very well for [*sic*] Wilmet really found her mother-in-law quite as congenial as her husband and sometimes almost more so' (MS PYM 17, fol. 15).

The most celebrated pair of spinsters in Pym's fiction is Harriet and Belinda Bede of *Some Tame Gazelle*, who suffer only minor annoyances and portray all that is best in a sisterly household. They create a picture of perfect felicity, as when the two sisters and their single women friends engage in an impromptu frolic: 'At tea they were all very gay, in the way that happy, unmarried ladies of middle age often are' (*STG*, 169). This scenario reflects the blessings of the single state, but the characters' schoolgirlish behaviour strikes a slightly ironic note; it suggests a sort of immaturity which accompanies the more pleasant aspects of their relationship with each other. Spinsterhood can reflect an arrested development where, as is typical in the entire novel, the group of Oxford undergraduates continues to play out its perpetual larks and frictions. Harriet and Belinda seem to reinforce these traits in each other in their conversations about the other characters.

Still more interesting than her treatment of relationships between women is Pym's emphasis on the joys of solitude. Many of her single characters strongly resist allowing someone else to move in with them. Mildred in *Excellent Women*, for instance, has recently been left by her friend, Dora Caldicote, and reflects on the relief that she feels not to have the inevitable frictions anymore; the milk-jug cover still acts as a reminder of differing opinions, and symbolises Dora's fussiness and Mildred's exasperation. Later in the novel, when Winifred comes to Mildred and asks to move in with her, or, rather, assumes that she will be able to, Mildred displays an immediate reaction against this proposed invasion. She values her solitude immensely. Similarly, in *No Fond Return of Love* Dulcie expresses apprehension about Viola coming to live with her, anxious that Viola's presence should not cause her to have to change. Dulcie determines to 'begin as one meant to go on' in the

matter of shared meals on the occasion of Viola's first meal with her
(*NFR*, 71). She further envisions separation within the same
household as her ideal. At one point she fantasises about herself,
Viola, and her niece Laurel all preparing hot, milky drinks on their
separate gas-rings.

In *Quartet in Autumn*, when Letty is forced to make new living
arrangements, the question of property and of maintaining sole
rights to one's private place becomes immediate and crucial. Marcia
rejects the notion of inviting Letty to live with her, as Edward
shrinks from the idea of asking Norman to live with him. The end of
the novel stresses this, when Letty considers refusing Marjorie's
offer to share a country cottage with her, and the novel closes with
her delicious sense of having some choice in this important matter.

A large number of spinsters (or bachelors) in Pym's novels live
alone, and would even take steps to defend their solitary
households. Mildred in *Excellent Women*, Ianthe in *An Unsuitable
Attachment*, Emma in *A Few Green Leaves*, Marcia in *Quartet in
Autumn*, Leonora in *The Sweet Dove Died*, Prudence in *Jane and
Prudence* – each treasures her solitude. Prudence emphasises the fact
that she would not know what to do with a husband in her
exceptionally well-arranged flat. This fastidiousness about remaining separate becomes the basis for Pym's exploration of the subject
of men and women living together. Curiously, the home remains a
woman's province so entirely that when couples unite, the woman
often provides a home for the man in question. Mark defines the
domestic situation of Catherine and Tom in *Less than Angels* in
anthropological terms: ' "It would be a reciprocal relationship – the
woman giving the food and shelter and doing some typing for him
and the man giving the priceless gift of himself . . . It is commoner in
our society than many people would suppose" ' (*LTA*, 76).

The relationship he refers to is an odd ménage in several ways, as
Catherine is independent (in the end too independent for Tom's
tastes) and lives alone for much of the time anyway. In their
'uxorilocal' relationship, Tom has moved in with Catherine in her
own flat. When the novel opens, Tom reappears after two years
away in 'the field' in Africa, and in his moving into the flat again
Catherine views his return largely in terms of the change it will make
in her household. She thinks of Tom's discarded thesis pages
littering the floor, and the reappearance of the small African statues
which he owns and which she abhors.

When Tom actually arrives to take up residence again, she seems to value his company mostly because he provides a passive audience. She chatters on at him about the bay leaf she is putting in the beef dish, or the stone lions they see on their walk through the suburbs to the Swans' house for tea. Catherine senses that she annoys him by her fantastic turn of mind – she knows this irritates him, for Tom expresses his displeasure. Further, in sexual terms it seems a passionless relationship. Tom is not particularly kind to her, or even, it seems, attracted. Her bohemian clothes repel him, her inventiveness bores him, and her calmness during his loss-of-faith crisis (regarding anthropology, not religion) angers him. All of these cumulative discomforts for Catherine underscore the fact that she is a supplicant for Tom's love, receiving only the 'priceless gift' of the man, in Mark's terms, in return for a fairly inclusive gift of home and hearth.

Other heroines offer different gifts in exchange for a man. Mildred in *Excellent Women* intends to proofread manuscripts and to cook meals for Everard, Jessie Morrow in *Jane and Prudence* offers certain unspecified and highly suspect favours to Fabian, Dulcie in *No Fond Return* gives academic skills in order to 'help' Aylwin in his work; both Ianthe in *An Unsuitable Attachment* and Leonora in *Sweet Dove Died* offer places to live to John and to James.

Some of this bartering can be linked to a maternal urge, as in Harriet Bede's 'cherishing' of young curates in *Some Tame Gazelle* (*STG*, 7). More often, however, it is an expression of the nature of romantic love, which is characterised by illusion, infatuation, devotion on the part of women and indifference on the part of men. Pym invariably focuses on the 'uncertainties of loving', which provide a source of endless frustration for her spinsters, due to the inevitable fickleness or apathy of men. And this condition becomes chronic for her female characters because she presents a vision of love as it affects people throughout life. Though Pym's scope has been criticised as being limited in its lack of a portrayal of sexual passion or intensity, it is broader in another way: Pym shows love in the context of the ordinary woman's life, taking for her subject love in middle age, and moreover, in her heroines' imaginations, as they tend to think about romance more often than to live it out.

She understands the difficulties of love at this awkward age; it is a convenient myth that older people have no romantic feelings, a view she satirises in her comment on Deirdre's naïvety in *Less than Angels*. Her middle-aged spinster aunt, Rhoda, displays obvious attraction to the married clergyman Father Tulliver, seeming 'almost flirtatious', to Deirdre's disgust. The narrator observes at this point that 'She was as yet too young to have learned that women of her aunt's age could still be interested in men; she would have many years to go before the rather dreadful suspicion came to her that one probably never does cease to be interested' (*LTA*, 150).

By exploring infatuation in this middle-aged, spinsterly context, Pym displaces the subject sufficiently to approach it from a new perspective. One of her primary subjects is unrequited love, since excellent women often stand little chance of charming those they admire. And the disappointment inherent in this rejection is sketched in a way that avoids inviting either excessive pity or contempt for her heroines. In keeping with this aim, Mildred in *Excellent Women* represents the theme of a woman deluding herself into thinking that a man cares for her when no such felicity is possible. Her love for Rocky offers a prime example, as when she berates herself sharply for entertaining false hopes of him: 'I pulled myself up and told myself to stop these ridiculous thoughts, wondering why it is that we can never stop trying to analyse the motives of people who have no personal interest in us, in the vain hope of finding that perhaps [they] may have just a little after all' (*EW*, 221). In portraying this grief ironically, Pym risks making Mildred sound bitter and waspish; or, worse, self-pitying. Yet this sense of malevolent fate is balanced by Mildred's realisation that, in some sense, she has overstepped proper bounds by falling in love with a married man and by constructing false expectations.

Her feelings for Rocky are obvious enough to others that even at an early stage in her acquaintance with him Julian, the vicar, rebukes her as if she were beginning an affair. He first accuses her of having fallen in love with him, and then solemnly approves her objection that she cannot think of him because Rocky is already married: ' "So many people nowadays seem to forget that it should be a barrier" ', Julian says (*EW*, 44). Thus Rocky clearly poses a threat to Mildred from the time of her first acquaintance with him. Later, when she lets slip her remark about Rocky being ' "just the kind of person I would have liked for myself" ', William Caldicote is similarly shocked, and admonishes her with a recommendation not to marry anyone (*EW*, 69). The exchange gains significance for two reasons: first, because Mildred's infatuation lies so near the surface that it escapes on occasion almost despite her. Further, William's admonition reveals opposition of a different sort, regardless of the moral aspect involved. No one else wants her to be in love. More than the fact that Rocky is married, the others are shocked by the very mention of the fact that she has strong feelings.

The most curious part of Pym's treatment of this problem in *Excellent Women* is the fact that Mildred competes not only with Allegra, who becomes engaged to Julian, but with Helena, who is Rocky's wife. Since Mildred does not want to marry Julian, losing him to Allegra does not matter; but she has lost Rocky to Helena before the novel begins. As if to redress the balance, Mildred ends by marrying Everard, who is the prize coveted by Helena. This sort of exchange of suitors echoes very closely the kind of plot tactics Pym used in her earlier fiction, where the hero is later made to regret his indifference and the heroine is rewarded with a better man than the one she originally wanted. But this exchange is more subtle – one hardly notices it. For one thing, Mildred's marriage to Everard is not revealed until the next novel, *Jane and Prudence – Excellent Women* itself remains open-ended. At the close of the book Mildred contemplates a 'full life' between performing thankless tasks for Everard and playing the 'excellent woman' (slightly less excellent) to Julian (*EW*, 256). Her long experience as vicar's daughter makes her ready-made to continue in a slight modification of this role as vicar's wife, should she marry Julian. She would also be adept in dealing with the missionaries Everard meets in the course of his work in Africa. But what she really wants is to join Rocky in his country cottage, where he suggests they sit outside drinking an amusing little wine – a party which never takes place.

The exchange of Everard for Rocky is made still more subtle because Mildred's love for Rocky never emerges openly; her infatuation for him appears only indirectly. Interestingly, her only comments on love as it regards herself stress the fact that she feels she has not loved on a grand scale, and in consequence feels that she has missed an important experience. After Mildred's first crush, the banking clerk from a dim past, Rocky dazzles her. He actually appears to be charming, and his superficiality contributes to this image. He affects Mildred profoundly, transforming her during the course of the novel by his interest, nonchalant and glib as it seems. She dresses more attractively, as her friend Dora notices when visiting Mildred after a long absence. Mildred also talks more under Rocky's influence. Describing an afternoon tea with him she adds: ' "he made me feel that I was gay and amusing too and some of the things I said were really quite witty" ', which is an unprecedented admission from her (*EW*, 75).

Thus Rocky's arrival causes Mildred to stage a mild rebellion against ageing, or resigning herself to life without love. For Belinda in *Some Tame Gazelle*, one evening of Wordsworth with Henry every thirty years or so is sufficient; for Mildred, life is not so simple. She is secretly loathe to agree with Dora that after the age of thirty one does not care about one's looks any more. This objection has all the greater force because Mildred has formerly tried to hide herself in this role, labelling herself 'spinster', 'vicar's daughter' and 'excellent woman'. Even so, stirrings of unrest surface, as she envies Allegra's apricot-coloured make-up and Helena's snappy black dress. She attempts to become more like them; she buys a new hat and 'Hawaiian Fire' lipstick. Mildred Lathbury represents a study of middle age with hidden and unexpressed depths. Rocky Napier moves her to unaccustomed dissatisfaction, and disturbs her sufficiently to make her declare at one point that she wished she had not met him or Helena. In this novel Pym skilfully integrates the dual themes of the spinster's attempt to avoid emotion and the man's inevitable indifference to the heroine. The stirring of memory and desire which April brings is indeed cruel.

In a darker version of this conflict, Wilmet in *A Glass of Blessings* is similar to Mildred in her hopeless love for Piers. It becomes increasingly obvious from the direction of her fantasies that she is growing obsessed with him through the novel. The detective urge surfaces in her, a trait which always signals love in Pym's women characters: Dulcie in *No Fond Return* finds love 'a powerful incentive' for such research (*NFR*, 44). Wilmet longs to meet Piers' flat-mate and to see where he lives; she consults city maps one evening in order to plot a journey to his address. She is also moved to extravagant gestures when she is with Piers. At one point in the novel, she sees him in the park, and plans to run behind him and put her hands over his eyes, further confessing a desire to plunge in among the lupins. Piers literally steps aside to avoid Wilmet's gesture of welcome.

Where romance in *Excellent Women* is prohibited by Rocky's marriage, Wilmet's love in *A Glass of Blessings* is still more hopeless. The object of Mildred's affection may have a wife, but as she and Allegra agree, one ' "*does* see these broken marriages" ' (*EW*, 127). Yet the conventions of marriage do not pose the primary barrier for Wilmet and Piers, though Wilmet has a husband. She cannot begin to qualify for Piers' true romantic love because she is the wrong sex.

A woman's love for a homosexual man represents the most

extreme example of men's indifference to women's sexual attractiveness. Pym's novels explore the problems inherent for women
infatuated with homosexuals. These relationships in turn become
representative, since nearly all her male characters are indifferent to
women, and homosexuals represent only the most decisive men in
this regard. As a whole, the novels reflect the frustration women feel
in never being able to enter a man's world, or to be seen as
significant to men. Men are proof against feminine wiles and
seduction; women characters can only hope to tame men by feeding
them and enticing them to stay behind bars.

A primary stumbling-block for the woman in these cases is the
man's self-sufficiency. He does not need her. This frustration
extends to other matters besides sex alone. Pym wrote a revealing
reflection in her diary regarding Richard Roberts, the younger man
she became passionately fond of when she was in her fifties; this
sheds light on her view of the subject as a whole, as she reflects on
the difficulty of what gift to offer him: 'One couldn't really give him
anything that he hadn't already got. Not even devotion and/or love.
It gives one a hopeless sort of feeling' (*VPE*, 225). This need to give to
one's beloved forms the main theme in *A Glass of Blessings*, where
Wilmet longs to make a difference to Piers: ' "I hate to think of you
being depressed" ', she tells him, continuing, ' "If only I could help
you in some way!" ' (*GB*, 162). She later concludes that she has had
an effect on him: ' "I felt that Piers really needed me as few people
did" ' (*GB*, 163). This flattering view of her own womanly powers is
not entirely without precedent, stemming as it does from a time-
honoured chivalrous tradition which holds that 'lovely woman'
provides inspiration to man and civilises him by her graceful ways.[9]

Still, there is a fascinating twist to this role in Wilmet's
condescension towards Piers. She primarily intends to teach and
not to serve. Further, despite her insistence on her naïvety, she
make adroit and forceful attempts to direct Piers to do what she
wants.

Her failure to make something of him is underscored by the fact
that Piers does actually change, but that his transformation is due to
Keith in the role of lover rather than to Wilmet. Further, while she is
deceived by Piers on all points, the illusions are of her own making.
Her fundamental error is illustrated by her belief that the
anonymous Christmas gift she receives from Harry, another
admirer, is from Piers instead. Her constant meditation on the
significance of the gift reveals, more than anything else does, her

infatuation with him. The inscription on the box reads: ' "If you will not when you may, / When you will you shall have nay" ', and this becomes doubly ironic in light of her relationships with these two men (*GB*, 96). Coming as it does from Rowena's husband, Harry, the gift extends a direct invitation for amorous dalliance. He plays on a time-honoured *carpe diem* seduction theme: 'gather ye roses while ye may'. Wilmet's substitution of Piers for the suitor is a fundamental mistake, for he offers her nothing. This is not a question of timing, or of loving before it is too late, though Piers parodies Harry's insistence when he rings Wilmet one evening to demand that she come out with him that very night. With Piers, the problem lies not with timing, or with Wilmet refusing while she 'may', for he never intends to offer her romantic love.

Wilmet's suffering from this rejection consists largely of a feeling of private humiliation. As in Mildred's infatuation for Rocky in *Excellent Women*, no one else knows of her love or of his betrayal. He hurts her when he flaunts his relationship with his homosexual lover, Keith, and tells Wilmet coolly that she is not 'to blame' for what he perceives to be her ungenerous character: ' "Some people are less capable of loving their fellow human beings than others" ', he tells her (*GB*, 199). This is doubly cruel, since Wilmet longs to be intimate with him and to be ' "lovable" ' (*GB*, 190). Piers' rejection humiliates Wilmet. Still, she has been prudent in her love and has not revealed her feelings to him or to others. Thus it remains a private grief, not a public embarrassment. In this instance, then, the man's indifference proves not to be too disastrous, and Wilmet is able to create a relationship which includes both Piers and Keith. In addition, she becomes drawn further into the church community and turns more attention back to her marriage. The moral she points to herself is that her life can still be a 'glass of blessings' without Piers (*GB*, 256). Her relationship with Piers is central to the novel, but remains subdued, woven into a larger scheme.

In a later novel, Pym focuses exclusively on the theme of woman's love and man's indifference in a full-scale study of one such relationship. *The Sweet Dove Died* examines the relationship between an older woman, Leonora Eyre, and a younger man, James. The book unites several of Pym's earlier themes in a stark, almost nihilistic treatment. Its main subject is possessiveness, illustrated by a tag from a Keats poem which Ned quotes to Leonora. The 'sweet dove' in captivity died of grieving: ' "Oh, what could it *grieve* for? / Its feet were *tied* with a single thread of my *own hand's* weaving" '

(*SDD*, 146, Ned's italics). Where Harriet in *Some Tame Gazelle* is seen feeding curates, and later appears in *An Unsuitable Attachment* leading a ' "tame curate" ' on a leash in Rome, Leonora goes one step further by imprisoning her dove in a cage (*UA*, 150). She arranges during James's absence on a trip abroad that he will move into the upstairs flat in her house on his return – another uxorilocal relationship in Pym's fiction. The novel depicts James's efforts to free himself from Leonora, which he does aided by his homosexual friend, the infamous 'Ned the American'. The dove does not die here, but escapes this particular captivity.

From James's point of view, Leonora's attempts to arrange his living quarters, furniture and finally his life and loves, seem restrictive. He notices bars on the window of his new flat – the room was formerly a nursery – and these emphasise its claustrophobic atmosphere and Leonora's maternal oppressiveness. Later on, he feels entirely confined when he lies ill in bed and Leonora has brought him a tray of food. He thinks: 'There was no escape from anything, ever. Now she was urging him to eat a few grapes' (*SDD*, 149). From Leonora's point of view, however, she seeks less to possess James than she does to give to him as one would to 'some gentle dove'. Still, her unwanted generosity becomes a form of manipulation, as can be seen when her overly extravagant birthday gift saddens and dismays James.

The Sweet Dove Died can convincingly be viewed as a *roman-à-clef*, with Pym as the Leonora figure and Richard Roberts, her young Bahamian friend, as James. Some superficial resemblances can be noted: Roberts did, in fact, collect *objets d'art* and at one time ran an antique store. Pym actually bid in person for (and obtained) a pair of china birds at an auction at Sotheby's, on behalf of Roberts' mother. Pym's letters and diaries evidence her anguish over the falling off of the relationship. More to the point, Pym herself drew a direct correlation between the novel and this relationship. In 1978 she wrote to their mutual friend Robert Smith in high spirits because *The Sweet Dove Died* was, after numerous rejections, at last accepted and published. She implies in her letter that this event provided a fitting end to – even a reward for – her earlier struggles: 'Little did I think that anything as profitable as this novel would come out of it', she writes (*VPE*, 321).

Despite this specific reference to the actual event, it seems to me that there is little direct correlation between the two friends and the two fictional characters. In converting this experience into art, Pym seems to have drawn from some of her cumulative feelings of cynicism about love which arose from consistent disappointments, and not to have taken her two major characters directly from this relationship. At most, Leonora seems to typify one particular aspect of Pym's character, serving as a counterpoint to her self-portrait in Belinda of *Some Tame Gazelle*.[10] As for the character of James, he is so bland as to have scarcely any definitive qualities at all. His main trait is passivity and a corresponding desire to please everyone. It seems most likely that Pym split Richard Roberts into the two characters of James and Ned, both of whom hurt Leonora in different ways and show different varieties of egotism.

Regardless of its origins, the novel is problematic in its treatment of romantic love and sexual passion. It is invariably stark and at the same time forced; in some ways it reads as if Pym were attempting to include some of the sex and modern 'swing' that had made the 1960s turn away from her 'kind of writing'. James, for instance, goes to bed with Phoebe Sharpe and later with Ned; still, Pym does not portray sex as a powerful or attracting force. James is passively pulled into the orbit of his two successive lovers, and does not seem to feel physical passion for either of them. Ned's great advantage to 'Jimmy' lies solely in his homosexuality; he is actually more manipulative and competitive for James's affection than is Leonora. In leaving Leonora, James abandons one captivity for another.

When she was writing *The Sweet Dove Died*, Pym referred to the novel in a letter to Philip Larkin as 'sinister and unpleasant' (*VPE*, 244). It represents an attempt to dramatise the maxim she set to admonish herself in relation to Richard Roberts, in other words, not to care any more, a lesson which Leonora must learn. Men will not, finally, submit to being tamed or cherished. James illustrates the tenet expounded by a minor character in the novel, a Miss Culver, when she tells Leonora: ' "The odd thing about men is that one never really knows . . . Just when you think they're close they suddenly go off" ' (*SDD*, 118). Still, despite its didactic tone, the book shows great poignancy and delicacy in depicting Leonora's grief. Both Leonora's suffering in this novel and Wilmet's in *A Glass of Blessings* offer variations on this recurring theme of unrequited love in Pym's work: the uncertainties of loving ultimately lead to the shock of certain rejection. Male indifference reaches its highest pitch in these two novels.[11]

Curiously, the men who generally attract Pym's heroines often seem flabby or shallow. One wonders why Emma in *A Few Green*

Leaves cares anything about that 'dull dog' Graham Pettifer, or why Leonora should love the consummately ordinary James with such intensity (*FGL*, 197). The alleged charmers in Pym's world – Rocky Napier, Fabian Driver, Tom Mallow and Aylwin Forbes – can each be classed with Rocky as 'really a shallow sort of person', as Mildred thinks of him. Despite these drawbacks in their objects of devotion, women cannot deny their fascination. Pym's relationship with Henry Harvey at Oxford seems to have exemplified this same attraction and hanging on against all odds. Pym declared in her diary at one point that she had finally become tired of this kind of relationship: 'I am beginning to feel the weest bit hostile towards Henry, and to think that the glamour of being his doormat is wearing off some' (MS PYM 102, fol. 54). In truth, she did not give up even then. Her heroines similarly tend to persevere in love, or, conversely, to allow themselves to be hung on.

Because of this inevitable disappointment, Pym's heroines must negotiate a way to live, to 'accept' their 'situations' of not being loved, and to create what cosiness they can from it.

Pym's fictional universe revolves around the fact that women must develop emotional restraint in romantic love. It is particularly difficult for them to retain their dignity as spinsters because everyone else either wants to deny them marriage (Mildred and Ianthe), to get them married (Emma, Penelope, Prudence), or in any case to define them exclusively in terms of marriage. In order to show how Pym ties the threads of spinsterhood and romantic love together, I shall conclude this chapter by considering *An Unsuitable Attachment*. This novel offers an astute, comprehensive study of singleness, and at the same time it also attempts a portrait of a romantic relationship which leads to marriage. In this it is unique among Pym's novels. Other of her heroines may marry or plan to marry, but in this novel the author depicts the entire courtship, including the wedding. More importantly, Ianthe is said to experience love in a deeply passionate sense – in a rare moment of abandon, she allows it to 'sweep over her like a kind of illness' – and she moves from spinsterly solitude to married companionship (*UA*, 147). Pym experiments in this novel with her conception of the spinster by focusing on Ianthe's transition and its effects on herself and on the community around her.

Ianthe begins the novel as a reserved, decorous spinster, recently freed from living with her widowed mother. She conceives of herself as an excellent woman, one of the ' "pillars of the Church" ', as Sophia enthusiastically describes her (*UA*, 195). Yet Ianthe also secretly thinks of herself as being like Emmeline Summers, the heroine of Elizabeth Bowen's novel *To the North*. This comparison points to the tendency in her that will lead to her loving John; Emmeline is similarly awakened from contented singleness to passion. Her lover, Markie, takes Emmeline's hitherto icy heart by storm. *To the North*, in Bowen's inimitable style, is an elegant, ironic, sophisticated novel; and in comparison, *An Unsuitable Attachment* seems mild and timid in its portrayal of romantic passion.

Where Emmeline is described as being elegant, remote and like an angel, Ianthe is simply a little faded. The other characters dislike her because she seems to them too good to be true; the reader may feel that Ianthe is dull. She represents single life creditably. As a spinster, she arranges her life well: she buys a small house and furnishes it attractively (she has ' "nice things" '), and heats the rooms properly (*UA*, 106). She fixes adequate meals for herself. Emmeline in *To the North* is similar to Pym's heroine in some respects; but while Ianthe works as a librarian, Emmeline, more exotically, runs a travel agency; and while Ianthe is a fairly ordinary 'excellent woman', Emmeline proves intriguing and ultimately hardly knowable at all – and, further, capable of dramatic passion. At the close of *To the North*, Emmeline destroys both herself and her seducer, while the end of *An Unsuitable Attachment* finds John putting up shelves in Ianthe's house preparatory to their marriage.

Emmeline never conceives of herself as a spinster, or indeed of the single state as a denigrating or peculiar position. Early in the novel she wonders if she will ever love, doubting that any relationship could offer more delight than that found in solitude: 'Nothing could be as dear as the circle of reading-light round her solitary pillow', she feels.[12] Her seduction by Markie is portrayed brilliantly, as it springs from her innate singeleness of purpose. Ianthe, on the other hand, exemplifies the typical spinster in Pym's fiction; when she falls in love with John, it entails primarily a change in her domestic life.

Most of the major characters in *An Unsuitable Attachment* are unmarried: Rupert Stonebird, Penelope Grandison, Ianthe Broome, Sister Dew, Mervyn Cantrell, John Challow, Daisy Pettigrew and Edwin Pettigrew. Even minor characters like Miss Grimes, Lady Selvedge and Sophia's aunt in Italy represent a shady sort of singleness. The only marriage present when the novel opens is that of Mark and Sophia, and their relationship is marked by Sophia's childlessness and compensatory doting on her cat, Faustina: ' "she's all I've got" ', says Sophia (*UA*, 138). Ianthe's uncle Randolph and his wife, who live in the fashionable district of Mayfair, are a parody of Mark and Sophia. While Sophia has her cat, Randolph's wife, Bertha, turns entirely in upon herself in hypochondria.

The novel provides, from one point of view, a study in the single life. The characters have some family ties, of course; Rupert always tries to establish relationships with precision from this perspective. ' "Penelope is the vicar's sister-in-law . . . And Ianthe is a canon's daughter" ', he explains at his dinner party for anthropological colleagues (*UA*, 128). The community of St Basil's parishioners is largely single and childless. Other single characters find their sexual pleasure (if any) in slightly odd ways. The aunt in Italy has her paramour, the 'Dottore', whom Sophia describes to Ianthe as her aunt's great friend, in fact, ' "the most, as Penny would say" ' (*UA*, 191). Lady Selvedge has, for her part, been bested by a more glamorous woman and divorced by her husband.

When the novel opens, Ianthe has limited her life to pleasant, manageable proportions, and her subsequent love for John takes her by surprise. Her counterpart, Penelope, forms a contrast to Ianthe's placidity. Like her fictional counterpart in the *Odyssey*, she shows patience and cunning, although Pym's character works, ironically, to attract suitors rather than to stave them off. In her egocentrism and cynicism about love, she combines vulnerability with hardness. The irksome nature of male indifference is transformed into a positive wrong here, as Penelope rails to her sister Sophia about her former lover's callousness: ' "It's a comfort when people do what they ought to do. Not like him", said Penelope bitterly' (*UA*, 15). Sophia, whose name means wisdom, tries to comfort her sister with the assurance that the man in question ' "wasn't good enough" ' for her, thus supporting female dignity (*UA*, 15).

This seems a typical dialogue in Pym's novels on the subject of unrequited love. But Penelope is unique among Pym's later heroines because she voices her hurt and anger so freely. She recalls Pym's earlier heroines, such as Flora in the unpublished Finnish novel, who rails at the apathetic Gervase. The later novel provides a more realistic setting for this rehearsing of outrage to occur; the man who did not 'do what he ought' never appears in the novel, and Penelope finds herself able to complain only to her sister. Their dialogue also hints at a seduction or use of sexual favours to attract and attach a man in the manner of Jessie Morrow in *Jane and Prudence*; but Penelope suffers the ill effects of being jilted more drastically and, moreover, fails to hold the man. Thus, in contrast to the too-perfect Ianthe, Penelope is irritable and unpleasant in her agonising over men. In the ongoing search for a husband, Penelope plots her attack with a measure of crudity which arises from desperation. She wears outlandish clothes to attract attention, and walks past the Anthropological Institute where Rupert might be found in hopes of a chance meeting. She does not love him in a romantic way, but rather shows, in her growing attention to him, the increasing desperation resulting from a seemingly hopeless search for a suitable husband. She suffers initially from 'humiliation and hurt pride' rather than from a disappointment of the heart, and those shocks of rejection continue throughout the novel (*UA*, 14).

Pym makes the character of Penelope unattractive and peevish in order to invite sympathy for her primarily because of her difficult position. Unrequited love can embitter women, or drive them to this state of distraction. Further, Penelope suffers keenly in the novel from Rupert's rejection notably because her conception of herself is acutely involved in his treatment of her. During their walk together in Italy she begins to weep because she realises he does not care about her, but his assurance that he thinks of her as a ' "jolly little thing" ' is the blow which humiliates her profoundly (*UA*, 182). Penelope longs to attain grand, tragic proportions. But no one takes her or her grief seriously. She weeps for herself, not for Rupert's love. Penelope illustrates Jane's observation in *Jane and Prudence* that 'the pride of even young spinsters is a delicate thing' (*JP*, 73). Spinsterhood seems a hopeless state to Penelope, not only because of pride, but also because of her need for love and affection.

Many of the single characters in the novel contemplate marriage, generally viewing it in a detached and studied manner. Rupert concludes one evening while visiting Ianthe in her house that he might like to marry her because he would like to have her always present as a decorative object. Further, she reminds him repeatedly of his mother. Mervyn Cantrell, her fellow library worker, goes so far as to propose to Ianthe because he would like to possess not her, but her things. He constantly appraises her furniture and belongings in this light; like the gentlewoman that she is, Ianthe has ' "nice things" ' (*UA*, 27). Only John Challow seems to want Ianthe herself, which is perhaps why she accepts him as a husband.

Oddly enough, Ianthe seems to be attracted to John in a maternal rather than romantic sense. When she goes to visit him in his boarding-house room when he is ill, she seems mostly struck by the squalor of his surroundings. She is indignant on his behalf: 'John loved beautiful things, she felt sure; it must be painful for him to live in such surroundings . . .' (*UA*, 116). And when the two do marry, naturally their arrangement is uxorilocal: the man comes to live in the woman's house.

Despite John's apparent interest in Ianthe, a trait which sets him apart from other men in Pym's novels, he strikes a jarring note in the courtship by his glibness. He is ingratiatingly familiar, always pressing personal questions on Ianthe. As the one male character in Pym's novels who does not seem indifferent to women, he shines by comparison with the other men in this regard. He seems less greedy than his rival Mervyn, less remote than Mark and less apathetic than Rupert. When Daisy Pettigrew meets the two lovers together after their engagement, she notes approvingly that John seems to gaze at Ianthe with obvious devotion. Love as portrayed in this novel is not always unrequited; if it is an illness, like flu, it is a benign disease and not a wholly crippling malady. For women in particular, it is a necessity; Sophia asks Mark, in all seriousness, ' "What is there for women but love?" ' (*UA*,152–3). Still, the romance between Ianthe and John seems thin and meagre.[13] The novel's title suggests that the book is about an 'attachment' rather than a passionate affair. The author implies by the qualification of 'unsuitable' that the couple in question are not suited to each other, but that they are so much in love that they determine to marry despite the opposition of various neighbours and relations. The parish as a whole seems to stand against the marriage.

But even this opposition fails to spark much controversy or create such tension as would reveal a strong spirit of determination in the lovers. Ianthe and John determine to marry and then do so, with a depressingly sober and conscientious consideration of the consequences. In marrying her hero, Ianthe becomes another variation of the modern Jane Eyre figure; Sophia confides to Rupert that she wished someone had stood up to prevent the marriage in similar manner during the wedding ceremony. But men remain protected by convention; everyone knows that they are inferior or unreliable, yet no one can accuse them.

The objections which other characters raise to the marriage illustrate a central theme in Pym's work: society regards spinsters as non-persons. In the others' view, Ianthe's house and possessions ought to be sufficient for her. Sophia finds herself shocked to discover that the 'trivial round, the common task' is not, apparently enough for Ianthe. Moreover, Pym suggests that Sophia's is a selfish viewpoint. In her speech to Ianthe in Italy, Sophia stresses not the joys of spinsterhood but Ianthe's usefulness in the parish, and her being a person ' "whom the church certainly couldn't do without" ' (*UA*, 195). Ianthe responds by recollecting that until recently she had entertained the same view of herself. She only realises the possibility for change in her love for John, and thus in this instance romance can be seen to exert a transforming power.[14]

The result of this attachment is that the grand passion between John and Ianthe does not seem very firm or promising. Perhaps the reason for John's 'unsuitability' is to emphasise not the blindness of Ianthe's infatuation – which is not entirely blind, as she can see fairly clearly what he is – but to underline her ability and right to choose her own life. The others are jealous of her attentions going elsewhere. Sophia and Rupert agree that Ianthe disappoints them by marrying because ' "one had one's own idea of her" ' (*UA*, 247). So the novel becomes less a depiction of love overcoming all obstacles than of spinsters choosing their own lives.

Pym presents a slightly eccentric view of love. In some ways, it seems that she severely diminishes the whole topic – how could people in love feel as little about each other as Pym's characters seem to do? But from another perspective, the study of romantic love in her novels rings with authority and conviction. Unrequited love is her great reality, and spinsterhood her true subject. The difficulties of middle age loom large, from a simply logistical point of view. By this time in life, she implies, possibilities are narrowing. As Dulcie reflects in *No Fond Return*, when she learns of Aylwin's marriage: 'People usually were married, and how often it *was* "in a sense" ' (*NFR*, 16). This bemused recognition suggests the tantalising possibility of breaking up a marriage in order to establish a new tie. But Aylwin's marked preference for young girls of nineteen over cultured lady indexers of an uncertain age shows this likely to be a vain hope. This is so palpable a reality in Pym's fictional world that her romantic happy endings tend to seem unconvincing.

In her depiction of scholarship as it relates to romance, Pym satirises her early adolescent extravagance in love in her middle-aged heroines. A tangential theme which proves no less important in her fiction is that one must subdue this tendency to love. Her spinsters learn to be decorous and 'drearily splendid' (*VPE*, 121). In a speculation and self-admonition in her diaries, Pym formulates a summary of this aspect of her work by observing that women must learn emotional restraint. Her particular mode of restraint consisted of drawing back into self-mockery – creating Belinda, and later Leonora, to embody and satirise parts of her own character. The giddy undergraduate chasing after Henry Harvey in the Bodleian Library is not after all so different from the lady novelist in Barn Cottage, knitting with a cat on her lap. She has a firm and shrewd sense of what infatuation is, and how it afflicts its sufferers – and further and most importantly, Pym does not follow the convention which decrees that passion disappears after the age of thirty. She captures this perspective in an observation prompted by reading an L. P. Hartley novel, which she noted in her diaries: 'Once a man, or a woman, for that matter, has tasted the heady brew of a strong personal attachment, especially in middle age, it becomes a necessity, an addiction' (MS PYM 66, fol. 9). This holds true for many of her characters, and explains the motivation behind their devotion in loving.

The author does not hope too much of relationships between people, as is clear from Letty's reflection in *Quartet in Autumn*, when she decides that people can only imitate the pigeons outside her office window, picking off insects. Still, the possibility of romantic attraction is ever-present, no matter how unlikely it seems. The tenuous relationship between Marcia and Norman in the same novel, for instance, illustrates this possibility. The two seldom say anything to each other. But something definitely binds them – from beyond the grave, as it were, Marcia engages Norman in an uxorilocal arrangement. He plans to move into the house she has left to him in her will.

Older women in Pym's novels do continue to be attracted to men – or at least some do. And Pym charts this nebulous but persistent pull: even spinsters have feelings, much as they may guard their solitude and strive for elegantly arranged lives. Some of her characters assert that spinsterhood is a positive, chosen state. In refusing his proposal, Harriet tells Mr Mold in *Some Tame Gazelle*, ' "I'm afraid my sister and I are *very* confirmed spinsters" ' (*STG*, 138). Pym's characters require, in all humility, 'something to love'; some tame gazelle, some gentle dove or some tortoise-shell cat can fill this role. Failing even this consolation, the furthest extreme of emotional deprivation can itself constitute its own positive state. Letty in *Quartet in Autumn* wonders if possibly 'the experience of "not having" [might] be regarded as something with its own validity?' (*QA*, 25). The cosiness of women friends is comforting, but not entirely fulfilling. One must endure the 'uncertainties' of loving, if one is to love at all – it is never a sure thing with men. Sometimes they just 'go off', as Miss Culver tells Leonora.

Thus Pym contributes to our view of life by speculating on this problem: singleness, rejection, loving, having, not having. And she sweetens it with a comic vision, by laughing at the steadier perspective which might, after all, come with time. One does attain more serenity, perhaps, as Belinda Bede has demonstrated from Pym's very first novel. The author describes a typical romantic relationship in her diaries with wry wit: 'Her memories of him were associated with delicious meals . . . is that how it turns out as one grows older? Interesting study – or does it depend on the people. Some with tears others [sic] with chocolate mousse in Balliol –' (MS PYM 40, fol. 20). Pym seems to have cherished both kinds of memories. She began as 'Sandra' and became a 'spinster', and this self-created transformation from romantic to ironist forms the heart of her novels.

4
High Church Comedy

As a chronicler of parish life in 1950s England, Barbara Pym stands unrivalled. Not since Anthony Trollope's Barchester novels about Victorian England has the Anglican Church received such minute and detailed treatment in fiction. The recent resurgence of interest in Pym's novels owes much to her recreation of a vanished upper-middle-class world, of which the church is an integral part. Each of her ten novels mentions the church in some connection, and several contain a clergyman as a major character and a vicarage and parish church as a setting. In a century in which satirisation of the church grows increasingly sharp and virulent, Pym's mildness seems surprising. Compared to the bizarre picture of the clerical world found in the work of Evelyn Waugh or A. N. Wilson, her fiction strikes one as tolerant and genial – and perhaps suspiciously shallow as a result.

Her approach has annoyed some readers. One contemporary reviewer spoke disparagingly of Pym's novels as comprising a comic vision that is 'elegantly grey rather than "high" – unless that adjective refers to their type of Anglicanism'.[1] This judgement is largely a matter of taste, and might possibly be altered by the recollection of the Archdeacon Hoccleve's 'literary' judgement day sermon ('Eliot! And for the evening congregation!'), or by Jane's view of the vicar Nicholas Cleveland: 'Beamy and beaky, mild, kindly looks and spectacles' (STG, 118, JP, 129). Indeed, another reviewer states that 'unlike most of the high comedy known to me, hers is funny'.[2] Moreover, Pym's themes bear critical examination for their treatment of religion in this particular setting, as her approach reveals depth as well as astuteness.

Pym's clerical world seems old-fashioned in its simplicity. The Church of England exists for time immemorial, past and future. Her fictional England is a place where people are, in Robert Smith's words, divided 'into those who do and those who do not attend their parish church'.[3] This view which Pym offers is reinforced by the fact that she stays largely among the laymen. An archdeacon figures prominently in her first novel, and a canon and his wife visit the vicarage in her third; but aside from these brushes with greatness, the lower orders of the clergy and their parishioners hold centre stage. The author concentrates on the daily tenor of religious life, on the humdrum nature of many of the tasks necessary to keep the church running, and on the very ordinariness of the people in it. And such an approach, which focuses on the surface, yields insight into the Church of England as it is rooted in national consciousness.

Contrary to popular myth, Barbara Pym was not a vicar's daughter, as some reviewers of her work have assumed. One might easily conclude that she had been one, judging from her convincing portrayal of Mildred Lathbury, the narrator of *Excellent Women*, who defines her entire character by her father's calling, and from the uncanny sympathy which Pym shows as a novelist for the Anglican Church. Her connection with Anglicanism was strong and enduring. In a biographical note about their childhood, Pym's sister affirms that the church was an integral part of the girls' early years. (Their father was actually a country solicitor.) Barbara Pym affirmed the importance which the church assumed for her personally in several interviews and talks late in life. She remarked on more than one occasion: 'Best things in life for me – English Literature and the Anglican Church – and I would hardly know which order to put them in' (MS PYM 95, fol. 32).

The Anglican Church forms a pervasive background in Pym's novels, as it formed one in her life. Pleasant, unobtrusive, comic and mild – the 'dear old C. of E.' is all this in Pym's fiction. She does not engage in the biting social satire which Dickens and Trollope pursued in their portrayal of the church. As reformers, they wrote energetically about such subjects as the misappropriation of charitable funds or the moral character of clergymen. Barbara Pym chose squabbles in the Parochial Church Council as her subject instead. She points up the little frictions among the ladies of the church over flower arranging or alludes cryptically to an 'unpleasantness between Miss Jenner and Miss Beard' in *Some Tame Gazelle* (*STG*, 64). As opposed to creating dramatic verbal confrontations, she achieves her most glorious comic moments when no words are even spoken: 'nothing "overt"', reports Mr Oliver to the vicar in *Jane and Prudence*, regarding the last PCC meeting: 'nothing had been said but the feeling was there' (*JP*, 64).

This indirectness is very much in keeping with Pym's fictional world and with her way of presenting it. Her subject is 'the little things in life', the small absurdities; and her works are 'miniatures', as Philip Larkin defines them. So it is a natural choice. What could provide a neater microcosm of society than a parish church? Her writing style reflects this obliqueness and delicacy. The gentle treatment which she accords the church is characteristic of her habitual understatement. One would not expect the agony and soul-searching of a Dostoevsky character in a Pym novel; nor yet would one look for the irony and terror of Joyce's Stephen Dedalus, who shivers over visions of hell and approaches the sacraments with trembling. The matter of salvation for her characters is an embarrassing, slightly puzzling necessity that is best left undiscussed; not because it is untrue or unimportant, but because it is ultimately seen as a matter of faith, which cannot be argued rationally.

A passage in *Excellent Women* illustrates this muted approach to theological issues. Mildred feels certain that the congregation gathered for a noontime service can benefit from the sermon, which her friend Mrs Bonner summarises disparagingly as ' "a lot of talk about *sin*" ', adding that she ' "can't believe we're really so wicked" '. Mildred describes her own spoken and unspoken response to this objection: ' "No, but we have to be made to realise it", I said unconvincingly, for we certainly seemed harmless enough' (*EW*, 51). Although Mildred cannot effectively argue for the theological tenet of total depravity, she can point astutely to the essential difficulty of faith: appearance is different from reality. Faith involves believing in the unseen; in this case, in the wickedness of harmless-looking people. The clergy as well as the laymen illustrate a measure of deception in this matter, as its 'emphasis on the humanity in which we all share' in *Quartet in Autumn* indicates (*QA*, 205).

Still, although its members seem to exemplify this paradox, the church as a visible institution remains crucial to attaining an understanding of spiritual truth. When Mrs Bonner goes on to speak in favour of the worship-in-a-garden school (' "I always feel the presence of God much more when I'm in a garden or on a mountain" ', she says), Mildred tries to forestall her (*EW*, 52). This conversation at cross-purposes typifies the characters' wariness in discussing the question of belief. In effect, Mrs Bonner does not really want answers, while Mildred's reluctance to lead the discussion further speaks for her sincerity. She refuses to argue about the issue because it does mean something important to her.

Throughout the novel, no serious intellectual discussion of religion takes place, emphasising a general indifference on the part of outsiders. Mildred, Helena and Rocky agree that the 'ardent convert' Everard Bone ' "knows all the answers" ' (EW, 54). But no one seems to want to know what the answers are, and the church remains, in Rocky's phrase, comfortingly ' "just where it is." "Wherever that may be", Helena added' (EW, 54).

Exactly 'where' the church is remains deliberately vague. And because of this unassuming acceptance of the Church of England as part of the natural order, it blends into the background of Pym's novels until it merges indistinguishably with their general setting. Its very pervasiveness tends to camouflage its centrality in Pym's fictional world and also its complexity. Its stability is emphasised by the fact that no one tries to defend it or to define its position further, much less change it. Through the church the author probes the essence of England itself, particularly in its relation to the Oxford Movement of the nineteenth century, which emphasised ritualism and antiquarianism.

She relates various themes through it – part of the 'miniaturist' aspect of Pym's fiction works to relate all of her themes. Thus the church serves to unite and provide a stage for a discussion of several universal concerns – love, death, learning, art, social class – yet also to distil them into a peculiarly Anglicised blend. Love finds ironic expression in the church, consisting usually of 'excellent women', Pym's term for churchly spinsters, doting on clergymen. This was an early subject in her work, as the early unpublished novel *Civil to Strangers* shows: a vicar advises all clerics to marry, insisting that a single curate is the ' "prey of every spinster in the parish" ' (MS PYM 5, fol. 150). Death is intimately connected with the church; memorial services are solemn occasions, and graveyards become a favourite spot in which many characters walk and pose. The traditional figure of the gentleman scholar cleric in eighteenth- and nineteenth-century England is parodied in Tom's dabbling in historical research in *A Few Green Leaves*, and in Archdeacon Hoccleve's literary flights of fancy in *Some Tame Gazelle*. Art and aesthetic taste become nearly inseparable from the essence of the church in the gourmet establishment which Father Thames enjoys at the vicarage in *A Glass of Blessings*. And distinctions between the classes may be obliterated temporarily within the parish hall, but any infringement of this privilege is soon stopped, as Mildred's cleaning women, Mrs Morris, discovers in *Excellent Women*. The Church of England provides a setting for larger conflicts and issues, yet it also remains a separate entity in itself.

In some sense, circumstances dictated Pym's choice of subject because of the specific group she chose to portray. Traditionally, upper-middle-class England is closely tied to the Anglican Church, so historical accuracy suggests that it be included in her fiction. Philip Larkin praises Pym's creation of the 1950s ambiance in England and comments on what he terms her 'unpretentious adherence to the Anglican Church'.[4] Her adherence to and also her treatment of it is unpretentious in that she generally incorporates religious issues as they relate to the church's day-to-day workings and to the lives of her characters. She represents the church in her novels more in social or historical than theological terms in order to make it serve as a metaphor for England and as a container for the preservation of British culture, aims which are primary throughout Pym's fiction.

For Pym's characters, Anglicanism provides a point of pride and identification, as in *Excellent Women*: ' "I was always church", [says] Mrs. Morris proudly' (*EW*, 23). The parish church forms a natural extension of the characters' lives. Even those who do not believe are conscious of its presence. Pym defines the church by describing what it appears like to outsiders and also by showing its response to antagonistic forces. For those who do not attend church, it still forms a constant background: Leonora in *The Sweet Dove Died*, for instance, is bothered and 'always' made to 'feel guilty' by the religious programmes which her neighbour Miss Foxe listens to on the radio (*SDD*, 26). Prudence in *Jane and Prudence* appropriates the church for one of her innumerable romantic fantasies, picturing herself first as a Roman Catholic, 'a black lace mantilla draped over her hair, hurrying into some dark Cathedral' (*JP*, 201). Before the fantasy has run its course and been rejected, she concludes: 'Perhaps the Anglican way was the best after all. It was the way she had been brought up in' (*JP*, 202).

Anglicanism symbolises all that is homely and essentially English to her, and this is true for several other characters as well. Rupert Stonebird jokes about his upbringing as a vicar's son in *An Unsuitable Attachment*, remembering his mother 'at the urn', and feeling that 'it would have seemed like living his life backwards to enter voluntarily a church hall full of women and cups of tea' (*UA*,

35). Dulcie in *No Fond Return of Love* comes the closest among Pym's characters to picturing herself joining in the community offered by the church from the outside. Though she is an unbeliever, she seriously considers Fr Neville Forbes's invitation to become part of his congregation; she imagines the flat she might have, the various church committee meetings she might attend, and the duties she might assume. In the end it seems distasteful to her: 'all that church work, with so little reward, might well become an intolerable burden – a thankless task, indeed', she decides (*NFR*, 251). Significantly, she also admits to herself that by joining the church she intends to substitute one brother for the other as an object of devotion, Neville for Aylwin. She rejects Neville's invitation to join the church in favour of Aylwin Forbes's proposal to marry. But the fact that she considers the choice at all indicates that the church could become a part of her life, and that as such it holds possibilities for those who are unbelievers.

Thus for polite agnostics, the church stands as a cosy, unthreatening presence linked with childhood memories – and with adoration of the vicar. For the parishioners themselves, the church represents a staid, firm, unremarkable presence. They go to church as a matter of course, and with very rare exceptions they seem to experience no great spiritual elevation from attending worship services. Still, the church can occasionally provide comfort through its solidity. Characters occasionally enter the church building alone in order to reflect, as Mildred does in *Excellent Women* during her moment of greatest crisis, when Rocky has moved out of the flat below hers. She goes to St Mary's in order to 'try to find a little consolation there' (*EW*, 167). Similarly, Tom the rector in *A Few Green Leaves* enters his church building in order to meditate. What the characters find in both instances are ladies who are cleaning the brasses or arranging flowers, as though in mockery of their desire for spiritual revelation. Mildred ends by feeling slightly foolish at Miss Statham's surprise and at her insistence that ' "it seemed a bit funny to be sitting here on a nice afternoon thinking things over" ' (*EW*, 168).

These episodes emphasise the prosaic aspect of the church. Both Tom and Mildred receive some consolation from having entered the sanctuary; yet the spiritual notion of standing on hallowed ground is undercut or at least offset by a solid physical sense. One is well aware of the cleaning, rubbing, polishing and flower-arranging that countless excellent women undertake. In addition to providing a sense of the empty building, Pym also alludes to the logistics which come into play when the congregation is present, by noting the self-conscious choice of its seating. Jane in *Jane and Prudence* tells Miss Doggett that 'clergy wives' have a specific role: ' "They have to be sitting there in their dowdy old clothes in a pew rather too near the front – it's a kind of duty" ' (*JP*, 69). Wilmet observes in *A Glass of Blessings* that the well-wishers who have come from St Luke's to attend Father Ransome's ordination are probably 'usurping the places of many of the regular members of the congregation' (*GB*, 251). The fact that the characters conceive of worship from such an ordinary perspective undercuts its sense of spiritual mystery and solemnity.

These irrelevancies and comic details assume great importance as they relate to the dignity of the church. *A Glass of Blessings* opens, for instance, with the sound of a telephone ringing during a church service – 'unsuitable', Wilmet feels (*GB*, 5). The novel reaches its climax as Bill Coleman's cigarette lighter efficiently strikes a flame on the Paschal candle. Such examples of slight incongruities abound. One of the strongest statements in all of Pym's novels which the church officially makes is the notice which Dulcie and Viola find in Neville Forbes's church in *No Fond Return*: 'Nobody, repeat NOBODY, is to tamper with the electric heating apparatus in here' (*NFR*, 104).

These comic details undercut the mystery of the rituals. How can the church seem holy and unapproachable when it is connected with such everyday matters? Moreover, how can clergymen be judged as good or bad when they are so ineffectual? And why should parishioners require exhortations to repent when they appear to be so shabby and harmless? The acuteness of Pym's perception lies in this apparent ordinariness and seeming puzzlement. She deals with religion in a kindly yet ironic light, and in creating a cameo which seems to describe only the surface, she is able to point to a number of important issues while hardly seeming to do so. Most importantly, she defines its essence by raising various objections against the church. The attacks are always minor, and occasionally even ridiculous; still, this subtlety proves effective in skirting a too-militant, too-passionate defence, while at the same time asking thoughtful questions. Barbara Pym's forte is high comedy – between tolerance and irony – and here she is at her best.

As earlier mention of Mildred's conversation with Mrs Bonner in *Excellent Women* indicates, Pym's characters evidence a profound reserve on the subject of religion. In *A Few Green Leaves*, Tom reflects that his excellent churchwoman Miss Lee would never doubt the Anglican faith because it would be unladylike to do so. She would be too 'well-bred' to trouble her rector, should she experience doubts (*FGL*, 202). In a diary entry in her own notebooks, Pym shows Letty of *Quartet in Autumn* commenting on religion with similar detachment: 'All Souls. If only, Letty thought, Christianity could have had a British, even an English origin! Palestine was so remote, violence on one's TV screen' (*VPE*, 275).

These responses reveal a curious slant in Pym's exploration of spiritual issues; almost a deliberate refusal to take the question seriously. Miss Lee seems shallow in her well-bred reticence, while Letty is nationalistic in a limiting sense. Christian faith as expressed by her Nigerian neighbour, Mr Olatunde, bothers her because it vibrates with exuberance and energy. These are not English virtues. She finds herself taken aback when she tries to describe her own 'sort' of belief to him, in a description that sounds like a refined brand of tea: 'How was she to explain to this vital, ebullient black man her own blend of Christianity – a grey, formal, respectable thing of measured observances and mild general undemanding kindness to all?' (*QA*, 66).

Two novels in particular show instances where Anglicanism is threatened and is called upon to defend itself: *Excellent Women* and *A Glass of Blessings*. The church sustains a mild attack in *Excellent Women* from the anthropologists; Helena shows contempt for it, although her hatred has more to do with jealousy because of her love for Everard than with any intellectual objection. Another interesting light is thrown on the church as viewed by anthropology in a snatch of dialogue from Pym's 'little notebooks', the basis from which she composed her novels. One scene shows a believer (who sounds very like Mildred of *Excellent Women*) arguing feebly against the familiar sociological argument which deplores preaching Christianity to people in other cultures. In the final version of the novel, only the first part of the conversation appears, spoken by Mrs Bone; Mildred's objection is omitted: 'A Lady talking about Africa and Christianity. "Of course the natives have their own religion which is much more ancient than ours. We really have no business to try and make them change it." "Oh, but it isn't the true religion", I said quickly and then felt a little embarrassed' (MS PYM 40, fol. 11). This dialogue rehearses the usual argument against missionary work. Yet in excluding Mildred's direct defence from the novel, and leaving 'all the answers' to rest unspoken with Everard Bone, Pym avoids ponderous explanations, while implying that they could be offered in full. As a result, her heroines can clearly be seen to worry about and even to speak of their convictions, and the fact that they are agitated by this argues for their sincerity.

It is not until *A Glass of Blessings* that the most serious challenges to the Church of England emerge, and other mystical alternatives begin to vie for attention. Wilmet, the heroine and narrator of the book, becomes the focal point for these conflicting demands or temptations, and the novel describes a subtle battle for Wilmet's soul. To begin with, this novel illustrates the role often played by the parish church in Pym's fictional world – it provides the unattached women with something to do. A constant undercurrent of her fiction is the refrain '*Something to love, oh, something to love!*' – and a second-best alternative to someone (though a clergyman often fills this role) is something to which to devote one's time and energy actively (*STG*, 17). The church fills this role for Wilmet; she has virtually no responsibilities, as she and her husband live with her mother-in-law. With house-keeping provided for, she has nothing to occupy her except to spend her own time and her husband's income. She begins the novel slightly outside the church circle, and in the process of being drawn in she is assaulted by various temptations which pose threats to the church: atheism, paganism and aestheticism.

These other influences are often linked to specific characters. The atheist faction is represented by Sybil Forsyth, Wilmet's widowed mother-in-law, and by Professor Root, who marries Sybil at the end of the novel. Their names reflect this classical influence; the Sybil of Greek legend is a prophetess who gives cryptic messages to the world, while Professor Root is, appropriately, an archaeologist, searching for past roots to present ideas. Wilmet imagines him and Sybil viewing Christmas in these terms, foreseeing: 'the dispassionate discussion of the significance of the festival, the Christian taking-over of pagan symbols and all the rest of it' (*GB*, 94). Sybil represents the voice of reason and logic throughout the novel. She defines her theological position from a strictly rational viewpoint: ' "I thought out my position when I was twenty" ', she proclaims, " 'and have found no reason to change or modify the conclusions I came to then" ' (*GB*, 14). This stance holds a peculiar attraction for Wilmet, who terms it 'courageous agnosticism' and admires her mother-in-law for holding such nihilistic views while she is nearing the end of life. In comparison with Sybil, her own religious belief seems faintly superstitious; she holds fast to religion as a hedge against death, valuing mostly its comfort and security.

Paganism impresses Wilmet still more than archaeological roots do. It is represented first by contact with nature, and later by the character Keith. Sybil's reverence for reason makes her unable to arrange flowers, and at one point she creates a table centrepiece out of dried leaves and branches that appears 'dead' (*GB*, 133). According to Wilmet, Sybil 'had somehow missed the point' in this endeavour (*GB*, 133). Wilmet, on the other hand, has 'a talent for arranging flowers', and arranges or admires sweet peas, laburnum and tulips throughout the novel (*GB*, 11).[5] Her most significant interaction with this vitalising force of nature occurs when she visits Mary Beamish at a church retreat house in the country. When Wilmet throws some pea pods on a compost heap in the garden, she imagines 'all this richness decaying in the earth and new life springing out of it . . . There seemed to be a pagan air about this part of the garden, as if Pan – I imagine him with Keith's face – might at any moment come peering through the leaves' (*GB*, 226). Oddly, this scene fails signally as an epiphany. Paganism here achieves little intensity or force, except as it bears on her ill-fated infatuation with Piers Longridge. The god Pan, in his manifestation as Keith, takes Piers for himself and leaves Wilmet with nothing except his own obnoxious and beautiful presence. Hence, he is a wicked sprite, serving only to point to Piers' homosexuality and not to fertility or love.

Thus paganism as either a classical, rationalist force or as a naturalistic force fails to pull Wilmet from the church. But when it appears in the form of aestheticism, it becomes the strongest means of creating disruption in the novel. Father Thames, Father Ransome and Wilfred Bason form a trio which plays out this conflict within the Anglican Church itself. Marius Lovejoy Ransome, as his name suggests, clearly possesses epicurean leanings. When he contemplates following his friend's example of going 'over to Rome', the influence which deters him from taking the irrevocable step is a low-class tea (egg and chips) on the occasion of his friend's admittance to the Roman Catholic Church. The vicar, Father Thames, shows a similar fastidiousness and refined palate. He ' "likes his glass of Tio Pepe before dinner" ', as Wilf Bason declares (' "as who does not?" '), and cannot 'take' Indian tea (*GB*, 238, 60). Moreover, he collects *objets d'art*, and this collection forms the basis for struggle in the novel and illuminates the shady middle ground between the impishness of paganism and the dignity of the Anglican Church. The statue that he brings back from Italy to adorn the church, for instance, is discovered to be too 'pagan' to be appropriate once it reaches England. One can apparently be led astray in the search for beauty.[6] Indeed, Father Thames's taste is felt to be a bit too rococo; Wilmet finds his Fabergé egg too sweet and fussy for her liking. Both Father Ransome and Father Thames possess superior taste, and Wilmet imagines the two of them competing in amassing greater and greater amounts of Dresden china.

The most flamboyant aesthete is Wilfred Bason, the vicarage housekeeper who forms a grotesque parallel to the two clergymen. Whereas Father Thames collects beautiful objects, Bason steals them. The first uproar in a series is caused when he covets and then wears fellow server Mr Coleman's specially tailored cassock during a service. As Bason's mild case of kleptomania is revealed further, we learn that he had earlier stolen a small jade buddha from the Civil Service office where he worked briefly, and he later ' "[pinches] the vicar's egg" ' or 'borrows' Father Thames's Fabergé egg (*GB*, 171, 183).

This strange series of objects which attract and fascinate Bason reveal an odd aspect of his character. His aesthetic tastes are (by himself) much touted. He may prepare 'almost a shepherd's pie' as a variation on fried octopus and other delicacies, but scorns it: ' "Twice cooked meat is something I don't think much of" ', he tells Wilmet (*GB*, 181). We have it on the very best authority that he is a remarkable cook. Adam Prince, the gourmet critic in *A Few Green Leaves*, reminisces several years later about the Father Thames ' "set-up at St Luke's" ', and highly endorses Bason's talents (*FGL*, 93). But Bason's increasingly dogmatic assertions about what is good and what is bad make it clear that he has merely appropriated for himself others' tastes in fine food in the same manner that he coolly takes their belongings. The jade buddha reveals a leaning towards exoticism – ' "the wisdom of the East" ', Sybil calls it (*GB*, 177). The incident of the cassock borrowing, which Bason has obviously noticed, though he claims he has not, typifies his chameleonic character and his desire to act different roles. He is a not very successful imposter.

Paganism as it appears in these different guises attacks the church during the course of the novel. But in the end most of the disturbing elements vanish, leaving Father Bode as vicar of St Luke's. Father

Bode, here to 'bide' or stay when the others leave, represents the saintly ideal of simplicity and humility. He alone among the ménage at the vicarage is content to make do with the status quo. While Father Thames yearns for an Italian villa and acquires Dresden china, and while Father Ransome (so regrettably unstable) considers going over to Rome, Father Bode shows no ambition for change. With typical economy, he asks the former housekeeper, Mrs Greenhill, to mend his pyjamas. The old is good enough. And he helps his parishioners; Mary Beamish describes him to Wilmet as ' "the best" ' in helping her after her mother's death, being 'full of *practical* sympathy' (*GB*, 126).

Thus atheism, paganism or aestheticism do not overcome the Anglican Church. The end of the novel finds Wilmet and Rodney moving away from an atheistic household to a flat which is closer to St Luke's, and Wilmet joining in decorating the church, with Father Bode installed in Father Thames's place.

A more serious challenge to the church's authority is the influence of the Roman Catholic Church. Pym treats the subject lightly – Jane Cleveland in *Jane and Prudence* makes a joke of Mr Oliver's change from the moderate parish church of which Nicholas is vicar to the neighbouring 'High' church of Father Lomax: 'Friend, go up higher', she thinks, on hearing the news (*JP*, 211). But the question raises a profound theological issue.[7] Mark Ainger in *An Unsuitable Attachment* considers it sufficiently important that he warns his congregation against Roman influence periodically. During his trip to Italy he contemplates a sermon to this effect: 'perhaps another "Why I am not a Roman Catholic" would be salutory for him as well as for them', he thinks (*UA*, 144).

At its historical roots, the issue refers most directly to the Oxford Movement in the nineteenth century, and particularly to the figure of Cardinal Newman. Mildred in *Excellent Women* at one point reads a biography of him and expresses ' "great sympathy" ' for him (*EW*, 141).[8] The isolation Newman endured as a result of his leaving the Anglican Church is parallelled in the corresponding figure of Marius Ransome's friend in *A Glass of Blessings*, who cuts himself off from his Anglican community by converting to Catholicism. On leaving the Church of England he has nothing left but a solitary holiday, where he ' "will take long walks over Exmoor and try to think out his future" ', as Marius Ransome says (*GB*, 210).

Pym's constant referral to this peculiarly Victorian religious issue emphasises the anachronistic nature of her treatment of modern

England. Over a century after the Oxford Movement began in 1833, her characters still worry about Romish influence and fear the implications of incense and other ritualist trappings of worship.[9]

Catholicism also exerts an appeal to Pym's Anglican characters because it represents a cosy group. The episode in *An Unsuitable Attachment* which sets Mark Ainger onto his favourite topic anew is observing the group of Catholic priests and nuns who are travelling with the party from St Basil's on the same flight to Rome. The Catholic party buys a suspicious number of 'little bottles' of spirits on the plane, and on arrival are accorded obviously favoured treatment at the airport, being whisked off by fellow churchmen (*UA*, 142). Such ostentation is not English; it is not in good taste, and seems finally as unsuitable as the attachment between Ianthe and John, which is intended to form the largest incongruity in the novel. To further satirise the danger represented by Catholicism, a fellow passenger in the subway speaks disparagingly of nuns to Ianthe: ' "It gives me the creeps and I know it frightens the kiddies. I mean it's *not very nice*, is it" ' (*UA*, 136).

These comparatively minor objections obscure the fact that 'higher' worship comprises a threat in the minds of several characters. The danger suggested by a leaning towards 'Rome' stems from a distaste which may even be fear of an institution and customs which are 'not English'. For many Anglicans it is not even a question of externals: nuns who wear habits, or forms of worship. The Anglican 'High Church' itself is characterised by elaborate rituals and processions, incense, even masses in Latin – in effect, by worship which seeks to involve the sense and the spirit in contemplation of God.[10] Not that all Anglicans would like the means. Yet neither are they all luxury and sensuality. Father Lomax in *Jane and Prudence*, for example, insists that his parishioners follow the more rigorous disciplines of the Catholic faith as well, including confessions and obligatory masses (*JP*, 55). Yet many of the characters fear it as subversive because it works against a sensible, sober view. Exaltation is suspect; it can lead to too serious a commitment, perhaps even to joining a nunnery. The Anglican hallmark is moderation and temperance.

Another important result of the Oxford Movement, or Tractarianism, is the interest it sparked and to some extent created in looking to the past for inspiration, and in the renewed reverence for ritualism. This did not spring directly from the Tractarians, but worked in tandem with it. The heated Victorian controversies about elaborate sacramental worship still reverberate in Pym's fiction of the 1950s. A further result of the antiquarian aspect of the Oxford Movement was the renewed interest in church buildings, which are so lovingly decorated by excellent women in Pym's novels. One church historian, sympathetic to the Tractarians, writes in 1925 about this influence, and the fact that the church building enshrines an 'invaluable heritage': 'The tender reverence with which we are accustomed to treat our old church buildings at the present day, the trouble we take and the expense we incur in their preservation and restoration, are largely an outcome of Tractarianism, and of the spirit revived and generated by it.'[11]

Barbara Pym's comedy is related especially to the High Church, not least over this question of 'Rome'. But it is not merely High Church, and it shows a keen awareness of feeling in her time about an institution, the Roman Catholic Church, possessing somehow a mystique that was suspiciously alien.[12] A Romish influence serves to define what is English by contrasting it with that which is foreign. Thus Pym creates a tension between the two elements of 'Anglo' and 'Catholicism'. The 'catholicity' or universality of the church remains a firm tenet for her characters Mark and Sophia Ainger in *An Unsuitable Attachment*. Yet the Anglican way is always 'best after all' (*JP*, 202). The comedy lies in the conflict between over-seriousness about the issue, with its resulting pompousness, and the still more shocking stance of indifference and agnosticism. Pym's evident affection for the church allows her to satirise it with warmth rather than with rancour, and this results in a shrewd comic perspective.

Another element that relates closely to the church, though not in an antagonistic way, is English Literature.[13] It does not compete with the church, but forms a dialectic with it. For the author personally, the two were strongly linked, as her remark about the Anglican Church and English literature indicates. Both together comprise the 'best' in life, and she 'would hardly know what order to put them in' (MS PYM 95, fol. 32). For many of Pym's characters, the two create a dialectic where each reinforces and redefines the other. Poetry and fiction offer a structure or meaning similar to that provided for her characters by religion; while it does not usually replace religious belief, it invariably works together with it. In addition, the picture of the church offered in fiction by other authors plays a significant role in shaping her characters' conception of it. The church incorporates texts into itself and also views itself critically as it is reflected in literature.

The importance of English literature in Pym's novels can hardly be overstated, and its significance to her treatment of Anglicanism proves no exception. Pym connects the two together at an early stage in her writing. In a long satirical poem composed while she was still in her teens, she created the following vignette, where a 'curate on a motorbike' enters:

His sermons are the passion of the Town,
Snippets of poetry to help em down [*sic*].
Too much Theology makes ladies ill,
His motto is, 'Give sugar with the pill' (MS PYM, fol. 14)

This little scene cleverly mixes the two ingredients in a symbiotic relationship which works to the detriment of both. Theology comprises the 'pill' – a salutory but bitter remedy – while poetry forms the 'sugar' – a delightful yet frivolous aid to the necessary philosophy. Henry Hoccleve in *Some Tame Gazelle* later brings this preaching strategy to a pitch of absolute perfection, with the result that his congregation heeds neither the poetry nor the theology. His 'famous sermon on the Judgement Day' alarms his audience at first, until they detect his familiar *modus operandi*, of a series of long quotations strung together with a few explanations from the archdeacon: 'It was just going to be one of the Archdeacon's usual sermons after all. There had been no need for those uncomfortable fears', the congregation concludes (*STG*, 109).[14]

Poetry acts as a constant counterpoint to faith. Mildred in *Excellent Women* quotes a line from a hymn or a Rosetti poem interchangeably in order to embellish her point. The importance of literature is further illustrated by a conversation in *A Glass of Blessings*. Wilmet seems alarmed and threatened during a conversation about poetry with her friend, Mary Beamish, appearing to be almost as embarrassed as if they were actually discussing matters of faith. Wilmet draws back in horror when Mary quotes a line from a de la Mare poem, and immediately denies her own interest in poetry, insisting that she prefers flighty novels instead. Wilmet's discomfort stems less from reverence for poetry itself than from its personal significance to her – this makes it something not to be spoken of. Wilmet feels outraged that she must share her source of meaning with anyone else: 'I could not bear to think that she might have read my own favourite poems', she complains (*GB*, 84).

Poetry also assumes significance because it represents an extension of Victorian thought in a post-Matthew Arnold era. Pym shows the effects of Arnold's substitution of art for religion. Her characters derive much of their philosophy of life from art. Those who do not believe, like Dulcie in *No Fond Return*, express deep sympathy with Arnold's poetry about isolation, particularly with 'Dover Beach'. Those who are Anglicans similarly hold poetry in high regard. Winifred Malory, the vicar's spinster sister in *Excellent Women*, keeps 'by her bed a volume of Christina Rosetti's poems bound in limp green suede' (*EW*, 40). Thus English literature and the church fill the same role. Both provide a structure for living that can be imposed to give expression, coherence and stability to a sometimes desolate existence.

Literature assumes importance to individual characters within Pym's fictional world, and also to the author herself in creating that world. She justifies her own method by contrasting her presentation of clerics with that of other authors. One specific example occurs in *A Glass of Blessings*, where Sybil describes to Wilmet the satirisation of the clergy in a play which she has attended:

'But how the audience loved it! How they roared with laughter when the vicar entered through the french windows at the back of the stage.'
'Was it funny, then?' I asked.
'The vicar's entry? Not particularly, He just stood there, holding his hat in his hands and blinking through his spectacles. He reminded me of your Father Bode, but it brought the house down.' (*GB*, 175–6)

In constructing this scene, Pym implicity defends her own treatment of the clergy by contrast with that of the playwright. First of all, the choice of a figure such as Father Bode as a target for satire rings hollow in the dramatic production. It is made to seem vulgar – not because the man does anything irreverent, but because the writer trades on the cleric's calling alone in order to make him comic. Pym's own presentation of this sort of character creates a much more complex – and interesting – figure. His saintliness is made endearing in Pym's novels by her allusion to his humanness: forgoing the customary two teaspoons of sugar in his tea during Lent constitutes a real penance, regardless of what it reveals about his aesthetic tastes. Further, she suggests in Sybil's comments that writers can easily satirise clergymen by virtue of their calling: the entry was not funny, yet the audience laughed. Conversely, Pym presents a more searching view of the humanity of the clergy which none the less respects its high calling and the difficulty of its task. Pym also suggests the possible danger of reading – or misreading – about the church in fiction in *Jane and Prudence*. When Jane and her husband first arrive at their new vicarage, Jane expects the villagers to behave in the manner of a Victorian novel:

> 'I feel that a crowd of our new parishioners ought to be coming up the drive to welcome us', said Jane, looking out of the window over the laurel bushes, 'but the road is quite empty.'
> 'That only happens in the works of your favourite novelist', said her husband indulgently, for his wife was a great novel reader, perhaps too much so for a vicar's wife. (*JP*, 15)

In addition to illustrating Jane's fancifulness, this passage also creates an illusion for the reader that Pym's novel is 'realistic' in comparison to Trollope's, which is fictional because so well arranged; his parishioners enter on cue. But the most interesting aspect here is the effect of Jane's illusory expectations within the realm of the novel. Though she has become disillusioned with the life she originally pictured for herself from such reading, she still feels that she has failed in life because she compares herself to fictional characters, or to the art of another age. She models herself on earlier heroines, conceiving of herself as one of those fictional Victorian clergymen's wives who were 'gallant' and 'cheerful' and who 'ran large houses and families on far too little money and sometimes wrote articles about it in the *Church Times*' (*JP*, 8). Her romanticised view of poverty is not offset by Trollope's more sober one. His ideal clergyman proves himself ready to forgo worldly goods, but his act is seen as a sacrifice and a hardship. In *The Warden*, the first of the Barchester novels, the main character resigns his post as warden of a hospital because of a fine moral scruple and point of conscience. In doing so, both he and his daughter relinquish a large salary and are forced to live on more slender means. Moreover, in the case of the Crawleys in *The Last Chronicle of Barset*, poverty is never presented as anything other than a crushing load and a terrible degradation. Mrs Crawley, to whom Nicholas later compares Jane, suffers cruelly from being poor, and this comparison forms part of the ongoing dialectic between the church and literature.

Finally, in a spirit of comic genius, Pym satirises the stories which the church tells about itself. In *Excellent Women*, Mildred read a serialised story in the parish magazine which soars into realms of absurdity, centring on 'some just cause or impediment which prevented the clergyman from marrying the girl', and so on. (*EW* 218–19). The connection with the Victorian serialised novel is marked here. The story as she summarises it reads like a parody of a Dickens' plot, with a mystery that is intended to create suspense and to tantalise the reader. The set-piece above all illustrates Pym's love of the ridiculous, and her consciousness that the Church of England does not provide a promising setting for fiction, and can all too easily become melodrama. Further, her own portrayal of the church verges on this sort of absurdity – her characters do snub each other at jumble sales, and her clergymen do abstain from marriage. In effect, Pym satirises her own choice of subject here, and adds one more perspective to the continuing dialectic between literature and the church.

Another influence on the Anglican Church – in this case an adverse one – is simply attrition. Pym documents this change most fully in *A Few Green Leaves*, her last novel, where the congregation has dwindled drastically. Tom, the rector, reflects that he can 'rely' on only a few people to attend Evensong (*FGL*, 6). More significantly, he has largely been replaced in his priestly function by the medical doctors in the village. Emma, the heroine of the novel, observes that there are long lines at the surgery but not at the rectory; no one wants spiritual advice. The threat posed to the church's function by the medical profession in Pym's last novel is anticipated by her reverence for Dr Strong in *Quartet in Autumn*, when Marcia's last moments before death are illuminated by the high priestly figure of the surgeon. Tom Dagnall's is not the only empty church. Father Gellibrand in *Quartet in Autumn* thinks regretfully of the impracticality of a 'Kiss of Peace – turning to the person next to you with a friendly gesture'; both Father Gellibrand and Edwin perceive the ritual as a kind of mockery since it can only be carried out among the sparsely scattered group of five or six in the church (*QA*, 15).

The Anglican Church does come into its own on occasion. In *A Few Green Leaves*, the church has been almost abandoned by the community as a whole, yet the rector presides with dignity over the funeral of Miss Lickerish, as the entire village gathers for the service. In performing these rites, Tom gains an equality with Dr Gellibrand – both meet on equal ground in the mausoleum, and in ushering Miss Lickerish into the next world, Tom has the final word when she moves beyond the help of a physician.

The church is buffeted by several elements – paganism, atheism, aestheticism, 'Rome', English literature, attrition and a corresponding reverence for the medical profession. Still, many of these factions become assimilated in the church rather than destroying or replacing it. Further, their very casualness in affecting church life points to a dilemma. No malevolent force seems to be intent on harming the church through these influences; where do they come from, then, and can the process of continued dissolution be reversed, or is it inevitable? The observations which Pym makes about social change in the novels are not particularly new or striking in themselves, but her subtle treatment of them illustrates their insidiousness and, ultimately, their profoundly human nature. The enemy is not Wilfred Bason, with his penchant for beautiful things, nor is it Martin Shrubsole, the young village doctor in *A Few Green Leaves*, who would like figuratively to replace Tom Dagnall by moving into the rectory. If the Church of England has withered, no one can be blamed. There is no villain in the case.

Pym charts a decline and fall of the Anglican Church. Throughout her novels, vicarages that were once full of children now house single clergymen or childless couples, and no one can be persuaded to come to Evensong. Moreover, people outside the church must now support it. This situation occurs as early as Pym's first novel, *Some Tame Gazelle*, where Ricardo donates marrows to the garden fête and attends the Anglican Church in hopes of ingratiating himself with his beloved Harriet. In Pym's last novel, *A Few Green Leaves*, it is discovered with some astonishment that one of the ladies who regularly 'does' the flowers never attends services. Several characters in the novel who likewise do not attend church appear at the vicarage to offer jumble.

Curiously, clergymen in Pym's novels seldom seem to worry about the diminishing numbers of the congregation or the decreasing influence of the church in the world. This placidity suggests either naïvety or apathy. Yet at the same time, it shows an unshakable confidence in the Anglican Church as an institution destined to outlast all time. Within Pym's fictional world, this confidence stems from a consciousness of what the church contains, and thus of what can enable it to withstand battering from without. It need not fear adverse cultural influences because its primary purpose is in fact to enshrine them – the Church of England acts as a repository for England's past and continues to collect new additions for its storehouse of knowledge. The Anglican Church is deeply rooted in tradition, and in national consciousness. Its dominion extends to the vicarage, to the graveyard and to a whole complex of thoughts, feelings and ideas. And as such, it becomes a container for the heart of English civilisation by gathering together a vast number of physical items, intellectual ideas and spiritual ideals. What it contains determines what – and 'where' – the church is.

First and foremost, the church contains paraphernalia. The solid physical aspects of the church building are often mentioned in Pym's novels, including brasses (polished by 'excellent women'), an eagle lectern for the reading of Lessons (brass or wood), pews and kneelers (usually not assigned, although characters have favourite ones) and heating apparatus (the regulation and enjoyment of which are jealously guarded). Hence the buildings take on a physical surface in which mundanity and ordinariness is stressed. The church may be hallowed ground, but it still demands a steady offering of fresh flowers and tins of Brasso.[15]

In addition to these fixed items, festivals and holy days invite offerings of flowers, fruits and vegetables. The church is presented as predominantly a woman's world. The precise rituals attached to decorating the church for such occasions parallel the strict hierarchy and territorial feeling observed among clergymen in neighbouring parishes.[16] The woman who assumes the role of overseeing the decorating of the church is as exalted and powerful in her own sphere as an archdeacon would be in his. The doctor's ascendancy over the cleric is reinforced in *A Few Green Leaves* by the fact that Mrs Gellibrand, the doctor's wife, takes charge of the group of women who are arranging flowers for a festival. Her indifference deeply wounds Daphne, the rector's sister, who is keenly aware that her own position as vicar's sister is being usurped: 'It was hurtful, that kind of thing. Tears came into Daphne's eyes as she stood there, waiting to be told what to do' (*FGL*, 79).

The church also collects parishioners, those of greater social stature naturally being regarded as the greatest prizes. Archdeacon Hoccleve in *Some Tame Gazelle* attempts unceasingly to secure Lady Clara Boulding for his own congregation exclusively. Members of

Nicholas's congregation in *Jane and Prudence* feel cheated because Mrs Lyall, their MP's mother, attends the Roman Catholic church; they console themselves with the thought that ' "*we've* still got Mr Edward" ', her son (*JP*, 20). Nicholas himself feels that he has failed grievously in not preventing Mr Oliver's loss to Father Lomax's higher church, confessing to Jane that he feels he has ' "failed there" ' (*JP*, 212).

In a parody of jumble sale collections, Father Thames in *A Glass of Blessings* collects antique *objets d'art*. The parish hall sports several (chipped) Della Robbia plaques, and the church itself contains statues. The church also collects gravestones and memorials which assume great significance for members of the congregation. The graveyard is often chosen as a fitting background for characters wishing to strike a contemplative pose. The archdeacon languishes among the tombs in *Some Tame Gazelle* in order to mark his connection with the eighteenth-century model of the scholar clergyman, quoting bits from Young's 'Night Thoughts' to whomever will listen.[17]

The graveyard serves a similar function in *Jane and Prudence*, when Fabian Driver places a photograph of himself on his wife's grave in lieu of a marker, thus revealing his sublime egotism, as her grave becomes a monument to himself rather than to his dead wife. Further, he reflects with satisfaction on his fantasy of a plaque placed in the church to honour himself. Mildred's meditation in the sanctuary in *Excellent Women* shows her drawing comfort from the contemplation of such memorials, even though they are recent – 'no weeping cherubs, no urns', and so on (*EW*, 167).[18] Memorials put one in mind of one's own mortality, but also of the piety of past ages, and the church's function as an archive for the purpose of instruction is evident here.

The church's most assiduous and ongoing collection is that of jumble. Since it does not receive sufficient money for its expenses from donations alone, it accepts those items which no one wants; all clothes sift down eventually to the final denominator of the jumble sale table. In addition, all of the flotsam and jetsam of the Victorian period seems washed up onto jumble sale tables, particularly in *Excellent Women*. The Victorian fondness for photographs is reflected in the large number of them sent to the sale. In addition, the Victorian penchant for household decorative objects surfaces in Lady Nollard's famous stuffed birds, always a popular item. Mildred remarks to Winifred that the Nollards' house ' "must be quite bare of birds"', judging from the number she routinely donates (*EW*, 43).

Jumble sale items are second hand and distinctly second best, forming the opposite extreme to the antique *objets d'art* which connoisseurs collect. In a further distinction, the gifts given to clergymen are always new and of the best quality. *Some Tame Gazelle* stages a minor popularity contest which is based on the offerings given by various excellent women to their clergymen. Father Plowman openly competes with Archdeacon Hoccleve on this score, glorying in the wealth of his own offerings and infuriating the archdeacon by casually giving him an extra pair of slippers, which his huge taking renders excessive. Harriet Bede makes a life-time profession of doting on curates, and a steady offering of fresh fruit, cakes and pots of home-made jam finds its ways to the lodging of the resident curate. Such gifts achieve immense significance in the rivalry for clerical favour; Olivia Berridge's gift of a pair of hand-knitted socks to the curate secures him as her husband.

These examples illustrate the tangible outward side of church life, which in turn reflects its corresponding collection of intangibles as well. Because this physical matter embodies and symbolises the past, its accumulation forms a record or history. Thus in an existential sense, and in its sacramental role, the church regulates the significance of time past and present. The church calendar gives meaning to the year, as Edward's consciousness of the round of festivals and special days demonstrates in *Quartet in Autumn* (*QA*, 73–4).

The Church of England also collects texts and records. Archdeacon Hoccleve constructs his famous 'literary' sermons almost entirely of quotations from poetry, while Tom in *A Few Green Leaves* pursues historical research in consulting seventeenth-century burial records in church registers. He attempts to imitate Anthony à Wood in preserving details of twentieth-century culture by keeping a journal of his own and by interviewing the villagers. Thus the church contains the past and English heritage by preserving them and by continuing to regulate time's cyles.

The church also collects souls – in a very circumspect way. In Trollope's *Last Chronicle of Barset*, Mrs Proudie tells her husband, the bishop, that the church ought to be pre-eminently concerned with caring for ' "the souls of the people" '. This phrase terrifies him: 'The bishop shook in his shoes. When Mrs Proudie began to talk of the souls of the people he always shook in his shoes. She had an eloquent way of raising her voice over the word souls that was qualified to make any ordinary man shake in his shoes.'[9] Where Trollope satirises excessive zeal in the particular character of Mrs Proudie – she does, in fact, cause a great deal of trouble in the novel through her forcefulness – Pym touches on the theme extremely lightly. Julian Malory in *Excellent Women*, for instance, exhorts Mildred to ' "say a word" ' to her unbelieving neighbours, fixing her 'with what [she] privately called his "burning look" ' (*EW*, 16). But Julian is sincere as well as comical, and evinces a kindness which Mrs Proudie so notably lacks. This contrast emphasises the difference between the two centuries, as well as between the two authors. Julian's methods are gentle and persuasive, though they can also be direct, as when he confronts Helena and says he hopes she will return to Rocky. Mrs Proudie's way of proceeding, on the other hand, is harsh; she intends to humiliate others and succeeds in this aim.

Pym's clerical world is fundamentally different from that of Trollope's, which assumes church allegiance as a matter of course. No conversions are necessary in Trollope's Victorian provincial England, since everyone is at least nominally part of the church.[20] No conversions are possible in Pym's novels. Father Ransome tells Wilmet in *A Glass of Blessings* that he only visits regular parishioners of St Luke's, as there is no hope of persuading others to come. Mark Ainger in *An Unsuitable Attachment* finds similar unsuccess in his work among the West Indians in his London suburb, who decline to attend church at St Basil's. Rupert Stonebird and Everard Bone both convert strongly and dramatically, but these decisions are private and almost accidental. Interestingly, both of these conversions are seen in light of their Anglican upbringing. Everard speaks for himself and Rupert in *An Unsuitable Attachment*, when he says that they 'recovered' their 'childhood faith' (*UA*, 128).

Another intangible entity collected by the Anglican Church is confessions. Because this institution is a mark of 'High' leanings, it is not always well received by the parishioners. Daphne shudders in *A Few Green Leaves* when she recalls that Tom had once tried 'to introduce that kind of thing – most unsuitably – in the village', a movement which the offended villagers firmly resisted (*FGL*, 22). The confessional is only as effective as its supplicants allow it to be – both Father Thames and Father Bode hear confessions in *A Glass of Blessings*, but Wilfred Bason, who sins in a specific way by stealing Father Thames's Fabergé egg, is never called to account for his theft.

He is treated with indulgence. Since the confessional symbolises the discipline of the church which attends its privileges, this episode once again underscores the dangers inherent in aestheticism. In a comic twist, the function of the confessional is displaced to the vicarage, where parishioners rush to tell the latest bit of news. In *Jane and Prudence*, Miss Doggett flies directly to the vicarage when she suspects Jessie's attachment to Fabian. In *A Glass of Blessings*, the practice seems to have grown to such proportions that Father Thames apparently becomes annoyed. He posts a sign on the vicarage door instructing supplicants not to ring 'unless on *urgent* business' (*GB*, 106).[21]

The church gathers thoughts, confessions, ideas, news and spiritual meditation, providing a centre for these to collect and to crystallise. Thus it becomes a repository for the past, as well as for history as it unfolds.

The church never attains omnipotence in Pym's fictional world. In contrast to Trollope's Barsetshire novels, where the church comprises almost the entire sphere of influence, except for the remote yet effective powers in London, Pym sets her Anglican Church among various foreign elements, where it forms an unobtrusive part of the fabric of English village life. Moreover, the church is so central to provincial culture that it can even transplant such a culture to the metropolis. Mildred remarks in *Excellent Women* that her experience of London is almost identical to that of the village she came from in the country, and that 'perhaps it is only a question of choosing one's parish and fitting into it' (*EW*, 11). Even in London, the church itself remains a constant presence in Pym's novels. Its quietness and loss of influence in the larger world tend to obscure its centrality and its function as preserver of English culture. As the constant comparisons with 'Rome' suggest, the Anglican Church is, above all, British. The gravestones, memorial tablets, flower arrangements, excellent women and cossetted clergymen form part of the nation's backbone.

Pym's love of trivial details which appears in all of her novels extends to the minutiae of church life. And in this modern era, particularly, the opportunity for grand statements and displays of heroism have, she implies, vanished. In *Jane and Prudence*, when Nicholas mourns Mr Oliver's departure from his congregation, Jane comforts him with a philosophical reflection: ' "What can any of us do" ', he asks, ' "with these people?" ' Her answer mingles humour and resignation: ' "We can only go blundering along in that state of

life unto which it shall please God to call us", said Jane' (*JP*, 212).
The two continue to rehearse their disappointments by drawing
comparisons between their situation and that in Trollope's *Last
Chronicle of Barset*, concluding that ' "it hasn't turned out" ' like that
(*JP*, 212). Nicholas teases his wife by comparing her to Mrs Crawley
– ' "How you would have stood by me if I had been accused of
stealing a cheque" ', he says – but there are no Josiah Crawleys to
play martyr in Pym's clerical world, and no Barsetshire
communities to persecute them (*JP*, 212).

Trollope concludes his six-volume study of Victorian clerical life
with the following apologia:

> . . . my object has been to paint the social and not the professional
> lives of clergymen; and . . . I have been led to do so, firstly, by a
> feeling that as no men affect more strongly, by their own
> character, the society of those around than do country clergymen,
> so, therefore, their social habits have been worth the labour
> necessary for painting them . . .[22]

Although Pym follows in Trollope's footsteps by writing about the
inner workings of the church, she does not share his assumption
that clergymen 'affect' those around them 'more strongly' than
anyone else does. Her clerics exert little direct influence on society,
though those within the church may look to them for guidance. In
writing about the Church of England, Pym focuses on its
parishioners as closely as she does on its clergymen. She moves
easily through different aspects of church life, from the vicarage to
the sanctuary to the parish halls full of 'chipped Della Robbia
plaques [and] the hissing of gas fires and tea urns . . .' (*GB*, 229). She
offers a comprehensive view of church life from a deliberately
limited – but significant – perspective, declining to recreate
Trollope's broad scope. His fiction ranges from the racking poverty
of the brickmakers and their wretchedly poor parson to the grand
wealth and power of the bishop's palace. For her, such
inclusiveness is not appropriate. Pym does not pursue, as Trollope
does, the goal of social reform in her novels, nor is she intent on
exposing shocking injustices. Father Thames of *A Glass of Blessings*
refers once to the imminent formation of a study group which will
' "go *very* thoroughly into the South India business" ' – but,
typically, the group never materialises (*GB*, 8).

Still, the quietness of Pym's vision of the church world enhances rather than detracts from a sense of its crucial place in the framework of the novels and of its significance to England. The Anglican Church as she presents it lacks spiritual intensity. Yet it gains in stature through its persistent, even magnificent presence. The church becomes a fixed entity for Pym's characters, who see it with eyes accustomed to its familiarity and dulled to its significance. Pym characteristically describes her fictional England by diminishing her subject. This tactic is particularly noticeable in her treatment of anthropology and of the church; in addressing these subjects she could easily transcend the immediate bounds of England. In the spiritual realm, the twentieth century has its share of martyrs to recall, and anthropology offers infinite possibilities for the exploration of social issues and of other cultures. But she chooses instead to show the ascendancy which the church gains in her characters' imaginations because of habit and dumb physical presence. Its very comfortableness and ordinariness ultimately form part of its power.

As for the matter of religious faith, the novelist cautions a similar reserve. The best course is not to say too much; how can one express the inexpressible? When Deirdre in *Less than Angels* declares at the dinner table: ' "I don't really know that I believe in it all anymore" ', she senses immediately that it is 'rather childish and in bad taste' to discuss such a serious matter with such flippancy (*LTA*, 79). One may either believe or not believe – reticence is all. Furthermore, Anglicanism can transcend even disbelief and achieve a solemn dignity of its own. Pym creates a High Church comedy which succeeds because it is, above all, comic. The novels offer a human comedy rather than a divine one, and they offer a detached and amused perspective rather than an intense one. Yet this approach yields its own interesting speculations. As Father Ransome observes, ' "it's the trivial things that matter, isn't it?" ' (*GB*, 86).

5

Anthropology

From one point of view it was simply an accident of circumstance that Barbara Pym began to write about anthropology in her novels after 1950: in 1946 she started work for a group of anthropologists at the International African Institute in London. From another perspective, the discipline suited her writing style so exactly that it became a natural extension of talents she already possessed, and furthered her development as an artist. Returning from her term with the WRNS in Italy during the Second World War, she began work at the IAI, initially doing tasks such as indexing and proofreading, and eventually becoming an assistant editor of the journal *Africa*. The job immersed Pym in a new field of study and introduced her to a new set of people. Taking what was close at hand for subject matter in her novels, in *Excellent Women* she created characters who were anthropologists, such as Everard Bone and Helena Napier, both of whom had ' "[trailed] round Africa" ' collecting data, and she set some of her scenes in a building which housed learned societies (*EW*, 9). In addition to providing material for her novels through bringing her into contact with anthropologists, the discipline of anthropology itself became increasingly important to Pym as a novelist. She grew to think of herself and to describe herself as employing its research techniques in her fiction. In interviews and talks near the end of her writing career she spoke of engaging in 'field work', of employing an anthropologist's 'detachment', or of practising a sociologist's 'technique of observation'.

Inevitable links existed between her anthropological work and her fiction writing, because the two competed for her time and attention. In letters to her publishers about work in progress she constantly refers to the slowness of her writing due to her full-time employment. In a letter dated 10 December 1949, Pym wrote the following to an agent who was trying to place some of her short stories: 'I hope to be able to send you some more stories before very long, but as I am working five days a week as an anthropological research assistant, I don't get as much time for writing as I would

103

like' (MS PYM 163/1, fol. 5). In a retrospective summary of her
writing career, she told a group of fellow authors that she had hoped
at one point to support herself entirely by writing fiction, but had
been unable to find a sufficient market for her work. Hence she was
forced to combine two careers.

In some ways, it was a comic marriage. Many of the drafts of her
later novels are composed on the backs of carbon copies of
correspondence sent out from the Institute. One side might consist
of the carbon copy of a letter from Barbara Pym, editor of the journal
Africa, acknowledging receipt of an article or return of proofs, or
inquiring to what address she should send the twenty-five free
offprints? It saves money to recycle paper in this way, she implied in
one interview; and it also bespeaks a certain modesty. The author
does not take herself as seriously as she did in her younger days,
when she extravagantly bought clean notebooks in which to
compose.

The Institute clearly valued Pym and her work. An obituary notice
of her death which appeared in *Africa* in 1980 is touching and
protective. Noting Pym's inability to find a publisher for her work
between 1961 and 1977, the article concludes that she abandoned
literary puruits entirely during this time and vowed she would
never write another novel (whereas she continued to write fiction
and to contact various publishers). It also assumes that she found
full compensation for the temporary eclipse in her literary fortunes
by devotion to her work: 'For the next fifteen years she held to her
resolve, directing her literary talents into her careful and
conscientious editorship of *Africa*.' And one does feel the honour of
undertaking this noble employment, as the writer goes on to
describe 'that scrupulously produced, prestigious and prized-by-
the-budding-scholar journal, the IAI's *Africa*'.[1]

The writer's tribute is most gracious, and his appreciation of her
novels warm. One feels she would have been pleased – and possibly
amused. Her editorial work was important to her; but she thought of
herself primarily as a writer. 'In any case I am not really happy
unless I am writing something', she wrote to Jonathan Cape in 1956,
in reply to his inquiry about work in progress. She further assured
him: 'so you can be quite sure that I shan't give it up!' (MS PYM 163/
2, fol. 307). The tension between office work and creative work
resulted in a curious blending of identities for Pym – she is both
anthropologist and novelist, or, combining the two, social satirist.
Her discussion of appropriating anthropological techniques in

writing novels seems at times naïve and simplistic; none the less it remains an important comparison because she thought of her own creative process in this light. Further, though it would be exaggerated to imply that work among the anthropologists made Pym into a successful novelist, her writing did undergo a distinct transformation after she began to work at the IAI, and this suggests at the least that anthropological influence was a positive one. In addition to other changes, the development in her writing can be observed particularly in the portrayal of foreign cultures in her fiction. Not only does her treatment gain in subtlety and authenticity, but it in turn enhances her picture of England.

Further, anthropology and fiction form an apt synthesis in many respects: Pym's innate love of detail and of odd quirks of civilisation, her scrupulous description, the whole enhanced by her sense of the absurd, made anthropology a fitting subject for comedy because she could employ a clever reversal. In the way that Rocky invites Mildred to 'observe the anthropologists' in *Excellent Women*, Pym similarly invites the reader to indulge in the same vicarious pleasure of watching those who make observation their profession. We can catch them at their own game. Thus she reverses an expectation by satirising the anthropologists, or observing those who observe others. Again, as in her treatment of other academic fields, she shows a wonderful and witty grasp of the competitive spirit of scholars and a corresponding consciousness of class structure, which is eminently appropriate to a discipline which thrives on kinship diagrams.

Another influence of anthropology on Pym's fiction can be traced in the change from her earlier work in her treatment of foreigners, particularly in an early novel set in Finland, and another which describes a trip to Hungary. In later novels, she shows more tolerance for other cultures and more subtlety in portraying them. In part, this graciousness is achieved through directing most of her attention to England itself and avoiding foreign settings. Yet at the same time, the focus on England is sharpened by the consciousness of a mysterious, heathen world which surrounds civilised England. It serves to define British culture more clearly, as well as to provide its own alternative target for satire. If the English seem silly on occasion, the French or the Americans are much more ridiculous.

Pym's fiction shows a definite strain of nationalism. But this is modified by the anthropologist's more detached and earnestly interested perspective. In the anthropologist's view of his profession, traditional concerns about governing the vast British Empire give way to the more analytic view of social scientists who seek primarily to understand, rather than to govern, distant lands. Pym's fiction reflects this perspective. The novelist, too, is more interested in culture than in politics. The para-culture to which she alludes becomes a significant background note, and never a primary subject. She does not follow her characters 'to the field', but only allows them to report their experiences later. Curiously, Pym's anthropologists become so focused on their particular corner of study that they seem to have no interest in their own native culture. Perhaps this is left to the novelist to explore.

Thus the anthropological strain in Pym's writing bears directly on her portrayal of English culture. She writes in the tradition of the realistic novel, acting as a social historian in her meticulous notation of detail and physical surface. She saw her own method of composing as observing life around her and taking from it the exact events which comprise her fiction. She prized the little notebooks in which she jotted down scenes and ideas which she then boiled up and reduced, '"like making chutney"'.[2] This replication of atmosphere, setting, food, clothing and numerous other details of the texture of life, serves as a record of life in England during the time she wrote. Yet it also provides more than a record of what people ate and wore at one point in time; the author shows its cultural significance. As a result, her portrayal of England is akin to the anthropologist's study of daily customs and rituals in his chosen culture. Whether specifically in the tradition of anthropology or not, Pym uses the novelistic technique of defamiliarisation, making the familiar seem strange by presenting it in a new light. Her emphasis on a narrow sphere of subject matter and on trivialities allows her to offer a particular perspective on her own culture.

Thus anthropology provides for Barbara Pym a world to describe; eccentric anthropologists and learned societies form a subset in her fiction. And it also reaffirms confidence in her instinctive way of describing it – anthropologists would agree that in interpreting the essence of society, the 'little things' are important. As Lord David Cecil observes, Pym provides 'an acutely observed record of English life in her time'.[3]

In Pym's early fiction, foreign cultures appear mostly in order to contrast with and to justify – ultimately to show the superiority of –

the English. For the most part this justification defends and exalts English women. The nice English girl is repeatedly contrasted with rapacious foreign men and sexy, designing foreign women. The young English person, male or female, has only to go abroad to Finland, or Budapest, or Italy, to be besieged by either rakes or temptresses. Much of this theme stems from a vital personal interest on the part of the author: Henry Harvey was abroad. Harvey, Pym's great love from Bodleian undergraduate days, left for Finland to lecture at a university after going down from Oxford. Her fiction from this period reflects definite nationalist leanings, as might be expected. Pym comforted herself in her diaries with the reflection that she was valued by her German admirer Friedbert, whom she had met on her student travels, if not by Henry: 'The Germans at least appreciate me if the English don't', she boasts (*VPE*, 41).

And in the same way, much of her early fiction is devoted to illustrating the tenet that English girls make infinitely superior wives. The heroine in Pym's unpublished novel *Civil to Strangers*, Cassandra, exemplifies this perfection both in her devotion to her husband – she is an ' "excellent housekeeper" ', as he acknowledges – and in her attractiveness to the Hungarian man, Mr Tilos, who moves into the village and begins to court her (MS PYM 5, fol. 148). (The Hungarians appreciate Cassandra, if the English do not.) At one point he gives a perfect homily on the excellence of British women as wives, confessing to himself that he has never met with their like anywhere before in the world.

Civil to Strangers illustrates not only the desirability of English wives, but their propriety as well. Cassandra's breeding and her nationality stand her in good stead as she rejects the advances of her suitor: ' "We don't have lovers in Up Callow" ', she tells him firmly (MS PYM 5, fol. 204). The overall attitude towards other cultures in this early work is perhaps best summed up in the reflections of a minor character, Mr Gay, who experiences 'sudden thankfulness' as he recalls his good fortune in being 'an inhabitant of Up Callow, and not of Budapest or Monte Carlo' (MS PYM 5, fol. 351).

In the same way that *Some Tame Gazelle* was composed ' "for Henry" ', much of Pym's other early fiction seems to have been written about him either directly or indirectly, and her portrayal of foreign cultures can be seen in this light (MS PYM 103, fol. 5).

Still, along with whatever other war-related changes affected the author, including unhappy love affairs and returning to civilian life in England, her work at the anthropological institute seems to have contributed to a sharper and more sophisticated view of society. Her middle fiction after this point – the revision of *Some Tame Gazelle* and the six novels which follow – are substantially different in tone from her earlier work. One may speculate on the changes in her outlook produced by contact with her employers; they provided her with subject matter, as the presence of several anthropologists in *Excellent Women, Less than Angels, An Unsuitable Attachment* and *A Few Green Leaves* indicates.

Some themes from her early work continue and are blended in to suit her new subject matter. Relations between employers and employees have some universal elements in common which affect office work in all disciplines. As in her treatment of the academic world in relation to Oxford and to English literature, romance remains closely tied to scholarship. For the anthropologists, this phenomenon assumes the same sad yet comic forms, because love inevitably means unrequited love: Deirdre's *tendre* for Tom in *Less than Angels* and Helena's passion for Everard Bone in *Excellent Women* are equally intense yet hopeless. As in Pym's treatment of other academic fields, women generally continue to serve men in minor capacities.

While one cannot accurately guage the effect of her work at the IAI on Pym's writing, some direct influence of anthropological subject matter and techniques can be traced in her 'little notebooks' and in her subsequent fiction. Much of the change in her style is as much literary as anthropological in influence; still, the two reinforce each other. Beginning with the revision of *Some Tame Gazelle*, which she undertook just after starting work in London, her style becomes sharper and crisper. Tedious comic bits and interminable quotations are pruned away, and foreigners in her fiction are no longer simply caricatures.

A specific incident which illustrates this change is the scene in *Some Tame Gazelle*, where the Bishop of Mbawawa illustrates his missionary work among a particular African tribe to the English villagers. After its metamorphosis in the revision of the novel, this episode becomes a high point of the book. Pym heightens the comic aspects of the slide show to the hilt – the bishop's quavering song and huge mask, Harriet's upside-down slide, the villagers' wonder and mystification. In addition, Pym employs her background of anthropological knowledge to further the comedy. Edith Liversidge accurately analyses one tribal custom which the bishop describes obliquely by naming it outright: ' "Phallic", murmured Edith, nodding her head. "Quite the usual thing"' (*STG*, 181). Pym also deepens her satire in this episode by emphasising the cultural problems which attend missionary work. Belinda wonders to herself whether the natives might not have been unnecessarily forced into adopting a European civilisation along with embracing the Christian religion. Pym's political satire is gentle, rather than scathing; still, she does raise the issue of the white man urging his own culture on that of the natives. Describing the British characters in sartorial terms throughout the novel – the archdeacon in soberly coloured socks, Harriet in her old tweed coat, Connie Aspinall in fluttering dresses, Agatha Hoccleve in 'good' silks – Pym extends the question of clothes to the Africans as well, who are seen in the slides to be ill-clothed for their climate and temperament.

The revised version of the novel, published in 1950, evidences a new precision and deftness of touch, which may be attributed in part to Pym's new interest in anthropology. Further, a more direct influence of the discipline can be traced in the conception of 'field work' which she gleaned from her anthropological colleagues. The 'little notebooks' from which she claims to have culled her novels from 1948 onwards usually reflected a wide variety of thoughts – spinsterhood, love and loneliness are frequent subjects, mixed with quick sketches of people and snatches of dialogue. Physical details abound as well, usually having to do with food. She might describe a short menu of greengages and French bread, for instance, or a 'revolting' one-dish meal in the oven made of potatoes and beans.

Perhaps the main connection between anthropology and Pym's creative process lies simply in the existence of these notebooks. Since she began composing them at roughly the same time as she began work at the IAI, they would be linked in her mind with that event. Some of the early notebooks contain remarks on academics, such as the following: 'Essays presented to Prof. X – why are they all so obscene?' (MS PYM 40, fol. 23). Yet for the most part, anthropology and novel writing combined in an harmonious whole, where no single theme seems to predominate.

In exploring the treatment of anthropology as a discipline in Pym's fiction, I shall begin with an example of the author's reference to anthropology in her late, unpublished 'academic' novel. The heroine, a young faculty wife named Caro, visits her sister, who is a sociologist living in London. While watching fellow passengers on a subway, Caro practises what she thinks of as her sister's 'technique of observation' as though she were 'storing up useful material' (MS PYM 23, fol. 124). Caro is largely interested in physical details of appearance; she notes a Burberry, a briefcase, greying hair in the other passengers around her. Yet she concludes her observations by speculating on the inner experience of her subjects, asking 'When did the joy begin to go out of their lives . . .?' This question combines a melancholy, emotional outlook with a scientific one. She seeks to locate a precise time. Yet the cause and effect she charts rests on a dubious romantic assumption, that the characters did possess 'joy' at one time.

A further problem in drawing such conclusions about others lies in how much one can know of another's life. Can Caro – or any novelist – or Pym herself – accurately understand and represent others? In order to mitigate this difficulty, Pym borrows from sociological terminology in order to validate her own work and her method of writing. She assumes that if one can see outward signs, one can accurately interpret their root cause and infer their meaning. Caro seeks to interpret meaning from external signs, as the sociologist might. But in this instance she sees herself as part of the flux and not detached from it; she shares 'life's journey', as she titles her subway ride, with her fellow passengers. This identification with the others invests her with some authority in analysing others' lives. Though her conclusions about others might rest on speculation alone, she knows her own experience, and thus can project beyond it.[4]

This approach emphasises Pym's minimising of her fictional world. She reduces it to recognisable quantities: the biscuit which Miss Trapnell offers Miss Clothier in *Jane and Prudence*, for instance, or the 'pale-blue-rimmed interestingly-shaped spectacles' which Prudence wears at the office (*JP*, 36). These details make the novelistic world seem solid and substantial. And as each of these details is intended to do, it symbolises some significant aspect of civilisation. The offer of the biscuit is ceremonial and ritualistic, as is the donning of the spectacles. These acts reveal something about the characters – their conception of themselves and their relation to each other. In the same way, the detailed description of the monotonous day-at-the-office which *Jane and Prudence* presents in this chapter typifies this aspect of Pym's style: details act as signifiers and as concrete examples of underlying, meaningful structures. The routine which her description of the work day catalogues in detail suggests an entire picture of office life.

Emma Howick's list of villagers in *A Few Green Leaves* shows another sort of anthropological influence similar to that of Caro's observations in the 'academic' novel. An anthropologist by training, Emma catalogues the members of the small Oxfordshire village into which she has just moved, according to their rank in the social structure. She sees them in terms of their roles – doctor's wife, vicar's sister, and so on. Pym lays bare the foundations of her novel by listing the cast of characters, much as she would do for herself in the early stages of composition, thus revealing to the reader the status of the various characters through this combination of description and analysis.

Thus Pym appropriates anthropology as a discipline in order to give shape to her own perspective. She implies that an anthropologist might proceed in this detached fashion and might pay similar attention to details and their significance. Further, this way of writing extends to her satire of the anthropologists themselves. She studies them as a group. Early in *Excellent Women*, Helena invites Mildred to hear Everard and herself deliver a paper at an anthropological meeting. Rocky makes light of the affair: ' "Yes, Miss Lathbury, you and I will sit back and observe the anthropologists", said Rockingham. "They study mankind and we will study them" ' (*EW*, 36).

Life in communities comprises Pym's primary subject, and this choice accounts in part for the fact that her books seem as though they are composed by a Victorian novelist writing – by some accident of time – in the twentieth century. Given their slight volume, her novels include a relatively large number of characters. Such abundance delighted her. ' "Oh, but I love a crowded canvas" ', says BP [*sic*]', Pym scribbled in an early draft of *A Glass of Blessings*, at the top of a page which lists characters as they are evolving in the novel (MS PYM 17, fol. 34).

Yet for the most part, the world she creates in her novels seems very small because it is homogeneous. Her canvas is crowded with the same sort of characters: upper middle class, educated, mildly intellectual and introspective. Pym's range seems limited when compared to the correspondingly vast canvases of George Eliot's *Middlemarch* or of Dickens's *Bleak House*, which reach from servant classes and beggars on the streets to aristocrats in stately houses. Pym narrows her field to a provincial setting, to a parish, to a suburb, and in the case of her study of anthropologists, to the premises of a learned society. Still, the world thus defined yields a study of social and moral distinctions as finely tuned as those of Pym's Victorian predecessors.

Where social classes are kept widely separated and distinct in Victorian fiction, Pym compresses consciousness of class structure into a deceptively narrow sphere. This reflects the changing times, to some extent; the Victorians seem obsessed with defining one's place in the scheme of things in terms of wealth and social class. Modern feeling may be equally strong, but it appears to be more subtle. Remnants of the old order remain in Pym's novelistic world, as in the predominance of distressed gentlewoman, or those who are displaced and homeless. Pym, like Dickens, thinks of the poor and needy. This breakdown in class structure is most clearly illustrated in *A Few Green Leaves*, where the loss of the landed family which provided a 'centre' to the village is keenly felt. *Quartet in Autumn* presents a study of a quasi-socialist society, where everyone is ostensibly protected by the 'safety-net' of the welfare state. And as early as *Jane and Prudence*, Mr Oliver argues about political views with Mr Mortlake and Mr Whiting.

But most important in Pym's fictional world is the survival of class distinction in such pronounced yet minute ways. One infers that Mr Oliver espouses liberal politics out of self-interest: he is poor. And this is immediately evident because he wears slightly vulgar clothes: his suit is of 'rather too bright a blue to be quite the thing', as Jane thinks (*JP*, 52). Hence, to be 'not quite the thing' discriminates between a higher and lower order. In the same way, the cadre of cleaning women in Pym's fiction hold a lower station. The Bedes' maid, Florrie, in *Some Tame Gazelle* is mostly colourless, but later figures of this type in Pym's novels are more outspoken.[5] Mrs Morris in *Excellent Women* and Miss Lord in *No Fond Return* occasionally overstep their proper bounds in relation to their mistresses; this indicates that their proper place is strictly defined, since it can be transgressed.

Less than Angels takes its title from Pope's poem which describes man's attempt to measure himself, and this sense of fitting station pervades Pym's fiction. Thus Pym compresses her distinctions between classes to such minute details as John Challow's pointed shoes in *An Unsuitable Attachment* (also not quite the thing, or not 'quite what men one knew' wore), or to Nicholas's wish for people 'of one's own kind' in *Jane and Prudence* (*UA*, 49; *JP*, 66). It can be as subtly displayed as the terms used by Canon Pritchard and his wife, when in the same novel they drive to the bishop's house in a 'motor' and stay to 'luncheon' (*JP*, 149). These are finely tuned distinctions, but unerringly rigid.

As for the place of the anthropologists in this scheme, they generally fit in with her other 'types', and move easily in the same intersecting circles of the novels' social world. Helena Napier of *Excellent Women*, Rupert Stonebird of *An Unsuitable Attachment* and Emma Howick of *A Few Green Leaves* all become absorbed into the suburb or village they enter when they move into new flats or houses. Still, anthropologists are marked as subtly though profoundly different from the other characters, and thus they fill a particular role in the novels and offer a unique target for satire. Their profession distinguishes them as outsiders because they study and analyse society. At the same time, they form a microcosm of the culture of which they are part, and as such are subjects who themselves represent English civilisation. While their attention is focused elsewhere – Africa or the Antipodes, Pygmies or Hottentots – they provide prime targets for the artist to observe. And Pym delights in the irony of doing 'field work' in such a 'primitive community' which itself does similar research (*EW*, 36).

A consideration of the anthropological community in *Less than Angels* reveals her conception of the anthropologist's place in society as a whole. The novel begins its study of anthropologists with a sherry party which commemorates the opening of a centre and library for anthropological studies. The fine Georgian building which houses the learned society has been obtained by Professor Felix Mainwaring, who has extracted funds for its purchase from a rich widow. The donor's name, Minnie Foresight, is ironic and apt; little does she foresee exactly what will result from her bequest. This puzzlement on the part of the benefactress points to one of Pym's recurring themes: the chronic misunderstanding between academics and society about the nature of scholarly research. On the one hand, scholars tend to react defensively to any hint of challenge or disrespect. Mildred observes Helena and Everard's displeasure in *Excellent Women*, for instance, when Rocky jests about an anthropological term which has sexual connotations; aside from objecting to the impropriety of drawing attention to it: 'It was obvious that [Helena] and Everard did not appreciate jokes about their subject', Mildred notes (*EW*, 97). On the other hand, anthropologists have a right to be defensive, since society tends to meet explanations of the value of academic work with deliberate obtuseness. No one cares to understand. Rupert Stonebird in *An*

Unsuitable Attachment reflects with near despair on the characteristic indifference shown by outsiders towards his profession: 'People were not really very interested in what one did, and a quick classification was all that was needed to distinguish an academic type from a farmer or a stockbroker' (*UA*, 34). Part of this indifference is related to suspicion and even fear. Other characters are afraid of the anthropologists, asking nervously: will they observe us? But the irony of the anthropologist's position is that he is like any other academic, interested in his subject and eager to discuss it with others who are also intrigued by it. Outsiders expect at once too much and too little from anthropologists.

In *Less than Angels*, the conflict between a sceptical outside world and an inner bastion of dedicated anthropologists extends to include discord within the ranks: the anthropologists compete with each other. In doing so, they comprise a microcosm of the larger British society which encircles them. Inevitably, given this corollary, class distinctions loom large. Addressing this facet of the academic community, Pym explores its ramifications both inside and outside the anthropological world, beginnning with Professor Mainwaring's satisfaction at having persuaded Mrs Foresight to fund his pet society. It is obviously in his role as gentleman, and not as scholar, that he has won her over to his point of view.

Thus the class system exerts an influence. To some extent, intellectual pursuits remain a gentleman's privilege and province. Pym parodies this hold-over from the past in Professor Mainwaring's own elegant tastes, which he contrasts favourably with those of his relatively shabby colleagues. When he surveys the guests at the sherry party at the beginning of the novel, he reflects with self-satisfaction on his superiority in matters of *savoir vivre*, concluding that his colleagues are not worthy of the best sherry. Not only would they be unable to distinguish between shades of excellence, they would not care which kind they were drinking. He continues his meditation with a note of *noblesse oblige* and aristocratic pity for those beneath him. 'After all, it was not his fault that his father had been able to educate him at Eton and Balliol, or that his youth had been passed in the spacious days of the Edwardian era' he reflects (*LTA*, 18). By contrast, he considers most of his colleagues ' "not quite out of the top drawer" ' (*LTA*, 18).

A younger anthropologist in the novel, Tom Mallow, provides a counterpart to Felix Mainwaring. The professor demonstrates an ability to combine the advantages of his social class with his profession. Tom represents the group of anthropologists who have deliberately 'detribalised' themselves, or denied the demands posed by the social system in order to pursue their profession. The two men respond differently to the privileges they receive in being born into the aristocratic echelon.

As the elder son of a landed family with a decaying estate, Tom seems destined by his lineage to carry on family traditions and to marry Elaine, the bride who has been chosen for him as suitably domestic and provincial. In pursuing a career in anthropology, and consequently spending much of his time in Africa, Tom succeeds in separating himself from his own clan, or in breaking away from the responsibilities as well as the privileges attached to his background. As if to emphasise his new role, he wears old and shabby clothes while in Britain, and native dress when in Africa. This sartorial adaptability allows him to blend in with both societies interchangeably, and to do so as easily as possible. Further, his lack of formality in dress effectively bars him from his past; dress clothes now feel strange when he goes home for a brief visit and must dress for dinner. One scene reveals how effective his disguise is: he goes for an evening walk in London and finds himself outside his aunt's house in Belgrave Square, where a debutante ball is in full swing. He hesitates about whether or not to enter – he is lonely and would like company – but a passing policeman dissuades him, because the officer clearly disbelieves Tom's claim that he belongs in such a gathering. He is not dressed for the part. 'Tom supposed, from the kindly, humouring note in the policeman's voice, that he must appear like some harmless lunatic found wandering at night . . .' and is bitter in feeling rejected and excluded from something that is rightfully his (*LTA*, 164).[6]

While Tom abandons his origins, class and the role he was born to fill, his fellow student Mark Penfold assumes those advantages which Tom discards. Mark symbolically attends the Belgrave Square party that Tom does not enter. He is as careless about the importance of his work as Tom is nonchalant about his class distinction, and thus Mark ascends the social scale while Tom figuratively descends. Mark ends by marrying an upper-class girl whom he meets at the fateful debutante ball, and enters her father's business. This arrangement provides a perfect example of advantageous 'uxorilocal' matrimony, where the husband enters his wife's residence and sphere of influence. Tom creates his own satisfactory uxorilocal arrangement by moving into Catherine

Oliphant's flat, unfettered even by the commitment of marriage. His aristocratic bearing continues to stand him in good stead even though he does not make use of it directly; as Mark concludes, in great envy, ' "Trust Tom to get himself well looked-after. I suppose it must be his ruling-class upbringing asserting itself" ' (*LTA*, 75).

Both men count the world well lost for the rewards of money or recognition they gain in return: Mark cheerfully exchanges his student garb for a bowler hat and a lucrative job, while Tom exchanges a full dress suit for corduroy sports jacket or native African costume. His sartorial transformation is so complete, in fact, that it leads to his death. Tom identifies so thoroughly with the culture he is studying that he is shot by police during a political riot along with a number of natives.

Pym seems curiously ambivalent about Tom's feelings about anthropology; the novel is unclear about what his ideals actually are. In terms of Tom's intellect and ability, he was intended, as Pym's notebooks indicate, to be 'a brilliant anthropologist, though one can't give specimens of his work' (MS PYM 44, fol. 22). But in the novel itself this original intention is parodied hilariously in a conversation between his two fellow students, Mark and Digby, who question Tom's 'brilliance' by declaring that they have never seen it materially demonstrated. Still more interesting, Pym seems to have feared that by causing her character to die in Africa, he would attain too much glamour and ultimately seem a martyr for his profession. In another notebook entry about Tom she worried that he might become a Lawrence of Arabia figure. Yet in the novel he fails to become a hero. The fact that his life is haphazardly snuffed out, rather than ending in a blaze of glory, seems fitting in light of his earlier feelings about anthropology. He returns to Africa at the end of the novel in order to escape from the complications of his relationships with women at home. He seems to run from problems rather than to an absorbing interest. His girlfriend Deirdre recognises that he wanted to go to Africa in order to escape from problematic relationships in England.[7]

There is a curious sense of anachronism in Tom's death, which is significant in terms of the author's portrayal of anthropologists. She perceives the discipline as becoming increasingly scientific and detached.[8] Pym commented in a notebook: 'With Tom, in a way, the wheel has come full circle. He dies the kind of death one of his kind might have died in, say, 1907' (MS PYM 45, fol. 8). He does not perish as a martyr for the cause of anthropology. Moreover, the system seems sufficiently glutted that deaths are in some sense hardly noticed except as they make room for others. Digby's response on first hearing of Tom's death is to wonder what will become of the rest of Tom's grant money? Tom Mallow is most fully memorialised by the four women who meet to mourn him – incongruously – over lunch, rather than by his colleagues. His field notes, which his sister Josephine offers to Deirdre, seem an intolerable burden to assume. In *Excellent Women*, Helena regards the death of older colleagues as a necessary removal of dead weight, citing herself and a few others (the ' "really worthwhile people" ') as the 'New Generation' who stand ready to take over: ' "It will be our turn soon" ', she tells Mildred (*EW*, 86, 89).

Competition is particularly keen among those in the middle ground. The older and disappointed members of the profession tend to complain the loudest about faulty workmanship in others, as they suffer the greatest need to compensate for their own personal failure. Alaric Lydgate of *Less than Angels* is the primary example of this. He writes scathing reviews of his colleagues' work while refusing to expose his own work to criticism by publishing almost nothing himself. Even so, Alaric remains a sympathetic character, despite his petty attacks on others; the reader senses the paralysing weight of his attic full of untouched 'field notes' and his inability to write them up. His final decision to burn them in the backyard evidences a peculiar sort of scholarly honesty; he tacitly admits by this act that he will never organise and present the material.

Pym's cynicism about academic research seems to have increased with time. Competition between colleagues becomes even nastier in a struggle depicted in one of Pym's late novels, untitled and unpublished, and referred to in letters to friends as an 'academic novel'.[9] The novel depicts a situation in which a university lecturer named Alan Grayston contrives to have a manuscript stolen from an unsuspecting party, a retired elderly missionary. He then uses the material – some local tribal folklore – to mount a scathing attack against the work of a colleague in his department, who has drawn erroneous conclusions through not having had access to this information.

The 'academic novel' poses a question of intellectual integrity in obtaining data. This situation parallels the earlier one in *Less than Angels* between Alaric Lydgate and Tom Mallow: Alaric's unused trunks of field notes might be of use to Tom in his research. They have both 'done' the same tribe. The competitive spirit in this case leads both men to refuse any collaboration and to stress the fact that their respective fields are different. The later 'academic novel' extends the ramifications of competitiveness much further; not only does Alan Grayston filch the manuscript, but he gloats over the clever use he makes of it in advancing his reputation. Thus in the later novel Pym focuses less on the ethical problem involved in stealing the material than she does on the use the scholar makes of it. The competitive spirit depicted here descends from the realm of the abstract pursuit of knowledge to private rancour and envy. Most notably, Pym's attitude seems to be cold and clinical compared to the warmer portrayal of anthropologists she offers in her earlier novels. This unpublished novel by no means constitutes Pym's ultimate vision of the academic world, but it does reveal her sense of a bitter underside to the profession.

Thus Pym examines the professional workings of the anthropologists, but always with an eye to the private realm as well. The two are equally significant sides of each other. Felix Mainwaring is at once gentleman, *bon vivant* and scholar. Tom Mallow poses simultaneously as dedicated anthropologist, dissertation writer, delinquent son and polished ladies' man. In a different sort of combination, Alaric Lydgate is presented as a lonely man as well as the author of caustic book reviews; he feels most comfortable when alone in his house wearing an African mask. In some cases the two aspects of private and professional become inextricable: the man and the anthropologist become completely identified. Rupert Stonebird of *An Unsuitable Attachment* achieves in everyday life the sort of camouflaged blending with his surroundings that the anthropologist needs for his work 'in the field'. He has developed an ability to hide in a crowd by reflex. On the occasion of Sophia's dinner party, he arrives at the vicarage already dressed for his role: 'He had changed into a dark suit as a kind of protective colouring, so that he could sit quietly observing rather than being observed' (*UA*, 39). Some of this withdrawn nature is due simply to shyness, which in turn draws him to this particular profession.

The heroine of the unpublished academic novel reflects on the subject of professional and private identities at a university dinner, where she speculates on the characters of her fellow guests, wondering if the academics around her are good husbands, fathers and family men. This echoes another tentative ghostly character who appears in Pym's notebooks around the time she composed *Less than Angels*, though he does not materialise in her novels: 'An unlikely-looking archaeologist being a very strong lover' (MS PYM 40, fol. 13). Thus the personal sides of professional lives are most important as they unite romantic love, a constant theme in Pym's fiction.

The most striking example of romance among the anthropologists is Helena Napier and Everard Bone in *Excellent Women*. Helena confides her esteem for Everard to Mildred, adding that academic work creates ' "such a bond" ' between the two of them. She catalogues her husband's comparative disadvantages in terms of work: ' "he knows nothing about anthropology and cares less" ', she complains to Mildred (*EW*, 26). Helena and Everard provide an interesting case because, though they parallel the other mismatched academic pairs of Prudence and Dr Grampian in *Jane and Prudence*, and Viola and Dr Forbes in *No Fond Return*, Helena is an intellectual equal to Everard. While the other heroines index and proofread for their idols, Helena coauthors a paper with Everard (though she does seem to be delegated a suspiciously dull task, in the assembling of the kinship diagrams). Everard treats her like an equal, which is perhaps better than as a secretary; yet he addresses her only as a slack or wayward one. He complains about their progress, as in the following rebuke: ' "We must *get on*", said Everard in an irritable tone' (*EW*, 36).

Helena cuts a dashing figure, comprising almost an unusual member of the typical Pym cast of characters. She knows how to dress, how to succeed professionally, how to read a paper at a learned society; further, she vehemently rejects the role of housekeeper, in an outburst which shocks the domestic Mildred: ' "I'm such a slut" ', Helena announces with pride (*EW*, 8). In his essay on Pym's novels, Robert Graham divides her heroines into roughly two categories: the excellent woman, represented by Mildred Lathbury, and the 'hard woman', typified in this novel by Helena. He observes that Helena belongs to the class of women who 'get what they want', and further, who receive more in consequence than they deserve.[10] Still, I would question this conclusion in light of what Helena actually obtains. She does not, finally, succeed in having it all. She clearly loves Everard (' "she has told me so" ', he affirms), yet does not move him to return her affection (*EW*, 145). Since anthropology and marriage with Rocky do not mix, she ultimately abandons anthropology. Moreover, it requires no particular feminist orientation to infer that Helena's initial revolt against domesticity stems from an effort to create a counter-role for

herself and establish her professional place. She declares that she is
a 'slut' as a housekeeper in order more fully to assume the mantle of
the professional woman (*EW*, 8).

Helena seems a problematic character in many ways. Though she
is hard and determined, she is also likeable and at times pathetic
because she is forced to choose between alternatives and to make a
sacrifice. One wonders how she fares in a country cottage with a
baby, as Rocky's last report to Rowena in *A Glass of Blessings* pictures
Helena. Marriage and anthropology become a dichotomy for her,
and perhaps constitute a difficult choice. Esther Clovis, on the
contrary, delights in breaking and reconstructing suitable working
marriages for her anthropological colleagues. She appears pleased
when Helena leaves Rocky midway through *Excellent Women*, and
Helena goes directly to Esther at the learned society when she leaves
him. In her flight from domestic difficulties, Helena leaves home
(her flat with Rocky) for work (the premises of the learned society),
and finally for childhood (her mother's home in the country). This
symbolic regression show her figuratively returning to childhood
and thus reversing her ascent and negating the professional place
she has established for herself. But life for women in Pym's fiction
remains incomplete without love, and thus work must be sacrificed
for marriage. Esther Clovis declares that Helena is better off single,
therefore being able to ' "devote [her] whole life to the study of
matrilineal kin-groups" ' (*EW*, 178). Helena agrees with Mildred
that this offers small consolation for the loss of a husband. Thus
private loyalties prove more important for her than professional
ambitions.

Everard Bone, by contrast, represents the opposite extreme in his
view of work and love. Apparently indifferent to all human
relationships except those among the tribes he studies, he becomes
defined entirely by his role as an anthropologist. Everard embraces
anthropology as his first love, in contrast to Tom Mallow in *Less than
Angels*, who literally dies in the service of his profession, but never
shows as much intensity or animation about it as Everard does.
When Mildred bows to the inevitable at the end of *Excellent Women*,
assuming the tasks of indexing and proofreading Everard's
manuscripts, she notices his excitement with surprise: 'I had never
seen Everard so enthusiastic before', she observes (*EW*, 255).

As a self-contained community, anthropologists in Pym's novels
yield 'opportunities for field work' in both private and professional
realms. As a group they form their own precisely defined social

structure, where Professor Mainwaring presides ('Comus and his rabble rout', as he says), and where all compete for grant money or academic reputations or love (*LTA*, 14). The anthropologists are a peculiar mixture; they are separate individuals holding themselves aloof and jealously competing with each other, and at the same time are identical members of an homogeneous social group. Their profession inclines them to inherent isolation, as they must go off alone to work 'in the field'. At one point in *Less than Angels*, Esther Clovis eulogises the anthropologist as ' "a dedicated being very much like a priest" ', a description of abstention in all forms which daunts the four students whom she intends to inspire (*LTA*, 205).

Professor Mainwaring takes up the suggestion by quoting the fragment of Pope from which the novel takes its title. This paradox of angel and brute man points to a basic dilemma in man's nature; devoted to his work, he also craves creature comforts.[11] Even Esther Clovis approves of marriage if it furthers the anthropologist's work. Academic research poses a conflict between the two demands of public and private. Thus Pym addresses the difficulty of balancing private and professional lives, and in her study of anthropologists captures some of the complexity of their task.

Pym parodies the discipline of anthropology itself by displacing its major thrust from the study of foreign cultures onto home soil. She scrutinises England – or her corner of it – as if it were a primitive tribe with strange customs and bizarre rituals. Tom in *Less than Angels*, for instance, at one point compares the rigid laws which govern marriage in tribal law to launching a British girl on the marriage market, and concludes that the principle governing both is much the same. In her novels Pym applies the pseudo-anthropological technique of observation and interpretation. As a result she defamiliarises the familiar, or makes the ordinary seem strange by approaching it as an odd phenomenon. She writes more in the tradition of the satirist than of the realist. And it would be a poor anthropologist who only described his culture and did not analyse or interpret it.

An air of wondering inquiry attends the observations of her narrators and of her characters, and in this framework Pym creates a fictional world around the premise of what its various signals mean. Occasionally, her characters project back into the past, as when Catherine Oliphant in *Less than Angels* notices the mosaics of peacocks in a cafeteria, and wonders why the diners do not set offerings before them: 'Obviously the cult of peacock worship, if it had ever existed, had fallen into disuse', she concludes (*LTA*, 7).

Each ritual gesture in Pym's fiction possesses both an intrinsic significance and a logical progression. Her narrators and many of her characters either imagine (or create) the meaning of an act or project beyond it to a 'suitable' or 'appropriate' sequel. Pym assumes an orderly world. And her narrators seem intent on ferreting out the meaning behind the little acts and conversations and glances that comprise it.

Mildred of *Excellent Women*, for instance, has such an habitually vivid imagination that the least provocation sparks a response. When Everard rings up to invite her to his flat for dinner (' "I have got some meat to cook" ', he tells her) she refuses the invitation, inferring that she would have to cook the meal as well as to eat it and deciding that she is too tired to cope with preparing a meal (*EW*, 218). But after the phone conversation is over, she launches into a full-scale howl of sympathy for Everard, creating and embroidering an exact picture of what he might now do with the joint; left to his own devices: 'He would turn to the section on meat. He would read that beef or mutton should be cooked for so many minutes per pound and so many over. He would weigh the little joint, if he had scales' and so on, as she envisions the scene (*EW*, 220). Mildred puzzles out meanings behind actions or words by extending them beyond what she can see. This episode reflects several aspects of Mildred's character, including her tendency to assume responsibility for others – especially for feeding them. But it also illustrates the workings of her vivid imagination and curiosity.

England is thus seen as a civilisation with a strict and solemn order for preparing and consuming food. The preoccupation with meat which runs through all of Pym's work, especially *Excellent Women* and *Jane and Prudence*, typifies this aspect of the author's anthropological bent. Everard's mother Mrs Bone, who appears in *Excellent Women*, is as superstitious as one could imagine any primitive savage to be. She tells Mildred she fears the ultimate triumph of the Dominion of the Birds, declaring: ' "I eat as many birds as possible" ' and expressing satisfaction that ' "at least we can eat our enemies" '(*EW*, 149). The solemnity about eating infuses an element of cannibalism into Pym's study of England. Similarly, in *Jane and Prudence* the butcher assumes the role of a select Levite priest, who shares out the offal on a fair basis. Curates and clergymen all through Pym's novels are offered roast chicken, which is seen as their due, in some obscure yet powerful way.

Pym's interest in food assumes a documentary significance, as she records the daily tenor of life in the kitchen, including such mundane details as shopping for food, preparing meals and washing up afterwards. Attitudes expressed towards food by the various characters show much about their natures – in *Excellent Women*, Mildred is a careful if unimaginative cook, while Helena is slapdash. Helena comes to grief as a direct result of careless housekeeping; at one point, to Rocky's horror, she sets a greasy frying pan down on a wood table, which in turn sparks his anger and precipitates her flight. Mildred, by contrast, appears in a glowing light to Rocky by coming into her own at this juncture in the domestic crisis. She prepares lunch for the newly-deserted husband, which earns his unqualified approval: ' "[Helena] couldn't even *wash* a lettuce properly", he said, "let alone prepare a salad like this" ' (*EW*, 156).

Foods possess varying significance in themselves. Pym always has an ear (or palate) for what is suitable for an occasion, and stresses this ritualistic significance. Examples from the novels abound. Mildred's meal of fish after hearing of Julian's engagement is sober and fitting: 'Cod seemed a suitable dish for a rejected one', she thinks, and eats it 'humbly', without any sauce or relish (*EW*, 134). Conversely, brandy is for 'emergencies' only, Mildred says, and for Ianthe of *An Unsuitable Attachment*, another excellent woman, it is always associated with disaster. In a similar vein, coffee is the proper beverage to serve after a meal – in *Jane and Prudence*, Jane wonders if she might offer tea to Father Lomax, the visiting clergyman who is due to arrive after dinner. Throughout *Jane and Prudence*, men are vigorously alleged (by women) to ' "[need] meat" ' (*JP*, 51).[12] And Mildred in *Excellent Women* is driven to assert at a church meeting that one needs tea 'always', at any conceivable time.

The fussy attitude adopted by some male characters towards food acts as a comic sidelight on their finicky (usually homosexual) natures: one thinks of Wilfred Bason in *A Glass of Blessings* (an ' "Anglo-Catholic and fond of cooking" '), William Caldicote of *Excellent Women* (' "Will there be *anything at all* that one can eat?" ' he asks upon viewing a restaurant menu), or Mervyn Cantrell of *An Unsuitable Attachment* (who cannot 'take' restaurant food) (*GB*, 31; *JP*, 205; *UA*, 26). Conversely, a properly regulated interest in food can also indicate a keen sensibility and attendant *savoir faire*. Everard Bone, for example, orders a meal for himself and Mildred in *Excellent Women* with excellent results and very little 'fuss', compared to William's previous performance at the same restaurant, and receives high marks for it.

The descriptions of menus serve partly to provide a particular atmosphere – the characteristic settings for Pym's novels include the kitchen or the restaurant table – and also function as clues to the characters' tastes and natures. One is what one eats in a Pym novel, in more ways than might be imagined.

Thus eating is seen in its larger sociological context and as a metaphor for characters' emotional states. It is presented as part of the universal tradition of gathering friends together for ritual meals. And it is important just as a joke as well. In one letter to her friend, Robert Smith, Pym accepted a dinner invitation enthusiastically; she and her sister Hilary would be delighted to come to dinner, '(meals being the most important things in our lives at present)' she adds (MS PYM 161/2, fol. 25).[13]

Clothing in Pym's novels assumes the same kind of importance as food; the reader knows the characters as much by what they wear as by what they eat. Barbara Pym herself showed a long-standing interest in clothing. She took great care with her own wardrobe, sewed some of her own dresses, and claimed to regret the diminishing interest in high fashion during the war years: 'We shall get shabbier and shabbier', she wrote in mock despair to Henry Harvey in 1942 (*VPE*, 110). At the least, clothes reveal the kind of image a character wants to project about himself, and dressing also reveals errors in good taste, especially among men. The too-pointed shoe, the ill-cut suit, or the shade of too bright a blue can betray unfortunate sartorial judgement amounting almost to a moral lapse. For women, dress is often most important in the attempt to attract men. Penelope in *An Unsuitable Attachment*, for instance, deliberately chooses to wear outlandish clothing in order to 'provide a complete contrast' to Ianthe, an excellent woman of faultless taste whom Penelope considers to be a rival for Rupert Stonebird's attentions (*UA*, 124). And Rupert does notice Penelope because of her costumes. Thus clothing is important for what it is intended to communicate or express.

It also indicates just how far a woman is prepared to go in order to attract a man's notice. Comfort must often be sacrificed in order to achieve elegance, as when Harriet in *Some Tame Gazelle* wears more fashionable high-heeled shoes that cause her difficulty in walking. In an effort to appear striking and attractive, Harriet continually tries to alter her clothes in various ways – a vee-neck or shorter sleeves to a dress, or the unlikely addition of leopard-skin trimming to a coat.

Cosmetics similarly possess ritual significance; on the evening of the village whist drive, Prudence in *Jane and Prudence* appears in green eye-shadow, to Jane's dismay and Nicholas's admiration. Jane interprets this gesture in an anthropological spirit, seeing it as a necessary preparation which unmarried women must undertake: 'What hard work it must be, always remembering to add these little touches; there was something primitive about it, like the young African smearing himself with red cam-wood before he went courting', she thinks to herself (*JP*, 84). Prudence overbalances later in the novel, startling the young undergraduate, Paul, by her appearance and wondering if she seems 'formidable' rather than 'feminine and desirable' (*JP*, 159).

To further underscore her investigation of British civilisation through an 'anthropological' approach, in *Less than Angels* Pym introduces a foreigner who plies his trade on the British. Jean-Pierre Rossignol is a French anthropologist who observes the culture around him in the course of his research at Professor Mainwaring's new library. He makes a separate study of London life 'in the suburbs' – and, practised anthropologist as he is, he skilfully conducts his own field work. When he is invited to Deirdre's house to dinner after church, for instance, he inquires about the family's habits, with the following results: 'The meal was highly successful and everyone liked Jean-Pierre, who put his questions about English suburban life so charmingly that nobody could possibly have taken offence' (*LTA*, 84). This is a marvellous study of the anthropologist actually at work – in his spare time, no less, he actively pursues information about the culture he temporarily lives in. Throughout the book, Jean-Pierre remains a foreigner, an outsider, a Frenchman with yellow gloves and a slightly odd way of speaking English. He insists on preserving anthropological detachment and makes it a point to ' "do the correct thing where possible" ' in social situations, as he tells Deirdre (*LTA*, 23). This anxiety to behave properly shows part of the anthropologist's dilemma; he can never be at home in the society he analyses.

The penchant to classify and to order information which Pym's anthropological characters betray is echoed in her own presentation

of her 'material' as a novelist. Her precision in noting details of dress
and food offers a picture of England in the 1950s and evokes this
vanished world. But it is more than the accumulation of physical
details which links her writing with an anthropological view; Pym
invests her observations of the surface of life with conjectures about
their significance.

One passage in *An Unsuitable Attachment* links anthropology and
fiction together in an illuminating comparison. At Rupert
Stonebird's dinner party, his guest Everard Bone remarks that the
novelist's art is like the anthropologist's work in that ' "both study
life in communities" ' (*UA*, 127). Pym's novels counterpoint various
characters in a way which gives an overall picture of the community
as a whole. By her own admission, as a novelist she '[loves] a
crowded canvas' (MS PYM 17, fol. 34). Her bits and pieces,
fragments of conversations and incidents fit together into a coherent
whole.

An implication of the comparison between the novelist and
anthropologist lies in Ianthe's unfinished response to the charge
that 'life in communities' is a dull choice of subject: ' "Even the most
apparently uneventful life . . . " ', she says, trailing off uncertainly,
because she thinks of herself and John here, and is unwilling to
reveal this (*UA*, 127). It is the uneventful lives which Pym
chronicles, as she analyses the patterns of her characters' lives; their
private rituals, their quiet reflections, their preference for dry sherry
or 'stewed' tea. Her subject is the 'little things in life'. And these
minute details assume significance as they reveal truths about the
basic structure of society. To an anthropologist, as to a novelist,
nothing is irrelevant. Further, Pym counterpoints her study of
Britain with a para-consciousness of other cultures which surround
it, and with the attendant expectation that foreigners are naturally
depraved. Mrs Bone in *Excellent Women*, for instance, asks Everard
which tribe in Africa is cannibalistic, thus implying that the other
people are the crazy ones. Even the specialist is occasionally unable
to see beyond his own particular interest: ' "No ceremonial
devouring of human flesh?" ' mutters the disappointed
anthropologist at Helena and Everard's lecture (*EW*, 93).

Thus Pym's novelistic approach draws some inspiration from an
anthropological approach and is enlivened by her wit and her sense
of the ridiculous. One of her notebooks cited a particularly revealing
sentence gleaned, apparently, from a handbook for
anthropologists: ' "It is important that not even the slightest

expression of amusement or disapproval should ever be displayed at the description of ridiculous, impossible or disgusting features in custom, cult or legend"' it announces (*VPE*, 189). Her narrator preserves the same sober demeanour throughout the novels, though always with a twinkle in the eye.

When Pym began 'turning into an anthropologist', as she described her new employment in a letter to Henry Harvey in 1946, it was a transformation which profoundly affected her novel-writing (*VPE*, 180). The job gave her close contact with an academic group – something to laugh at, if not something to love. And it seems also to have broadened her political horizons and deepened her social satire because of this new awareness. The political naïvety that she evidences in her visits to Germany before the Second World War gives way to a more thoughtful treatment of foreign cultures.[14] Naturally, her experiences in the Wrens in Italy account for much of this growing understanding of other cultures, and the Second World War cannot have left anyone who lived through it unaffected.

Further, the academic discipline of anthropology must have suggested to her as a novelist a fruitul and detached view of the microcosm as well. The small village is presented skilfully in her works in terms of its social structure, from the majestic advent of Lady Clara Boulding in *Some Tame Gazelle* to open the church bazaar, to Emma Howick's list of village 'types' in *A Few Green Leaves*. Work at the IAI seems to have suited Pym's fanciful imagination admirably. Hazel Holt, her colleague at the Institute for several years, has commented on Pym's ready wit in pointing out 'the ridiculous phrase' in the anthropological and linguistic studies they worked with together in their editorial jobs (*VPE*, 183). Anthropology gave Pym something to laugh at. Or, rather, she determined to laugh at the comic episodes in what must have been, at least at times, an exacting and tedious job. In the process, learning about the discipline of anthropology seems to have sharpened her vision and her writing.

Anthropology by no means dominated Pym's artistic vision. Roughly half of her novels after the point when she began to work for the IAI have little or nothing to do with anthropologists; and if the 'little notebooks' from which she drew ideas for her novels are an accurate indication of what Pym thought about while composing, her mind seems to have dwelt more persistently on emotional states than on quirks of behaviour in the anthropologists around her. Perhaps their comic aspects were so ready to hand when needed for a novel that she did not need to record them.

The point is that Pym was undoubtedly influenced by her fellow office-workers, and derived great satisfaction from exercising her favourite hobby of 'observing' those around her. At the same time, anthropology provided a vocabulary and point of reference; and her job offered a community to study and a setting in which a sensitive artist could work. Perhaps the influence of anthropology in Pym's work is most felt in the quick and observant eyes of her two first-person narrators, Mildred Lathbury and Wilmet Forsyth, who exercise to perfection the anthropologist's – or novelist's – art of blending into the background, observing and subsequently interpreting the civilisation around them.

6
The Artist as Observer

Barbara Pym's novels contend that the meek inherit the earth, and perhaps no other aspect of her work accounts so fully for the pleasure they afford the reader. Her comedy sets the downtrodden and little-regarded narrator and his audience in a position of moral superiority to the powerful, authoritarian characters in Pym's fictional world by exposing their weaknesses through the mildness of the 'excellent women'. Quiet resentment is a persistent undertone in Pym's heroines, though they seldom show it. This underlying sense of unexpressed anger charges her satire with vibrancy. Pym's women characters have ample cause to chafe, for they often find themselves in situations which constrict them and which emphasise their inadequacy in dealing with the world. They fail either to receive credit for what they have done or to get what they need. Further, other characters consistently humiliate or insult heroines such as Belinda of *Some Tame Gazelle* and Mildred of *Excellent Women*. And outwardly, they accept such treatment. These two, Pym's archetypal 'excellent women', invariably turn the other cheek, shoulder the blame and respond with deference to the latest display of rudeness or ill manners, as when Belinda apologises for not having offered sherry to her dinner guests sooner, 'thus taking upon herself the blame for all the little frictions of the evening'. She goes on to generalise: 'But it was so obvious that women should take the blame, it was both the better and the easier part . . .' (*STG*, 119).

Still – and this is Pym's particular genius – these women gain advantage over their oppressors by discerning their faults. Belinda's private realisation of her rival's meanness reverses her habitual sense of inferiority to Agatha Hoccleve. Mildred achieves a more complex gain not only by discerning the true characters of her adversaries, but by describing them to the reader. No one within her fictional world can understand her perspective. Thus *Excellent Women* is in part a confessional novel, an outlet for suppressed resentment and a palliative for isolation: Mildred illustrates Pym's use of narration as self-justification. Mildred uses art in order to deal effectively with life's disappointments, and in the process gains perspective on herself. Pym's later artist heroines, Catherine of *Less than Angels* and Wilmet of *A Glass of Blessings*, employ fiction for similar purposes. They initially suffer less resentment about their positions, and so can learn from creating without the bitter edge which haunts Mildred; on the other hand, their narratives correspondingly lose in force.

At the heart of each of these artists' techniques lies Pym's conception of the artist as primarily an observer, one who achieves a position of detachment in order to do the 'field work' which will provide material for a study of society or for a novel. The brilliance of Pym's fiction lies in her use of this material in an ironic mode, as she constantly poses a contrast between what seems and what is, between what others would have us think them and what they are. Thus her artist heroines gain an insight which goes beyond the chronic infatuation from which many of Pym's other heroines suffer. More even than the nostalgia and comfort they provide, in their role as 'books for a bad day', the novels' pervading irony is what draws us to them repeatedly.[1] Perhaps we all enjoy feeling secretly superior to those who show contempt for us, and find some of Mildred's situation in our own. We constantly meet the frustration of a lack of comprehension in others. This phenomenon, which the author registers in a comedy just short of cynicism, forms the staple of her fiction, and a main source of its delight.

Mildred's narrative technique stems from Pym's first novel, *Some Tame Gazelle*; its heroine, Belinda Bede, offers an early variation of Mildred Lathbury's 'excellent woman' character. Like Mildred, Belinda constantly apologises. Her personal feeling of inadequacy crystallises around the figure of Agatha Hoccleve; Belinda feels that she is neither as clever nor as competent as Agatha. Having been rejected by Henry during her Oxford undergraduate days, she has not ceased to admire him for the thirty intervening years prior to the opening of the novel. Nor has she ceased to feel inferior to Agatha, whom Henry has chosen as a wife rather than Belinda. Belinda assumes a direct corollary to this basic fact: Agatha is a better wife (and therefore a worthier person) than Belinda herself. The novel's comedy overturns this judgement and validates Belinda's character in both past and present.

The first reversal in perspective occurs when Belinda perceives that Agatha is not the faultless housekeeper that she has always assumed. The archdeacon announces incontrovertible evidence of gross neglect of wifely duties on Agatha's part publicly: moths have ruined his suit. And Miss Prior, the Bedes' seamstress, secretly informs on the shocking state of the vicarage table: ' "*Very* poor meals there ... Between ourselves, Miss Bede, Mrs Hoccleve doesn't keep a good table" ' (*STG*, 51).

This revelation acts as an epiphany to Belinda; Agatha's shortcomings begin to vindicate her own duller but more cautious character, though she remains humble in her newly-acquired self-righteousness rather than exulting in it. Further, she is astute enough to realise that her own fastidiousness would not have saved her from Henry's complaints. When he invites her to congratulate herself on her probable superiority had she been his wife (she would not have allowed the tragedy of the moths to occur), she perceives that he would have been equally annoyed by her preventive measures in the smell of camphor mothballs. None the less, her sense of Agatha's failings provides a small comfort in her sense of inadequacy, in the same way that the revelations about the state of the vicarage larder do.

The real *coup* in Belinda's revisionary perspective comes in her perception of the past: she learns that Agatha had proposed to Henry. This lessens the pain of Henry's rejection, since he did not choose Agatha over Belinda except by default; he was chosen. Most important, it reveals a shocking lack of delicacy and want of tact in Agatha herself. It is one thing to have made Henry an archdeacon 'by her scheming', but quite another to have proposed marriage (*STG*, 11). Thus Belinda's private realisation of her own decorous passivity as opposed to the vulgarity of Agatha's aggressiveness proves sufficient to reverse – or at least mitigate – her habitual sense of inferiority. Belinda earns a modest victory in self-esteem.

Belinda shows herself a lady at all points, taking no advantage of her new knowledge of her rival. Even so, there are more insidious undercurrents afoot. In her sister Harriet, Belinda has a double who accurately reflects her thoughts; if Belinda knows Agatha's secret, Harriet knows Belinda's as well. Inquiring about Belinda's tea alone with the archdeacon late in the novel, when Agatha has gone away, Harriet infers something quite near the truth: ' "he's been telling you that he's very fond of you, and hinting that he wishes he'd married you instead of Agatha" ', she says (*STG*, 155). She goes on to state that ' "everyone knows" ' that Belinda and Henry ' "love each other" ' (*STG*, 156).

Belinda Bede becomes a prototype for Mildred Lathbury in Pym's next novel, who tells a whole story directly from the perspective of the apologetic 'excellent woman'. Further, first-person narration makes possible the full expression of this dilemma of excellence that is little valued. Mildred understands her inferior social position. She also sees the faults in others, and in her narration she uses irony, indirectness and self-deprecation to illuminate thoughtlessness or cruelty in others while seeming only to emphasise her own weaknesses. Again, much of the pleasure of Pym's fiction can be found in the fact that her comedy makes the reader feel superior on behalf of the meek. Mildred's modesty disguises acute perception, and though she is outwardly apologetic for her slowness, she is inwardly shrewd.

An important parallel between Belinda of the earlier novel and Mildred lies in their conflicts with aggressive women. *Excellent Women* employs this theme with greater subtlety. Whereas Agatha proposes to Henry, her action at least has the merit of being straightforward. Allegra plots to catch Julian Malory by more circumspect and devious means. She sends an (initially) anonymous donation to the church for the repair of a damaged window, and later acquires a flat in the vicarage where Julian and his sister Winifred live. Interestingly, Mildred is offered the same opportunities as Allegra to attract Julian's notice. Early in the novel, Winifred begs Mildred as a personal friend to move into the spacious vicarage. Moreover, after the crisis of Allegra and Julian's engagement, Mildred imagines herself in Allegra's position, wondering what might have happened had she been the one to send the mysterious donation. Thus Mildred deduces by comparison that had she been less excellent and more devious, like Allegra, she might have been better served in the matter of a husband. These reflections lead Mildred and Sister Blatt, another excellent woman, to formulate the theory that catching a husband requires a particular skill: ' "Oh they have the knack of catching a man. Having done it once I suppose they can do it again. I suppose there's nothing in it when you know how" ', asserts Sister Blatt, and Mildred adds that it must be a learned skill like mending a fuse (*EW*, 120).

Agatha's excess in *Some Tame Gazelle* can be more clearly labelled a *faux pas*; her proposal is 'not done'. Yet it remains simple-hearted, single-minded greed, and in Henry's peevishness as a husband, Agatha receives full reward for her brashness. The hazy nature of

Allegra's aggressiveness makes it appear all the more evil because it is deliberately planned and executed treachery; she appears in her true character to Mildred on one occasion as a predatory fox with small, pointed teeth.

Neither Belinda nor Mildred denounce their rivals by using the information they obtain about them. For Belinda, private vindication suffices, and she only tells what she knows about Agatha to Harriet. Similarly, Mildred does not attempt to expose Allegra's character; and Allegra's unmasking and her subsequent break with Julian occurs unaided by Mildred. Justice prevails none the less. The wicked, in this instance, do not prosper. In both these novels, the 'excellent woman' figure sees her own shortcomings – or her inefficiency – in comparison to more confident women. Still, she receives some compensation for having been bested, in her secret knowledge of her opponent's shallowness. The vague, sweet character gains a private satisfaction in attaining a position of moral superiority, and in the consciousness of having behaved honourably while the enemy was, so to speak, in her power. Further, Allegra's deceit and overreaching has lead to her own downfall.

Belinda is able to share her news with Harriet, who, unaccountably, does not seem to spread the tale any further. Yet a problem remains for Mildred in deciding with whom to share her newly discovered perspective. Neither Dora nor Winifred would understand her anxiety. An episode midway through the novel exemplifies this dilemma, when Mildred and Dora have by chance seen Allegra and Julian holding hands in the park. When she ponders the implications of this, Mildred is so certain that those around her will not understand her anxiety that she briefly considers writing to the advice column of *The Church Times*. Her fears about Dora's reactions are well-founded, for Dora mocks Mildred, and later draws Rocky on to tease her about it as well. Significantly, the only person whom Mildred considers to be a possible audience for the disturbing news is Everard Bone, the man she eventually marries, who Mildred feels would listen and 'might even understand that it was a worrying business altogether' (*EW*, 107).

Barbara Pym's heroines, like Jane Austen's, must frequently conceal much of their knowledge of others. Therefore, in telling her own story to an unknown reader Mildred evokes a relationship where the reader becomes confidant.[2] And Pym's choice of her heroine as narrator fully illuminates Mildred's peculiar position as an 'excellent woman', which her style of modesty and indirection renders still more insightful.

Mildred conceals from the reader the fact that she is well aware of her understanding of others' faults – she consistently takes the blame when they are thoughtless or unclear. Further, she disguises her perception, constantly apologising for what she calls her obtuseness. She often describes herself in the role of confidante as 'stupid' or 'slow to realise' her companion's objection in conversation (*EW*, 127, 142).

In keeping with her style of indirection, Mildred alludes to her infatuation with Rocky obliquely, through negatives and denials – in short, through her consistent mockery of herself as a woman interested in men. The lady doth protest too much. 'As if anyone would care how I looked, or even notice me', she reprimands herself when she fusses over her appearance in front of Rocky (*EW*, 34). Mildred openly scorns herself here for being presumptuous; and this draws attention to her sense of her own worthlessness rather than to her desire to attract him. She employs a similar subterfuge when she goes downstairs to join the conversation in the Napiers' flat with Rocky, Helena and Everard. Responding to a slighting remark from Everard, she confesses: 'I forebore to remark that women like me really expected very little – nothing, almost' (*EW*, 37). Because she accepts this burden of self-denial, Mildred becomes completely submerged in her type-cast identity: Everard later refers to her as ' "a sensible person, with no axe to grind" ' (*EW*, 151).

But Mildred blames others for what is in part her fault. If they take advantage of her services in the role of intermediary, she invites them to. She simply keeps the axe well hidden, except to the reader's eyes; and the narration of the novel becomes her explanation of this position. In a sense, she is right to deny herself expectations; for a woman of her age and background, life seems to hold little more than a progressive identification with the elderly 'distressed gentlewomen' she now serves at the agency where she works. What Mildred does in her situation is to create a persona for herself of inquisitive spinster, much as Dulcie does in *No Fond Return of Love*, with her 'research' into others' lives.[3] Mildred defines her role in these terms early in the novel: 'I suppose an unmarried woman just over thirty, who lives alone and has no apparent ties, must expect to find herself involved or interested in other people's business, and if she is also a clergyman's daughter then one might really say that there is no hope for her' (*EW*, 5).

But Mildred uses her skills differently from Dulcie. Mildred waits to be invited to meddle in others' affairs, and passively waits to be given information, whereas Dulcie pursues it more actively. Most significantly, Mildred narrates her story, or makes art out of it, imposing order and coherence on her experience. She justifies herself by explaining and illuminating the narrowness of her position, and then by showing her choices in light of those restrictions.

One of her most persistent frustrations is in relation to Rocky; she must reveal her love indirectly because the infatuation makes her ashamed. She alludes to it obliquely through insisting on her own stupidity and plainness, which would not bother her so much if she did not care what he thought of her. Further, she presents her feelings for him in light of her defences against his charm. 'Rather a shallow sort of person', she repeats to herself as an antidote to infatuation, in addition to the more serious matter of his 'Italian girl friend' (*EW*, 116). In her feelings for Rocky, Mildred suffers under an illusion and yet at the same time realises that she is doing so. In effect, she tries to convince herself of the hopelessness of her passion by making light of it and ridiculing it in her narrative, a tactic which shows a more astute approach than other Pym heroines such as Prudence, Dulcie and Viola. In particular, Viola of *No Fond Return* rejects this kind of perspective altogether. She tells Dulcie that she is thinking of writing a novel, but bridles at Dulcie's compliment that Viola has ' "the gift for observing people and getting them down on paper" '. She replies immediately and with distaste: ' "Oh, it won't be *that* kind of novel" ' (*NFR*, 41).

As narrator, Mildred satirises herself with almost exaggerated humility, first inviting the reader to see into her life, and then typifying it in the least favourable terms possible. She mocks the dullness of her life, as in her description of washing hung up to dry in the kitchen: 'Just the kind of underclothes a person like me might wear, I thought dejectedly, so there is no need to describe them' she says (*EW*, 85). This invites disdain for her spinsterly, over-thirty state. Mildred wants to encourage the reader in this view, and to see through this how she views her life, which is in terms of a constant falling short. Mildred proceeds by comparing herself with others. She stresses the fact that she is not as educated or articulate as Helena, nor as smartly dressed as Allegra; neither is she as sweet as Winifred, though she also lacks Winifred's occasionally tiresome naïvety. Only Dora is dumpier than Mildred, and this realisation depresses her still further by association. (Dora's washing reveals underclothes 'even drearier than mine', Mildred says (*EW*, 106).) In short, Mildred is not the striking individual she would like to be, and thus adopts instead the subservient role of a woman who becomes the perennial 'vicar's daughter', as if to compensate in some way.

The irony about Mildred, though, is that she is aware of her double role; she is conscious that many of her attempts at consolation and the stock phrases she offers do sound silly or ineffective. In her role as confidante she insists on her own inadequacy; she repeats several times that 'people like the Napiers had not so far come within [her] range of experience' (*EW*, 27).

The self-awareness she betrays about her position as an outsider makes her interesting – in fact, the insistence on her dullness suggests her cleverness. She can easily detect when she is being snubbed, as when she follows Helena downstairs at the learned society 'feeling like a dog or some inferior class of person' (*EW*, 96). The reader sees Mildred's inner side, and experiences from her perspective what it feels like to be shoved aside. Unable to say exactly what she means in the context of her everyday world, stuck in a round of platitudes and polite insincerities, she can make intention and expression coincide to an outside audience. The central tension in the novel lies between Mildred's desires (which she is only beginning to acknowledge to herself) and what she is expected to be (a non-person, totally subservient).

Her astuteness is particularly well illustrated in situations where others wish to make use of her, as when Everard Bone invites her out for a drink and begins to talk obliquely about women being '"quite impossible to understand"' (*EW*, 142). Mildred chastises herself for not realising his real message sooner: 'I was to tell Helena that Everard Bone did not love her. I might just as well go home and do it straight away' (*EW*, 145–6). Pym constantly makes these fine distinctions, where Mildred is momentarily betrayed into thinking that she is being sought out for herself, and not for her potential usefulness to others.

One of Pym's notable accomplishments in this novel is the way she portrays strong emotion. It is the hidden truth of the novel that Mildred is a romantic, and the contrast between her and Helena stresses this. We expect passion or even wildness from Helena; it comes as no surprise to learn that she literally runs out of the flat when Rocky berates her about the frying pan on the wood table, or that she flies to Everard's flat another time and pours out her disappointments in marriage (unwilling as he is to listen) until late at night.

Mildred's actions are infinitely more restrained, and her description of emotional turmoil is correspondingly sedate. The episode after her lunch with Allegra, where she wanders into a department store and buys 'Hawaiian Fire' lipstick is particularly revealing. She identifies with women in the store: 'others like myself seemed bewildered and aimless, pushed and buffeted as we stood not knowing which way to turn' (*EW*, 130). Mildred's confusion here is the more poignant for her restrained description of it; her helplessness is a picture of profound depression. The fact that she can laugh at herself in the middle of it shows a trace of the earlier, witty Mildred, yet the passage remains an ironic acceptance of the fact that dramatic gestures are not suited to her outward image; she mocks herself with the description of the 'ludicrous' name of the lipstick and the 'depths of shame' she enjoys in taking her extravagant purchase home (*EW*, 131).

Mildred ages in this one scene to doddering, elderly aimlessness. She senses a whole life ahead of her of being an 'excellent woman' – i.e. someone beaten out in love and marriage and life by the less worthy but more efficient Allegra Grays of the world.

Curiously, this episode echoes a passage in one of Pym's personal letters, written years later, during the long period of discouragement over remaining unpublished. Feeling of no account in the world, she nevertheless asserts to herself that she has succeeded in something important: 'I thought, surging through Smith's in Fleet Street today, "I'm just a tired-looking middle-aged woman to all these (mostly young) people, yet I have had quite a life and written (or rather published) six novels which have been praised in the highest circles"' (*VPE*, 208). As for all writers, Pym's hidden identity as an artist was crucial to her self-esteem. Much like her character Mildred Lathbury, she felt herself to be tongue-tied and shy, inferior socially, yet correspondingly she came into her own as a writer. As early as her undergraduate years at Oxford, she wrote in her diaries that she wished she could make more scintillating conversation with Henry Harvey, but that she was definitely shown to best advantage with pen in hand.

She similarly glories in her role as hidden observer. In a letter to her friend Robert Smith, she describes a triumph of detection during a conversation with a clergyman; the speaker might be boring or foolish, but Pym enjoys a delicious revenge in her superior perception: 'Little, of course, does he realise who is drinking it all in!' (*VPE*, 261). Something of the same delight in describing a situation or creating a story can be found in Mildred, who has no one with whom to share her view. None of the other characters gets the joke.

She shares it with the reader. In this way she enjoys a vicarious revenge on those who oppress her by exposing them. The artist is like the anthropologist, who strives to sink into the background, observe those around him, then describe his findings to colleagues who can understand his terminology and the significance and implications of his discoveries. In a similar way, the artist communicates his sense of the comic or the absurd. He immerses himself in society and then applies his power of vision in describing the society to others. Mildred declines, for the most part, to rebel against those around her, but diverts her energy to the process of ordering her story and telling it to an unseen audience.

Given Mildred's desire to communicate, she must still resolve the question of how to convey the strong emotion which impels her to confide. Her reticence as a narrator finds particularly apt expression here. On the occasion of the Napiers' leaving the downstairs flat, for instance, Mildred fully realises the weight of her loss when she watches the van leave, carrying Rocky's furniture. This symbolises his departure from the building which contains both of their flats. She remarks only: 'The effects of shock and grief are too well known to need description and I stood at the window for a long time' (*EW*, 167). She does not dramatise this – confide that she wept, or attempt to describe the depth of her sense of loss. She deliberately impersonalises and understates her grief, alluding drily to the 'effects' of bereavement.

In a similar way, she displaces or diverts the reader's attention (and her own) when a crucial emotional scene with Julian arises. He comes to find Winifred at Mildred's flat, after the dramatic scene with Allegra, where they break their engagement, and all but proposes to Mildred on the spot, having suddenly perceived her virtue: ' "But perhaps I looked too far and there might have been somebody nearer at hand" ', he says (*EW*, 211). Mildred responds as follows: 'I stared into the electric fire and wished it had been a coal one, though the functional glowing bar was probably more suitable for this kind of an occasion.' With the comic incongruity of setting, romantic intention and dampening response, it hardly occurs to the reader to wonder what Mildred is actually feeling at this dramatic moment, because her transition away from emotion is so subtle. She avoids telling the reader her reaction, and diverts Julian as well.

This scene is a master example of Pym's use of understatement. Mildred says that she wishes only that she had a superior kind of indoor heater, whereas she does in reality wish that Rocky were proposing to her rather than Julian. To further underscore this desire, she substitutes one man for the other in a dream that night, where Rocky stands by the heater in Julian's place, and asks Mildred 'to marry him' (*EW*, 212). As a further connection between romantic interludes and the common bond of the heater, Mildred ends the novel with dinner in Everard's flat, where she notes with approval that his heater has flames and hisses pleasantly. This bodes well for their future courtship.

This raises the question of the novel's ending, which is ambiguous in itself, though resolved in retrospect in Pym's following novel, *Jane and Prudence*, with the news of Mildred's marriage to Everard Bone. The final pages of *Excellent Women* suggest that Mildred will continue singly, as before, with her life made more 'full' because of her helping relationship to Julian and Everard. The earlier novel, *Some Tame Gazelle*, sets a precedent for the exaltation of the *status quo* as a desirable finale; Belinda feels that 'all change is of itself an evil' (*STG*, 251). By contrast to this, Mildred in *Excellent Women* tells Rocky and Helena that when they leave the downstairs flat, nothing will be the same: ' "People aren't really forgotten" ', she says (*EW*, 237). In Pym's first book, marriage constitutes a danger because it would separate the two sisters, Harriet and Belinda. Thus, when it is successfully averted, they can now continue to live together, to Belinda's relief, who ends the novel feeling that 'she could only be grateful that their lives were to be so little changed' (*STG*, 251). In *Excellent Women*, Julian's projected marriage to Allegra also poses a threat to long-established living arrangements for Julian and his sister Winifred. Even marriage itself, ironically, can dissolve, as when Helena and Rocky separate for part of the novel.

In light of this, Mildred's devotion to Everard and Julian seems both safely distant and secure, and thus much to be wished. Her relationship with the two men scarcely changes. She sees herself as 'protecting' Julian from the too-excellent women who are to share his house, and performing thankless tasks of indexing and proofreading for Everard (*EW*, 256). This plan looks like a continuation of her subservient role; Mildred always helps others and smooths away little difficulties in the parish. She seems content with her lot, but the 'full life' she describes retains an overtone of irony (*EW*, 256).

Mildred herself seems mildly bothered by her singleness, as a discussion with William Caldicote on the subject of marriage shows. Early in the novel, William states that Mildred (and he himself) should not marry because they ' "are the observers of life" ' (*EW*, 70). Mildred objects to this; she feels excluded, and stuck on the periphery. She alludes to this herself when she worries that because of this faculty, she will be considered 'an unpleasant inhuman sort of person' (*EW*, 70). Her greatest strength – detachment, keen vision – is also her greatest weakness, as it separates her from others. Does Mildred finally marry, then, in order to renounce this burden?

When Miss Doggett reveals Mildred's marriage in *Jane and Prudence*, Jessie Morrow offers a characteristically cynical appraisal of it, asserting that Mildred has forced Everard to marry her through learning to type: ' "That kind of devotion is worse than blackmail – a man has no escape from that" ', she scoffs (*JP*, 126). Mildred might have come to feel indispensable to Everard. At the end of *Excellent Women* she envisions herself undertaking a progression of tasks: proofreading Everard's manuscripts, compiling indexes for his books, then finally bending over the sink peeling his vegetables. The process might have seemed inevitable to her. The peculiarity of the marriage lies not in the fact that it should have occurred, for the two partners are well suited in some ways, as theirs is the perfect complementary relationship. Everard demands help; Mildred likes to give it. But Mildred does not love Everard – or certainly is not in love with him as she has been with Rocky.

At the same time, she does hint at the beginnings of an attraction to him in the pages of *Excellent Women*. When he invites her to dinner (to share his joint of meat) and she refuses, it later becomes, she says, 'necessary for me to know that I had been the first choice' (*EW*, 220). Still more significant is her walk past the learned society in hopes of seeing Everard, as she relates this directly to her former love for Bernard Hatherley, when she had hurried past his flat in the days when she loved him. She compares the two incidents in identical terms of motivation, as she is now 'doing what I had so often done in the days of Bernard Hatherley . . . is there no end to the humiliations we subject ourselves to?' (*EW*, 239).

Further, Everard shows himself unique in being virtually the only person in the novel who understands that Mildred has a point of view, but that she does not always say what she means. His seeming brusqueness and insensitivity is offset by this perceptiveness. Two minor but telling examples illustrate this. On one occasion when they are together in a pub, he observes that Mildred does not like the beer she is drinking, and brings her a gin and orange instead. He then asks her outright: ' "Why did you say you wanted bitter when you obviously didn't like it?" ' (*EW*, 142). This indicates that he expects to listen to what Mildred says, and that it is her responsibility to say what she means. Later in the novel, when Everard invites Mildred to lunch, she forsakes platitudes and even politeness, responding ungraciously – in short, she actually expresses exactly what she feels. In a rare stroke of intuition, Everard excuses her by referring to Rocky and Helena's separation: ' "I expect you are upset at all this happening", he said' (*EW*, 188). This seems remarkable simply because he allows Mildred to have feelings.

Thus Everard Bone as a husband for Mildred becomes not so impossible after all. Mildred consistently experiences difficulty in talking to him, in contrast to her usual flow of ready conversation. The fact that platitudes do not serve here bodes well for the honesty and forthrightness which Everard forces upon her.

Pym rewrites Brontë's *Jane Eyre* with a satiric twist. Her heroine does not overcome all odds in order to marry the romantic hero represented by Rockingham Napier, a weak and facile Mr Rochester, in *Excellent Women*. Instead, she ends by marrying a modern version of the St John figure. In Brontë's novel, St John invites Jane to marry him in order to assist him in his missionary work in India. Correspondingly, Mildred will go to Africa with Everard to aid him in his anthropological studies.

Excellent Women ends with a deliberate ambiguity, though Pym seems to have wanted to underscore the conclusion of Mildred and Everard's relationship, since she mentions the marriage in three subsequent novels. From what we see of the relationship in these later novels, it appears to follow the predicted course. In *An Unsuitable Attachment*, Everard briefly reappears, allowing the reader a glimpse of their marriage several years later. He still treats Mildred almost as if she did not exist, leaving her at home ill while he attends Rupert Stonebird's dinner-party, and remembering 'his sick wife, perhaps for the first time that evening' when it is time for him to return home to her (*UA*, 131). There is something rather sad about this indifference, and moreover, one feels cheated in missing Mildred's reappearance.

At the same time, much of the delight of Mildred's character is the pleasure of seeing her point of view. It is difficult to imagine her seeming as vibrant and witty as she appears in *Excellent Women* if she were only to be described by an outside narrator. The crucial importance of Mildred telling her own story her own way in *Excellent Women* lies in the fact that for once she gets to tell how it feels for her. This does not assume an unbiased view – on the contrary, her narration offers her own subjective perspective. But that is the point on which I want to focus. Pym is brilliant here: she makes it seem as if Mildred is not really aware of her situation. This camouflage leads readers to conclude that Mildred is still more subservient than she realises or admits. She may feel unable to do anything to change her situation, but she is aware of it. This light self-irony is a *tour de force* of narration. And that is what this perspective is meant to do; in reality Mildred does show that she knows she is cleverer than others, being one of the 'observers' of life. Mildred cannot share her insight with anyone in the novel, so she tells it to an outside audience.

The two artist–heroines who follow Mildred in Pym's fiction are Catherine Oliphant of *Less than Angels*, and Wilmet Forsyth of *A Glass of Blessings*.[4] Catherine is a distant cousin of the 'excellent woman' figure, as she is much more independent and bohemian than Belinda or Mildred of the earlier novels. She has less need than Mildred to express herself through her writing – in fact, she considers the short stories that she writes for women's magazines as simply a pleasant way to make a living, refusing to take herself seriously as an artist.

In a novel crammed with characters who are anthropologists, Catherine exemplifies the artist's technique of 'field work' which Pym borrowed from anthropologists as a method of gathering material. In her writing, Catherine functions as a parody of Pym's own novelistic style, particularly in her use of literary quotations. Most importantly, she progresses from an entirely detached view of life, which allows only for subjects which do not spring from her own experience, to personal, direct involvement with her art. In a short story which obliquely appears later in *A Glass of Blessings*, Catherine is seen to have drawn from a painful, real experience which occurs in *Less than Angels*.

Catherine writes stock romantic fantasies for women, embracing the conventions of the genre and offering her readers a happy ending. She imagines a typical story adorned in publication with a picture of a woman in a rose garden and a man 'handsomer than any real man could possibly be', in the same way that her stories are idealised (*LTA*, 27). In the short excerpt from which Mark reads aloud, Pym satirises her own novelistic style. The section he reads contains two lines from a minor Victorian poem, much as Pym herself might weave into her own text: '*Dear as remembered kisses after death* . . .' (*LTA*, 27). Since life imitates art, or Catherine's art could be supposed to imitate her own life, Digby asks her if the imagined scenario will become reality on Tom's imminent return from two years away in Africa. ' "Will you say that to Tom when he comes back?" ' he asks her (*LTA*, 30).

This crossing over from fiction to fact is prominent earlier, in another context within Pym's work. The literary woman like Prudence Bates of *Jane and Prudence*, for instance, often constructs patterns from fiction and expects to transfer them directly to life. Prudence is fond of love-letters adorned with suitable literary quotations, which enhance their elegance. Further, she creates romanticised scenarios for herself similar to what Catherine does in her short stories; at one point Prudence imagines a holiday with Arthur Grampian in which he appears on a beach during an imagined holiday, mysteriously bronzed and muscular. At the same time, she takes her literary preferences seriously, as a private matter of faith. When Geoffrey Manifold observes her reading a volume of Coventry Patmore over lunch and remarks that his poetry would be ' "just your cup of tea" ', she feels alarmed and exposed (*JP*, 45).

Catherine, by contrast, responds to Mark and Digby's inquisitiveness by disassociating herself with fiction. Embarrassed by the sentimentality of her story, she rips the sheet from which Mark is reading out of the typewriter and cries out that it is ' "not your kind of story" ' (*LTA*, 29). A realist herself, rather than a romantic, she implies that she, for one, does not expect her conversation with Tom to reach such literary heights. The choice of this quotation is curiously apt, as Tom does die at the end of the novel. Though she affects indifference to it, Catherine does betray a love for literature which surfaces instinctively. When Tom experiences his 'loss of faith' crisis in anthropology, she quotes lines from Arnold's 'Dover Beach' to comfort him (*LTA*, 106).

Pym also satirises – or perhaps defends – her own style of writing through Catherine's comment on transmuting life into fiction. She reflects on a possible subject for a story while sitting at tea in a restaurant; as an author she 'had to draw her inspiration from everyday life, though life itself was sometimes too strong and raw and must be made palatable by fancy, as tough meat may be made tender by mincing' (*LTA*, 7). Pym seems always to have had an ear for things which could be 'used' in a novel, and correspondingly for those which could not be so used. In one of her letters to Robert Smith, for example, she mentions a recent church-related scandal and adds that it would be 'much too strong for a novel' (MS PYM 162/1, fol. 19).

Catherine sees her writing as a profession, a way to make a living which is pleasant because she can pay so much attention to 'life' around her, and can refuse to feel guilty for lingering over her tea and collecting, in a covert display of field work, bits of material to 'use' in her fiction. Perhaps as a character she represents an ideal of the professional writer which was attractive to Pym herself, who was unable to find sufficient market for her fiction to allow her to abandon full-time employment.

Yet Catherine begins as rather a dilettante, and much of the novel concerns the fact that she matures as a writer: she ends by writing a story about an experience which happened directly to her, not one that she has simply overheard or observed in others' lives. The episode occurs the evening when she goes into a neighbourhood restaurant to buy a bottle of wine for supper and discovers Tom sitting at a table holding Deirdre's hand. The shock of betrayal is delayed, as Catherine finds herself first analysing the situation with habitual detachment, mechanically returning to her apartment, and then running out again in confusion. Catherine seldom seems to feel much; and in addition to her character generally being presented in this light, Pym's usual technique of depicting strong emotion in her fiction is to describe her characters' defences against feeling the full brunt of the hurt.

Catherine's subsequent actions – getting Tom out of her apartment, generally going on with life, meeting her editor with eye-shadow to camouflage eyelids swollen with crying – all illustrate her resilience and emotional hardiness. Further, the fact that she describes the event later in her fiction bears out Catherine's basic philosophy: the artist 'uses' bits of life in creating. The use of this particular incident in her fiction suggests an ability to process it, move beyond it and gain perspective. More importantly, the story reveals a new direction in Catherine's writing; she flaunts the convention of a happy ending in order to write about pain or, literally, reality.

Thus Catherine represents the commercially successful artist who learns to tell stories from her own perspective; she learns the truth which Mildred already knows instinctively. One's own feelings offer the best 'material' for writing.

Curiously, the two women in *A Glass of Blessings* who read Catherine's short story dismiss it as unrealistic. Rowena describes the plot to Wilmet while both are at the hairdressers', indulging in ladies' magazines. Is Catherine's telling of the story unskilful and unconvincing, then? What the readers seem to object to is the coincidence portrayed in the story; Wilmet protests that the whole scene is highly unlikely. ' "But what a far-fetched situation . . . As if it would happen like that!" ' She continues her speculations: ' "Do you suppose Catherine Oliphant drew it from her own experience of life?" ' (*GB*, 152). Yet the basic truth of the scene – a woman accidentally seeing proof of her lover's betrayal – is not only real in terms of Pym's fictional world, having occurred in *Less than Angels*, but universal. Wilmet will soon suffer a similar revelation herself.

Pym intends the reader's recognition of Catherine's vision of Tom to be ironic: Wilmet's own narration in *Glass of Blessings* centres around the fact that she will be betrayed in her turn. She finds herself mistaken about the motives and even about the fundamental characters of the people around her. For her the initial shock of recognition occurs when she first sees Keith and realises intuitively that he is Piers' lover. Her infatuation with Piers has blinded her to the fact of his homosexuality. The odd sequel to this drama shows Wilmet returning with Piers and Keith to their flat for tea, where she comes to pity Piers because of Keith's overprotectiveness. Once she grasps the basic principle of the two men's sexual relationship, the rest of the pieces fall into place, and she can describe them accurately.

As is true for Mildred in *Excellent Women*, much of Wilmet's narration in *Glass of Blessings* is shaped by the force of her love for Piers, as Mildred's is by her feelings for Rocky. Wilmet is different from Mildred in that she starts off the novel having everything: marriage, wealth, leisure, attractive appearance and beautiful clothes. She is a Pym fantasy heroine – her husband gives her pin money but considerately stays away emotionally.[5] Mildred and Wilmet are similar in each having a settled life, and the business of the novels is to knock the comfortable pattern awry, in both cases by the entrance of a forbidden, attractive man. The novels become love stories from the heroine's point of view.

Both of the heroines tend to hide from the reader the fact that they are infatuated, or to express it nonchalantly, as if the attraction did not really matter. In part, they are trying to convince themselves that their motives are unmixed, and that their feelings are strictly platonic in any case. This reserve is typical of Pym's heroines, but becomes of crucial significance in a novel narrated from the heroine's perspective. Pym chooses irony over sentimentality and shows her characters suffering from their illusions and self-delusions. It is as painful for them to admit that they are in love as it is to admit that they are not loved in return.

Wilmet's infatuation with Piers corresponds to her vision of others around her as well, as she points out herself in the conclusion of the book. Her conception of everyone is mistaken, as plans for marriages and ménages are revealed. Several events and plans are ostensibly a surprise to the heroine: other characters have all been 'doing things without, as it were, consulting me', she marvels (*GB*, 230). Wilmet may be self-engrossed, but she is not an egotist in the sense that she wishes to direct or manipulate others to her own ends. Her elegance and her detachment causes her in the end to feel simply left out of the party. The blow of others making their own plans knocks her off-balance because she aims at perfection, at a well-ordered life, and others' arrangements upset all her calculations. Wilmet is similar to Pym's other heroines Prudence and Leonora in her desire to keep her relationships sophisticated, cool and well-regulated. Yet when the men she is interested in do break the mould, and act on their own initiative, she is able to recover and to manage some perspective. Like Austen's Emma, whom she resembles in her blindness to those around her, Wilmet is an otherwise disagreeable heroine who is made into a sympathetic one. Pym achieves this by making the reader share in successive revelations and by showing Wilmet contrite; she admits that she has been mistaken.

At the same time, the novel's resolution strikes one as rather bizarre. Wilmet seems to end by benefiting in exactly the way she desires most. When she reappears in a cameo in *No Fond Return of Love*, she is seen by Dulcie and Viola touring a castle in Tavistock. Well-dressed as always, Wilmet is further enhanced by the fact that she is squired by all three men: her husband, Piers and Keith.

Moreover, she seems delighted by the arrangement, and Dulcie and Viola experience a slight stab of envy. Whereas Mildred is perceptive, although she appears to be dull, Wilmet does not seem especially innocent and yet fails to observe some fairly obvious developments. In the end, Wilmet is not as interesting as Mildred; the pose of innocence works so smoothly that she does not seem to express real feeling. She does describe occasional moments of exhilaration, such as during a walk with Piers, when she confesses: 'I was in the kind of exalted mood when all one's sensibilities seem to be sharpened, and I thought I had never seen anything so beautiful as the black persian cat crouching in a bed of double pink and white tulips . . .' (*GB*, 162). She displaces onto the vision of the cat her feelings for Piers, who is actually responsible for her exhilaration of the moment.

Wilmet flirts with more than one possibility of an adulterous affair, and a further problem in the novel lies in Wilmet's failure to perceive that she would betray her friend Rowena by entering into a flirtation with Rowena's husband, Harry. On a visit to their house early in the novel, Wilmet finds that Harry is holding her hand while the three of them are sitting in front of the television. Her response, though she is slightly shocked, is still largely self-centred: 'The silly old thing . . ., I thought; but then I felt flattered and a little guilty' (*GB*, 39). Later it appears that Rowena has guessed Harry's *tendre* for Wilmet, and is even rather proud of Harry's tendency to 'break out' in this youthful fashion. Rowena herself makes a romantic flourish: ' "One ought to be in *Venice* with a *lover!*" ' she complains, and indeed, all the characters in this novel are feeling their age a bit and anxious to do something grand before youth fades forever (*GB*, 149).

The irony inherent in Wilmet's narration of *A Glass of Blessings* lies in the fact that she describes the events around her through her own mistaken interpretation of them. The novel reads something like a mystery story, and like all good detective fiction, it is filled with clues to the reader. We learn through allusion, and finally through direct confirmation, that Professor Root will marry Sybil Forsyth, that Mary Beamish will marry Marius Ransome, that Keith is Piers's lover, that Rodney has been mildly unfaithful but does not really mean it, and that Wilmet's life (had she the wisdom to see it) is in reality a 'glass full of blessings' (*GB*, 256).

Yet this conclusion, or possibly the heroine herself, fails to convince fully.

Wilmet suffers to some extent as a fictional character because she lacks either Mildred's wit or Belinda's earnestness. She has more in common with Catherine Oliphant of *Less than Angels* than with the meek 'excellent women' of Pym's earlier fiction. One cannot as easily sympathise with her because Wilmet is so clearly a 'have' as opposed to a 'have not'. She does show a slightly fantastical turn of mind, which is akin to Mildred's 'talent for observation' (*EW*, 70). Many of the same kinds of observations surface in Wilmet's narrative as appear in Mildred's. The literalised metaphor of Father Thames and Father Bode boiling an egg, for instance, is inventive, as is the committee discussion of the rapacious desires of the elderly, who seem to ' "*need* meat" ' (*GB*, 20).

The point of Wilmet's character is that she is cold and egotistical, and must learn that she is this. Keith's assurance that he and Piers do not consider Wilmet 'unlovable' is a bitter blow (*GB*, 218). But the progression to self-enlightenment is more difficult to achieve successfully. Belinda of *Some Tame Gazelle and Mildred of Excellent Women* move from slights to vindication, from perceived inferiority to a comprehension that their 'nice' characters do have genuine value, though they will always be generally disregarded by society. Wilmet, however, is in a more difficult position. She must learn that she is less nice than she thinks she is. And the reader may find little satisfaction in watching Wilmet learn the existential truth that others exist independently of her and make their own choices. She comes to appreciate her luxuries, certainly; yet in some ways she does not seem to see the other characters more clearly at the end of the novel than she does at the beginning. At the least, it seems she will never be able to rid herself of the 'incubus' Keith.[6]

Her pose of innocence is puzzling, and leads one to suspect ultimately that she dons it simply in order to dupe the reader. Such naïvety followed by earnest resolves to do better in the future tend to make the narration of the novel tiresome. Wilmet justifies herself through the telling of her own story, as Mildred does in *Excellent Women*. But Wilmet's selfishness and obtuseness in what she says act to stress her failings rather than to redeem them. Still, she does move somewhere beyond her original conception of the world, and goes further than Prudence or Leonora, her nearest equivalents in Pym's world.

As in anthropological studies, the artist who wishes to observe must attain the correct position from which to view his subject. This manoeuvring suggests a strong connection with Pym's perception of the role of the detective or academic who does 'research' into the lives of contemporaries, as represented most fully by Dulcie Mainwaring in *No Fond Return* (*NFR*, 44). In other words, to find out valuable information, one must establish a position of superior knowledge and of detachment in order to be effective as an interpreter. Pym's version of the 'researcher' shows the character most often entranced with the object of research, since love is 'a powerful incentive to this kind of research', as Dulcie would acknowledge (*NFR*, 44). And much of what Pym's artist–heroines describe in terms of their intimate, daily experience is the effects of infatuation and unrequited love.

But the major difference between the artist and the merely educated-in-English-literature academic woman is that she can finally attain a truer perspective on herself and can set aside her own illusions. Mildred, Catherine and Wilmet all attain a more realistic view of their position towards the men they admire, while Dulcie, Prudence, Viola and others of the educated yet essentially dilettante group do not. By writing out and exposing their fantasies, these women can subdue them or gain perspective so as not to be ruled by them. They are not dependent on fortuitous endings or marriages to provide stability or meaning.

To give a biographical context to this question, Barbara Pym thought of herself as an artist, and gloried in her distinction as an acute observer. As the passage about the department store quoted earlier suggests, Pym constantly guaged herself against those around her, and saw herself alone against the background of an unknown community, giving account of herself. This kind of self-parody is illustrated in her humorous private account of the Booker Prize dinner where she received an award for *Quartet in Autumn*. She mocks herself in terms of her appearance, comparing herself to the other authors present: 'BP in her 65th yr. [*sic*] Tall, short hair, long black pleated skirt, black blouse, Indian with painted flowers (C & A £4.90) and green beads' (*VPE*, 311). In a similar self-parody on the novelist incognito, she staged a vignette in her diaries: 'In Witney waiting for the bus. Who is that woman sitting on the concrete wall outside Barclays Bank reading the TV Times? Answer: it is Miss Pym the novelist' (MS PYM 77, fol. 7).

She visualised herself in terms of her calling as an artist. It directly reflected her sense of worth as a person, or, rather, came to do so early on, when it became clear to her that her relationship with Henry Harvey would not result in marriage. The extent to which she saw herself in something of the role of a private detective is

illustrated by the episode in *No Fond Return*, where she projected
herself as a character in her own novel. The first joke occurs when a
copy of *Some Tame Gazelle* appears on the bookshelf in Dulcie's
bathroom. Later, when Dulcie and Viola have gone to a guest-house
in Tavistock, an unidentified character enters the hotel
dining-room:

> It was at this point that somebody came to the unoccupied table,
> but as she was a woman of about forty, ordinary-looking and
> unaccompanied, nobody took much notice of her. As it
> happened, she was a novelist; indeed, some of the occupants of
> the tables had read and enjoyed her books, but it would never
> have occurred to them to connect her name, even had they
> ascertained it from the hotel register, with that of the author they
> admired. They ate their stewed plums and custard and drank
> their thimble-sized cups of coffee, quite unconscious that they
> were being observed. (*NFR*, p. 176)

This scene suggests that part of the exquisite delight of being an
author is that one can glory in one's conception of worth, *incognito* –
and, of course, the novelist can 'observe' those around her.

This hidden position bears directly on the way Pym proceeds in
writing her fiction: her imagination seems drawn to this detective-
like craving for information, for finding things out, for being on the
inside and having a superior vantage point.

The method in this sort of vision begins with minute details and
deduces from them, or extends out from them along the lines of
what might be a likely or 'suitable' sequel. Pym's immense curiosity
led her both literally to spy on her neighbours and to ponder the
significance of the actions she observed. Her character Senhor
MacBride-Pereira in *No Fond Return* exhibits classic traits of this
tendency. Looking out of his window in suburban London, he
observes others and constantly poses the question of their
significance to himself: 'The things I see', he thinks, as he notices
Aylwin and Laurel outside Dulcie's house (*NFR*, 205). Later he also
witnesses the episode of the *marron glacé* between Leonora and
Phoebe in *The Sweet Dove Died*. He is punished for inquisitiveness, as
he is doomed to only partial knowledge of the episodes he observes,
'wondering what, if anything, he had missed' (*NFR*, 254).

Pym herself seems to have greatly admired authors, and collected
several biographies of literary figures. Her library at the time of her

death contained biographies of several writers, including Keats, Thomas Hardy, Henry James and Lytton Strachey. She was friends with several contemporary authors as well, as her correspondence with Robert Liddell, Elizabeth Taylor and Philip Larkin illustrates. She hesitated about her own papers being examined in similar fashion, referring playfully but none the less anxiously to Jake Balokowsky, the grotesque fictional biographer of Larkin's poem. When thesis writer Tullio Blundo wrote to Pym in the late 1970s requesting biographical information, Pym replied in a slightly offended tone, answering that a critic could only tell what she was like as a person by meeting people who had known her and by reading her diaries. And access to those, she added firmly, would certainly not be possible while she was still alive (MS PYM 147, fol. 83). Perhaps some of this reluctance to be known personally stems from natural modesty and reserve, but it might also reflect indignation at being so palpably left out of literary circles. Her relative isolation might have been as difficult to bear as lack of wider public recognition.

She coped with this, in some measure, by humour – as she coped with everything. On the occasion of having tea with Elizabeth Bowen, Pym described the afternoon in her diaries in self-mocking tones, adopting a deferential attitude towards her hostess: 'She is very kind and obviously feels she ought to know more about me than she can possibly know!' (*VPE*, 186). On another occasion Pym attended a talk delivered by Bowen at a Literary Society meeting, and recorded later in her diary her own peculiar fantasy about making a scene, and having to be escorted from the room. The main concern here has to do with Pym's own identity and her obscurity, as Pym imagines the sequel to her meditated revolt: ' "Who was that woman who made a scene?" someone would ask. And nobody would know . . .' (*VPE*, 249).

Like all writers, Pym regarded fiction as a means of saying something to others about her situation, of communicating her vision, as all artists do – but the interesting thing in Pym's work is that she seems so fastidious and detached from her subject matter, and yet at the same time it is highly autobiographical. At times she writes primarily to a single person, as *Some Tame Gazelle* is intended ' "for Henry" ' (MS PYM 103, fol. 5). She wrote for the public as well, of course, agreeing with Ivy Compton-Burnett that one would write for a dozen readers, though never for none at all.

Later in life, Pym wrote (in part) for her younger friend Richard

Roberts. A revealing passage from her notebooks which she sent to him as a letter illustrates this fine dividing line between art and life. She evidently created her small story from a real event: an awkward evening *tête-à-tête*, part of which was spent cooking sausages in the kitchen. Most of the vignette concerns the woman's thoughts about their relationship after the man had left to go home, remembering with shame her 'appalling domestic inefficiency and the meagre meal she had given him . . .' (*VPE*, 231). The main point concerns an earlier occasion still, 'the one for which she *really* needed to be forgiven' (*VPE*, 231). At the end of the letter she adds, in her own voice: 'So you see, my dear, how with a little polishing life could become literature, or at least fiction!' Thus in this letter – and to some extent in her fiction too – Pym apologises for what she is. She tries to get the man to see her side, how sorry she is, how inadequate she feels, how she would like to do better if she could. At the same time, by joking about it she asserts that she is still worth something. Comedy is for Pym a way of asserting dignity; and also of getting her own back. Though constrained to be polite in conversation, she can spell it out accurately in fiction. Writing is a revelation of her point of view.

Oddly, Pym's letter to Richard Roberts has uncanny affinities with Mildred's narrative voice in *Excellent Women*, though the novel was written several years earlier. It reflects the same sort of subject matter – inevitably, unrequited love – and the same response to it: trying to hold back from pursuing the beloved, the choking feeling of disappointment, the realisation that she cares more for him than he does for her. And although the relationship with Roberts seems to have been appropriated for the novel *The Sweet Dove Died*, Pym seems much closer to Mildred in this letter than she does to Leonora.

Thus the artist figure in Pym's fiction reflects much of Pym's conception of herself as an artist, which in turn formed a large part of her self-concept. At times Pym seems to have been concerned about the qualities of detachment which she cultivated. She tried to distinguish between degrees of distance, as she confided in her diaries: 'Being "interested in people" doesn't necessarily mean that one is a nice or a kind person. There might be too much of the detachment of the novelist or the sociologist in one's attitude' (MS PYM 72, fol. 6). Mildred, Wilmet, Catherine – and Pym – all deprecate themselves and do not outwardly boast of their insights.

None the less, the irony (and excellence) of Pym's work lies precisely here. For writing is a means of quiet, satisfactory revenge;

a matter of satirising oneself, yet also of exposing the vagaries and absurdities of others, particularly men. A strong belief in its efficacy prompted her to conclude in her diaries: 'What a pity more people (perhaps I mean women?) are not writers of fiction' (MS PYM 78, fol. 21). Pym's novels contain shrewd and telling satire. On occasion, they become too self-conscious and can lag. But they retain their final, most triumphant irony in consistently seeming to deny their revenge. Mildred remains docile and meek to those around her, enjoying the private joke of their peculiarities. And like her retiring heroines, Pym remains in the background – going shopping or to work, attending PCC meetings, humbly accepting an invitation to a literary talk – but all the time wondering 'what *if* . . . I really told them who I am?' For she does precisely that in her novels.

7

A Few Green Leaves as *Apologia*

In her final novel, *A Few Green Leaves*, Barbara Pym wrote from a unique position; in the glow of affirmation following the new recognition of her work, she was able to review both her life and her earlier novels. Though not in itself a wholly successful novel, the book is important because it shows Pym in her element as a social satirist, recasts or synthesises many of her typical themes from earlier fiction, and affirms her own personal choice for art and the novel.[1] It offers a counterpoint to *Some Tame Gazelle* at the beginning of her writing career, as if to show what life had taught her in between. This 'story of an imaginary village', as she christened the novel in her dedication, had its roots in Finstock, Oxfordshire, where she retired from London to live with her sister in 1974. Pym compared the two provincial novels in a notation in her diaries: 'When I wrote *Some Tame Gazelle* I didn't know nearly as much about village life as I do now' (*VPE*, 283). *A Few Green Leaves* incorporates several echoes of her life in Finstock, such as her sister Hilary's interest in local history and the actual presence of a mausoleum at the village church.[2] She wrote describing the novel to Philip Larkin in 1979: 'I am trying to finish and improve a country novel, a new one "based" on life here (but of course nothing like it, really?)' (*VPE*, 327). Curiously, this final novel is most strikingly 'like' the life depicted in Pym's earlier fiction.

The novel is singular in being the first novel in a long career that Pym wrote for a large admiring audience. She had already attained an established position as a writer, when her earlier novels of the 1950s had gained small steady following. But she was chagrined by the sixteen-year period in which her work remained unpublished, dating from the rejection of *An Unsuitable Attachment* in 1963. 'The embarrassment of being an unpublished novelist', she raged after a manuscript had been rejected yet another time, 'knows no bounds ...' (*VPE*, 288). But her 'rediscovery' in 1977 was gratifying in the extreme, and promised increasing public acclaim. The audience which was assured for *A Few Green Leaves* made the conditions under which it was written markedly differently from that of *The Sweet Dove Died* and *Quartet in Autumn*, which immediately preceded it. She wrote these two novels uncertain that they would ever be published, while her final book was conceived and written not only with the assurance of publication, but with the affirmation of her own excellence as a novelist. After she had been 'rediscovered' through the fortuitous *TLS* article in 1977 which drew attention to her work, Pym was interviewed on radio and television, taken to lunch by pleasant, young Macmillan editors, short-listed for the Booker Prize, approached by Dutton in the US, written about in London papers – in short, her reputation sky-rocketed dramatically, especially in contrast with her former near-oblivion.[3] In a biographical essay describing this period in Pym's life, Constance Malloy has described the delight which Pym took in her new-found fame, and the air of girlish expectation which infused Pym's letters and diaries of the time.[4]

This change in her literary fortunes was announced in what might be considered dramatic or even seemingly fictional style, and came as a complete surprise – she first heard that her name had been mentioned in *TLS* when a friend rang her on the phone. The event was significant enough to be recorded in her daily pocket diary as well as her more spacious writing notebook, appearing on 21 January 1977 cryptically as: 'B.P. in TLS. Paul Binding / Philip Larkin rang' (MS PYM 143, fol. 14). More important than the notice or honour attached to such publicity was the prospect of having her novels published once again. She adds an aside in her notebook which reveals this desire: '(During the [following] week letters from kind friends but no agent or publisher approaching.)' (MS PYM 76, fol. 14). This was soon changed. Most striking, besides the unexpected nature of such attention, was the background of provincial, domestic retirement against which it occurred. The author was, characteristically, in the middle of making marmalade when the telephone call came.[5]

The making of marmalade on a January afternoon typified much of her quiet, domestic life at the time. And it continued to define part of her response to all the subsequent fuss about her fiction generated by the 'rediscovery' of her novels sparked by the note in *TLS*. At a special session devoted to a discussion of Pym's novels held at the Modern Language Association Convention in 1982, panelist Professor Burkhart of Temple University commented on

Pym's possible response to the continuing publicity, had she still been alive at the time. (Pym died in January 1980.) Speaking for and concurring with Pym's close friend Robert Liddell, Burkhart stated that in his opinion, while her works were being praised, the author would most probably have been at home 'making marmalade'. This does not suggest excessive shyness – nor yet indifference to her sudden access of fame. Her 'rediscovery' as a novelist seems to have provided a profound source of satisfaction to her. But most important in her response to sudden acclaim was the writing of *A Few Green Leaves*; when acknowledgement came, and since time permitted, she took the opportunity to write another novel.

One hesitates to dwell too heavily on the circumstances surrounding Pym's change in reputation; it is easy to over-emphasise the Cinderella part of the story. Further, Cape's decision to reject *An Unsuitable Attachment* is by no means surprising in retro-spect. Even a brief study of sales figures and of the correspondence between Pym and Cape editors in the early 1960s would convince one of Cape's good wishes for their author (and of their reasoned business sense) – or so it seems to me. To some extent, Pym's publishing misfortunes reflected simply the fortunes of war.
of war.

Whatever the other implications of this situation are, the fact remains that the fabled 'rediscovery' of Pym's novels provided an inevitable background for the creative genesis of *A Few Green Leaves*: Pym wrote it out of some hard-won confidence. And sensing that so little time was left, she seemed to make the novel her 'final statement on life'.[6] Further, it is an intensely personal book in the sense that it suggests – at least in part – an *apologia pro vita sua*, offering a summary of all her essential novelistic themes and a comment – however indirect – on her personal life. In an interview Pym spoke of her art in culinary terms: working from her 'little notebooks' she 'boiled it all up and reduced it, like making chutney'.[7] In this final work she seems to have culled from her past novels as much from life around her: the novel 'reduces' precisely the elements she had always used in her fiction, and provides a sweeping, comprehensive view of her earlier novels. And in this drawing together, she simultaneously reviews her life, hinting at directions she might have taken, and justifying and explaining her choices. It also underscores her insistence on the importance of the trivial.

Her concern with the immediacy of death is also much in

evidence, and also with the judging of one's life in retrospect which can accompany its end. In addition, Pym uses the vantage point of the late 1970s to employ her powers as social satirist, especially in comparison with her middle period of fiction in the 1950s, which recreates post-war England in such minute detail. Times have changed, as she is quick to point out in her criticism of a 'synthetic' society. Thus *A Few Green Leaves* combines a recapitulation of former novelistic themes, a study of ageing and of approaching death, and a satire of provincial life. Pym wrote the novel from a unique position of confidence, and it shows wit, insight and graciousness. Fame did not spoil her, as it were, and after a life-time riddled with various disappointments, the modest yet affirmative tone of the novel speaks well for her.

In many respects, *A Few Green Leaves* seems absolutely typical of Pym's novels of the 1950s. A short list of its themes reveals the following staples in her fiction: the consciousness of literary past (especially Victorian) and extensive use of quotations, the important role played by the university, the relation of work to love, the largely unsatisfactory nature of romance and the abundant material for social satire offered by the hierarchy of a small village. The book further contains similar characters to those typically found in her earlier fiction: 'ineffectual' clergy, eccentric anthropologists, splendid spinsters, an observant artist (-to-be), an enigmatic cleaning woman, countless excellent women and a few feeble men. To complete the sense of recreation of her earlier fictional world, the author includes a collection of items intended for a jumble sale, and several scenes of women preparing meals in the kitchen. The richness offered by village life provides vintage Pym subject matter.

Modernity has crept into this more contemporary version of provincial life in the shape of freezers, televisions, bungalows and a complicated contraption for indicating how many milk bottles should be left for the travelling gourmet critic, Adam Prince. Pym takes account of shifts in social structure which have occurred since the comparatively sedate period of the 1950s. In the late 1970s, when the book takes place, marriage arrangements seem to be more casual, and the clergy is replaced in some functions by the members of the medical profession. In an earlier draft of the novel, Pym depicts a minor character Robbie Barraclough not only living with Tamsin, but having abandoned a wife and children in order to do so.

For the most part, however, *plus ça change, plus c'est la même chose*. In comparison with *The Sweet Dove Died* and *Quartet in Autumn*, which are distinctly urban, London novels with occasional forays into the country, *A Few Green Leaves* offers a return to a provincial setting which in turn reflects England's traditions and embodies its past. But what is still more suprising than the reworking of this familiar material is the way in which the author presents it. In her final novel, Pym returns to a style which recalls her middle fiction of the 1950s and early 1960s, from *Some Tame Gazelle* through to *An Unsuitable Attachment*.

Never radically experimental in form, Pym generally follows a traditional mode of writing, yet shows a marked change in tone in the different attitude taken by the narrators of these novels. *The Sweet Dove Died* and *A Quartet in Autumn* are chilling and stark, detached to the point of malice, whereas *A Few Green Leaves* might describe melancholy situations, but it does so with an essentially warm, comic approach. While keeping the central theme of *memento mori* firmly in view, it suggests a counterpoint of hope by arranging the majority of the characters around a heroine who looks forward to a productive and fruitful future. Emma learns to order her perceptions and makes a positive choice for the direction her life will take beyond the pages of the novel.

This is not to say that an optimistic ending is necessarily better than a pessimistic one. In addition, Letty of *Quartet in Autumn* and Leonora of *Sweet Dove Died* both end their respective novels with a similar enlightenment to Emma's: Letty will decide for herself where she plans to live during retirement, and Leonora chooses not to allow her overriding desire for James's devotion to goad her into renewing their former awkward relationship.[8] Still, the conclusion of *A Few Green Leaves* ties together more loose ends than those of the former two novels, and resolves the complex problem of Emma's future plans with more creativity; at the same time, its end seems fitting.

The novel is organised as a pastiche of vignettes which revolve around Emma Howick. Though she is not exactly a corresponding version of the author herself, she seems to embody a particular part of Pym's character, perhaps most clearly in her tendency mentally to review her life and gauge her accomplishments. As a corollary to Pym's personal life, Pym seems to have been especially struck by the death of her friend and contemporary, novelist Elizabeth Taylor, who died only a few years earlier, in 1976. She takes the occasion to

apostrophise on her own situation, comparing her own success to
that of Taylor's, in an agony of self-doubt: ' "Fame did not come, but
your life has made its own pattern." (me). [*sic*]' (MS PYM 72, fol. 19).
In *A Few Green Leaves*, Emma engages in a search for purpose, or
something to devote herself to in order to achieve distinction.
Though not excessively ambitious, Emma is none the less mildly
anxious about what she is making of her life. By training, Emma is
an anthropologist, boasting 'a few articles published in learned
journals', but apparently she has no striking insights and no passion
for her work. More to the point, her mother, a Victorian scholar,
seems sceptical of Emma's achievements, offering a constant,
unspoken reproach to her daughter. In light of Emma's character,
the alternative of an academic career might occasionally have
seemed a possibility for Pym herself to have pursued, as she worked
for a group of anthropologists for several years in a subservient role.
She wrote a revealing speculation in her diary before the unexpected
'rediscovery' – at the lowest point in her fortunes – wondering if
she had chosen wrongly: 'Better if I had followed an academic
career. rather than a novelist's – but it's certainly too late now!'
(*VPE*, 287).

Her character Emma Howick illustrates moreover the typically
frustrating position of the spinster: what she has done in a
professional realm remains insufficient without the added accomplishment of marriage. Her mother actively expects or wishes
Emma to marry, and even contemplates conspiring to 'bring her
together' with Tom as a suitable husband.

The figure of the early-middle-aged heroine who has not achieved
much distinction is paralleled by the older characters in the novel,
who are similarly unremarkable, but for whom it is too late to
change. Like the two books which precede it, the novel offers a
study of ageing; Dr Shrubsole specialises in geriatrics, an unfamiliar
work which sounds at first something like a joke. And the single
woman in varying stages of spinsterhood becomes its special focus:
Miss Lee and Miss Grundy, Daphne Dagnall and her friend Heather
Blenkinsop, Miss Lickerish, Isobel Mound, Miss Vereker – even
Magdalene Raven and Beatrix Howick hardly seem to have been
married in their present widowed state. The loneliness experienced
by several of these women leads them to adopt compensatory
measures: Daphne decides to get a dog, while Miss Lickerish keeps
cats and hedgehogs in her house.

Companionship between women who band together seems to

offer little more satisfaction than animals do; the two pairs of women who set up house together become locked in a battle of domination and submission. They represent a bleak reflection of the cheerful Bede sisters of Pym's first novel, *Some Tame Gazelle*. One curious aspect of the ménage of Miss Lee and Miss Grundy is the fact that Miss Grundy had once authored a romantic novel, in her younger days. It is not clear why she abandoned writing. Was Miss Lee too oppressive a presence? Did Miss Grundy lose hope and imagination? The failure of life to imitate art might have proved too disappointing for her to be able to continue writing romances. Pym suggests an ironic failure on the part of unobliging reality, when she emphasises that for Miss Grundy, at any rate, the handsome prince has never appeared. On the occasion when Miss Grundy trips in the garden at the Gellibrands' sherry party, Emma becomes her rescuer, and she further receives a sharp rebuke from Miss Grundy who had warned her not to wear 'those shoes': 'Miss Grundy had stumbled and nearly fallen on the rocky path. She, the author of a romantic novel, had found herself in the kind of situation that might have provided a fruitful plot; but it was not the son of the house who came to her assistance or a handsome stranger, but Emma, the anthropologist and observer of human behaviour' (*FGL*, 56).

Where Miss Lee and Miss Grundy are seen entrenched in a morbid relationship, Daphne's situation borders on the tragic because the novel portrays her in the process of entering into a similar bondage with her friend Heather. The two women plan to retire together to Greece, where they have gone on holiday together before, but Heather insists that they stay in England. Daphne's bright dream of hot Attic sun diminishes to the reality of a house in foggy London, while 'Thy Servant a Dog' becomes her demanding if unwitting master (*FGL*, 46). Daphne illustrates a curious case as a spinster; in her relationship with her brother Tom, for whom she keeps house until moving in with Heather, she demonstrates the dangers of excessive self-sacrifice and its attendant, gnawing bitterness. She resents serving him. Her anger recalls Mildred's impatience with pouring endless cups of tea and 'bearing burthens' in *Excellent Women*, yet without Mildred's perception that she is doing these tasks because she wants to. Daphne's example is poignant; sobering both because of the damage she herself incurs, and because Tom is also diminished and made further ineffectual by her mothering. When he ponders his sister's zeal in housekeeping, his response is a mixture of fear and indifference: 'If only women wouldn't work so hard, would spare themselves a little!' he complains to himself (*FGL*, 35).

Still another representative of spinsterhood, Miss Vereker, possesses a kind of mythical quality because of her attachment to old times and former glory. Pym's fiction is full of this kind of character: Miss Prideaux of *A Glass of Blessings*, who never tires of telling exotic stories about her former days as governess, Connie Aspinall in *Some Tame Gazelle*, who rhapsodises about her days as lady's companion in Belgrave Square, and even Miss Foxe of *The Sweet Dove Died*, with her valuable 'bits and pieces', who carries with her the dignity of being a 'distressed gentlewoman' (*SDD*, 110). Miss Vereker transcends the other women by bearing the unofficial title 'the last governess'. She is figuratively the last of the old order of the genteel servant classes, and also the last of Pym's contemporary Jane Eyre figures.

The other spinsters comprise a range of alternatives in living and arranging the single life. Miss Lickerish fills the role of village eccentric, and in her death provides a social event around which the author can crystallise the community. Thus one character has deceased '"effects"' cleared, which is one of the author's main preoccupations in the novel (*FGL*, 229).[9] Isobel, the headmistress who visits Emma with Emma's mother, acts as a comic version of the older woman who remains interested in men. She is obviously attracted to Tom, though refusing to admit as much to herself; yet at the same time she is perceived by everyone around her as too old for that sort of thing. But women never do lose interest in men, in Pym's fictional world. Ianthe Potts, Emma's friend from school days who works in a museum, is a younger spinster doomed to a life-time of loneliness; the man she loves turns out to be homosexual, making her situation 'hopeless', as romance appears to be for many of Pym's other heroines.

Beatrix Howick and Magdalene Raven illustrate the truth that age as well as death is the great leveller. Though they once achieved the status of wife and even of mother, they are now single again. Beatrix reflects some part of Pym's cynicism in her view of marriage as an obligatory but not necessarily enjoyable experience. Her husband 'had been killed in the war, and having, as it were, fulfilled herself as a woman Beatrix had been able to return to her academic studies with a clear conscience' (*FGL*, 8). In this view, a man is something to be got out of the way. These women are old enough to be settled in their roles, and as such to illustrate possible roles for Emma. The question then becomes what Emma will do in light of these examples: in her mid-thirties (the unspecified age of being just too old to wear Laura Ashley clothes) she still might shape a different life for herself.[10] Further, in comparison with the community around her she seems relatively young. Yet she hesitates about having to make any definite change or choice; while she resists facing the necessity to make plans, she is paralysed by her fear of not ultimately having lead a sufficiently 'distinguished' life (*FGL*, 57). Her concern with such matters is muted; Emma does not appear ambitious, and is perfectly ready to compare herself with those who are less fortunate than she is, such as Miss Lee and Miss Grundy and Ianthe Potts. Yet she yearns for distinction.

For the older characters who are already set in their paths, the necessity to acquire dignity and self-respect is still more important. In Martin Shrubsole's insensitivity to his geriatric patients, Pym satirises the common fallacy of regarding older people as less than human, and consequently of denying the relation of the soul to the body. While specialising in the physical health of older people, he shows no conception of their having lived past lives and of their still retaining cumulative hurts, disappointments and illusions from that time. An example of this attitude occurs at the beginning of the novel, when Martin feels that Daphne's emotional outburst should be physically beaten down: 'He felt that the drugs prescribed to control high blood pressure should also damp down emotional excesses and those fires of youth that could still – regrettably – burn in the dried-up hearts of those approaching old age' (*FGL*, 5). While the younger generation is coming on, and worrying about what it will make of itself, the older characters in the novel fight a feeling of narrowing horizons and of being unwanted.

In the context of these questions about purpose and past achievement, the centre of the novel is Emma's change from anthropologist to novelist, or from academic scholar to creative artist. This decision seems to represent on some level Pym's similar choice to write fiction. There is some foreshadowing of this early in the novel, when after an unsatisfactory lunch with Graham, Emma attempts to set the encounter in perspective: 'It might have been better if I'd been a novelist, Emma thought . . .', since she could 'use' the 'material' provided by Graham as a basis for fiction (*FGL*, 37). This seems to me a rather lame protest, but it does point to one of the themes which Pym attempts to illustrate in the novel. As in much of her earlier fiction, she asserts that a narrow or dull life can be made

more bearable by the cultivation of just such qualities of detachment
and observation as Emma shows and develops. In addition, Emma's
relations with men gain some direction at the end of the novel, when
she makes this choice, deciding to 'embark on a love affair' with Tom
Dagnall (*FGL*, 250).[11] Her choice to stay in the village echoes similar
resolutions for heroines in earlier novels, such as Wilmet in *A Glass
of Blessings*, who enters further into the church community in the
same way that Emma becomes integrated into the West Oxfordshire
village where she decides to stay.

She arrives at this decision through a muted yet painful period of
chronic disappointment. Throughout the novel, she struggles with
dissatisfaction in both work and love. Like several other Pym
heroines, Emma suffers a dearth of romance. Sharing the common
failing of Pym's academic women, she tends not to 'make the most'
of her appearance – a task Dulcie also neglects in *No Fond Return* – in
order to catch a man. It is never made clear whether such efforts on
their own would avail her much, although we see their negative
effects; unobservant as he generally is, Tom Dagnall is repulsed by
one particularly drab dress he sees Emma wearing. And there is no
doubt that she suffers by comparison with the elegant Claudia
Pettifer in glamour. What this ultimately illustrates is not,
somehow, that Emma should do more to make herself attractive,
but simply that life is difficult. It is not her fault that she was not
made beautiful. As for the necessity of having a husband, either
with good looks or without, in the novel's setting of the 1970s
Emma's needs are suggested to extend beyond the need to have a
husband simply for social reasons. Her singleness actually symbolises the spinster's plight of sexual frustration, as her consultation
about the rash on her hand with Martin Shrubsole suggests, in
rather a bold stroke of analysis for Pym.

Part of Emma's difficulty lies in the fact that no acceptable men
appear in order to court her; she lacks a romantic hero just as Miss
Grundy does. Thus she is mired in the typical dilemma of Dulcie and
Mildred and other heroines before her; she is professional enough to
want a man who is an intellectual equal, yet domestic enough to
want a man who appreciates her in the kitchen as well. A scene late
in the novel illustrates this paradox, when Emma tires of shop talk
during a conversation with fellow anthropologists Graham Pettifer
and Robbie and Tamsin Barraclough. Emma not only leaves the
house abruptly, but ends by enjoying a conversation about the
making of jam with Tom, the rector, after he meets her accidentally

and walks her home. In terms of their subsequent love affair and probable marriage, this domestic scene shows that the two seem a suitable pair, though theirs does not promise to be a compelling romance.

Even so, Emma is able to combine needs for both work and love in her determination to turn novelist and to pursue a love affair with Tom. The transformation to novelist can be easily made; she possesses all the hallmarks of an ideal novelist in the Pym tradition: quick observation, curiosity, detachment, even a formal training in anthropology. Further, she is a good cook. In the end, Emma wants both a marriage and a career; she plans to start a love affair and write a novel, since both are necessary to fulfilment. Further, by doing this, she implicitly accepts the community as her own, and makes a commitment not only to Tom, but to the West Oxfordshire village where she too will grow old.[12]

The novel's conclusion strikes a slightly odd note in relation to the projected 'love affair', both because so little is claimed for it (it 'need not necessarily be an unhappy one', in the narrator's words), and because Emma herself takes the initiative to pursue it (*FGL*, 250). Tom clearly admires Emma, but has shown himself so 'ineffectual' in a romantic role that he cannot pursue her. Though they seem to share some interests, their conversations consist largely of awkward pauses. Perhaps her resolve simply means that she will welcome his advances and encourage him in what he already desires. The conclusion of *A Few Green Leaves* is similar to that of *Excellent Women*, where Mildred looks forward to a 'full life', which, one learns in subsequent novels, includes marriage to Everard Bone. The two novels follow much the same progression. The correspondingly more glamorous male – Rocky Napier in *Excellent Women*, Graham Pettifer in *A Few Green Leaves* – makes use of the 'excellent woman' heroine to provide cups of tea or boiled eggs or to get a few groceries. In both cases, the men return to waiting wives, leaving Mildred and Emma to marry the duller yet steadier churchmen. It is less surprising that Emma should choose Tom than that she should ever have cared for that 'dull dog' Graham Pettifer, who has not even Rocky Napier's superficial charm to recommend him (*FGL*, 197). The comedy of his pseudo-courtship wears a little thin, as one learns progressively more of the ways in which he takes advantage of Emma and accepts a constant offering of food as his due.

The novel's closing is none the less an important affirmation of values for Pym, who seems preoccupied with the subject of death in the novel, and throughout the book asks questions about life and meaning, even to the extent of allowing one of her characters seriously to doubt the tenets of the Anglican Church. She considers both England's historical past and individual lives of her characters, and poses this measuring of past achievements against future possibilities for her heroines. In the process of figuratively getting 'Deceased Effects Cleared', she examines their nature in the same way that she details the pile of jumble which Daphne collects (*FGL*, 40).

The tendency of the isolated characters to judge themselves can be illuminated by a comparison with Philip Larkin's poetic treatment of this same theme. Barbara Pym has been called by one reviewer a 'female, prose Larkin', as Larkin is a 'male, poetic Pym'.[13] While this comparison perhaps simplifies their affinities too much, there is a distinct similarity between the two writers as they present the subject of the lonely protagonist who compares himself with others, or who guages his worth according to what he possesses. The departed figure of Mr Bleaney in Larkin's poem of that name, for instance, provides the mark against which the speaker of the poem – who has become identified with him – measures himself. The speaker compares himself to Mr Bleaney, having figuratively taken his place by renting the man's former room. His final question strikes at the heart of self-doubt; did not the former occupant of the room fear, as he does, 'That how we live measures our own nature'. How could he not have wondered if he was worthless when he considered his surroundings, 'one hired box'.[14] By extension, the protagonist himself measures the limits of his own existence and self-worth.

Similarly, in the poem 'Dockery and Son', the middle-aged speaker compares himself directly to a contemporary at Oxford. Where the Prufrockian poet feels sterile and useless, Dockery has by contrast taken hold of life and become fruitful by having a son. The poem ends with a sense of universal loss for everyone, faced with the grim necessity of spending life one way or another: 'Whether or not we use it, it goes . . .', the speaker concludes.[15]

This tendency to compare oneself with others haunts several characters in *A Few Green Leaves*. Tom feels ineffective in his role as rector, contrasting himself with the more slick and polished Adam Prince, a former Anglican priest. Emma adopts a pose of detachment in viewing the villagers, and in this way tries to keep envy (or pity) to a minimum; but even so, she feels chastened at the

Gellibrands' sherry party, where she compares herself with the other guests, and is forced to admit to Mrs Gellibrand that she did not attend Somerville, Oxford, but the much less prestigious London School of Economics. A few characters, most notably Beatrix Howick, compare themselves with an ideal of what they feel they ought to have done. Beatrix feels relieved to have got the expected thing out of the way – the experience of having husband and child. Daphne finds herself in an even worse situation, as she has fulfilled her ideal of helping her brother in his time of need, having rushed to keep house for him when he was newly widowed. But she discovers the ideal to be hollow. The outcome is a bitter realisation that the ideal was not worth the sacrifice. Tom does not care that she has devoted herself to him, and Daphne feels that she has wasted her life. For the most part, characters in the novel are not only isolated from each other, but are conscious of themselves as having succeeded or (more usually) failed according to comparison with others.

This pervasive theme of unfulfilled potential or misdirected zeal suggests a feeling of constriction; of being hemmed in and unable to move. To take the point further, it seems to reflect an aspect of Pym's life and her work. Both seem imbued with narrow possibilities and chronic disappointments. The restrictions from which her characters suffer are as much mental, or self-imposed, as they are objective and external. And this makes for an odd view throughout her fiction, where characters such as Marius Ransome in *A Glass of Blessings* claim that they have been ' "bruised by life as it were" ' – in consequence they appear both ridiculous yet unaccountably compelling (*GB*, 242).[16] What, after all, has been so terrible for them? A lame protest it is – and yet its seeming shallowness forms part of its impact; through the irony of this comment Pym seeks to forestall criticism of the narrowness of her perspective.

Pym's entire work constitutes, from one perspective, a concerted effort to react to life's inherent narrowness by limiting oneself. Her characters attempt to minimise: to make do with little. Letty in *Quartet in Autumn* tries to persuade herself that 'the experience of "not having" [might] be regarded as something with its own validity' (*QA*, 25). In a still more positive reworking of the same theme, Miss Grundy makes do with a 'few green leaves' in the church flower arrangements to compensate for the scarceness of blooms in autumn. In order to avoid feeling the indignity of life depriving them, her characters often seek to forestall fate by deliberately limiting themselves. Belinda Bede of *Some Tame Gazelle* makes do with one evening of Wordsworth (read aloud by 'dear Henry'), every thirty years or so, and Mildred Lathbury of *Excellent Women* urges herself not to have feelings, but only to observe the effects of other peoples'. Jane Cleveland of *Jane and Prudence* resigns herself to abandoning further attempts to write, and resigns herself to chronic failure as a vicar's wife. Sophia of *An Unsuitable Attachment* embodies Victorian melancholy and knows that life is sad. And so on. Pym's characters – especially her women characters – circumscribe and pose limits on themselves in an effort to hold at bay the worst that life can do to them; in a word, they are 'splendid'. Conceiving of themselves as fruitless and dry, the best they can do is to try to be well-ordered and precise, and to find what satisfaction they can in domestic pleasures. But the feeling of deep inadequacy seems never to be assuaged.

Like much of Pym's earlier work, *A Few Green Leaves* presents a group of characters in a closely-related community who then spend most of the novel talking to themselves. They experience small revelations and harbour faded memories; above all, their reflections are private. Thus Pym's final novel seems in a muted sense a series of Larkinesque soliloquies, filled with odd musings and haunted by disillusionment.

Pym's social satire flourishes in this novel in her portrait of late 1970s England, particularly since it draws on all of her previous novels at a twenty- or thirty-year distance. For an author so fascinated with detail and the physical surface of everyday life, the novel provided an opportunity to chart changes in British society since the post-Second World War days she recorded so scrupulously in her novels of the 1950s. The two preceding novels, *Sweet Dove Died* and *Quartet in Autumn*, capture some of this vision of changing times, as characters variously appear in hideous short skirts, or dine in coffee bars which contain trendy salad bars. But *A Few Green Leaves*, with its pervading consciousness of an historical past, offers her most searching study of English civilisation from this later perspective.

First in significance, Pym depicts a marked change in the old social order, stemming from the cataclysm of the First World War. The aristocracy has dwindled; the manor house, formerly the centre of village life, is now rented to outsiders, who do not know or care about the inhabitants of the village. The effect of the missing de

Tankerville family is one of vague loss and decentralisation. They
are still idolised in memory, and even the family which is now
renting the house gains some glamour by association; at one point in
the novel Miss Lee and Miss Grundy spy on the people who are
dining on the terrace. Still, a subtle substitution is in effect as well,
since Miss Vereker is missed more than the family members
themselves. The person most often mentioned and most exalted by
the ladies in the village is Miss Vereker, the former governess of the
de Tankerville 'girls', who exemplified all the best in feminine
accomplishments. As Miss Lee and Miss Grundy never tire of
recalling, Miss Vereker had a way with mutton, arranged flowers,
kept up the mausoleum, took her charges on picnics in the woods,
and did any number of gallant good works which maintained the
aristocratic style even when the family itself was content to let things
lapse.

The women of the village miss her because she was their link to
the Great Family. Moreover, this shift continues as the social order
in the village becomes modified in order to accommodate the loss of
the de Tankervilles. The villagers remain conscious of the past and
of tradition; they still walk on the manor grounds on 'Low Sunday'
because it is their privilege dating from ancient times. But clearly the
tribal headship of the village has descended to the rector and the
doctor, who, appropriately, lead the expedition to the grounds.
Dwellings continue to be important, as in the Old Order; as the
speaker in Larkin's 'Mr Bleaney' conjectures, one's dwelling shows
in part – almost too nakedly and clearly – who one is. Tom's
possession of the rectory marks him with some distinction, as is
shown by the fact that the younger doctor, Martin Shrubsole and his
wife Avice, covet the house and plot to try to displace him and move
into it themselves. Just as the de Tankervilles are now obsolete, the
church has fallen on hard times; the rectory is not full of children,
and even jumble sales are largely spurned by the lower classes.

In another contrast with former times, Pym compares the doctors'
dispensation of magic talismans in the form of prescriptions, and
the full waiting room at the surgery to the empty church and rectory;
as spiritual adviser, Tom has been replaced. Concern with spiritual
health is replaced by overriding concern with physical health,
although, ironically, much of what the two doctors offer their
patients is psychological advice. Others outside the provincial
setting share this concern as well; Emma's friend from London,
Ianthe Potts, shows an obsessive concern with her health and with

'preserving' herself for what life might still offer. The villagers often consult their physicians for reassurance more than for solely medical cures. Daphne primarily needs to feel important, and when Dr Shrubsole takes her blood pressure, she is comforted and inordinately pleased by this simple action. Emma comes to the physician ostensibly because of the rash on her hands, but its root cause is 'stress' caused by her disappointing relationship with Graham Pettifer; Martin mentally refers her to Avice for help, almost as if Avice were a vicar's wife who could deal effectively with such womanly matters. Similarly, Adam Prince instinctively seeks medical advice for his growing sense of isolation and loneliness, but is so proud that he cannot even bring himself to mention his real complaint.

Thus the characters seem to be more obsessed with physical health than with emotional spiritual concerns; yet much of what they seek is help in the latter. *A Few Green Leaves* illustrates the opposite of Jane's remark in *Jane and Prudence* that ' "People don't realise the importance of the body nowadays ..." ' (*JP*, 59). This situation has been reversed, and now the spirit seems to be neglected. Most importantly, the fact that the doctor now assumes the role of confessor stresses the inherent isolation of all the characters, who must go to Dr Shrubsole or Dr Gellibrand to tell their troubles.

Pym also registers another cultural change characteristic of the 1970s in this novel, in the rise of a synthetic consumer society. With her zeal for freezing a long list of items (' "We need the very biggest [freezer], what with meat and the veg and fruit from the garden, and ..." ' (*FGL*, 112)), Avice seems admirably efficient; and yet something is lost. She makes cooking into a business rather than an art, even when entertaining guests; Tom is dismayed at the meagre meal she offers him. Emma on the contrary, and much to her credit, still picks blackberries, makes jam from scratch and slices her cucumbers exquisitely thin by hand. When she serves Tom canned rice pudding, on one occasion, she is sufficiently ashamed that she does not 'reveal' to him that it had been tinned. In addition to a passion for quick preparation of food, other substitutions abound: saccharine for sugar, margarine for butter, polyester for cotton or wool and frozen food for fresh.

In a brilliant stroke, Pym parodies her own preoccupation with the physical, daily routine side of life in Tom's interest in those aspects of seventeenth-century culture. Tom as antiquarian does 'research' on both past and present, taking Anthony à Wood as a kind of model for the importance of such detailed information about customs of daily life. He sends helpers around to interview the villagers with tape-recorders (an ironically modern invention) to try to capture the immediacy, the day-to-day detail of life in the village for the benefit of future historians. But the difficulty with such an enterprise is that all the raw material that he gathers needs organisation, perspective and interpretation to make it interesting and intelligible. In contrast to this, Emma's anthropological training allows her to bring the proper perspective to what she observes in the village. Pym offers a sample page of her scratch 'field notes' on the West Oxfordshire village, where she lists the important people in the social structure and speculates about them according to their positions. This list further assumes significance as it bears on Emma's meditated transition from anthropologist to novelist, as Pym often seems to have begun her novels in exactly this way, with a list of characters followed by short descriptions of each.

A strong sense of anachronism pervades all of Pym's fiction, and *A Few Green Leaves* incorporates this more than any of her other novels. It plays an especially important comic role in this novel because it becomes confused, as different perceptions of the past tangle together. Victorian traditions and ideals are sustained (with a critical modern eye) by Beatrix Howick, and by the ubiquitous presence of the local landed gentry, even though they have virtually disappeared. Victorian values and social structure are constantly seen to underly the twentieth-century village, with its automobiles and televison sets.

In addition to this profusion of Victoriana, Pym creates two other parallel pasts which vie with each other: the seventeenth century of Anthony à Wood, which Tom exalts, and the 1930s pre-war England which Miss Lee, Miss Grundy and Mrs Raven worship. The comic jostling between the two time periods creates the effect of a palimpsest. The rector seeks excellent women to aid him in historical research, but is unable to inspire them to share his vision of a glorious English past. They invariably evade his enthusiasm for the seventeenth century, discussing instead the period of pre-war tension and rationing, which they can personally recall. Both interests become conflicting obsessions. Impatient with the dull present, Tom longs to take the holiday of a trip back to the seventeenth century by time machine, whereas the ladies constantly relive old times by sharing memories of the old days which they can still vividly remember as part of their own experiences.

Pym juxtaposes these two conceptions of the past in a comparison which embodies the essence of British culture: the England of Wood's diaries is a brave, new world, a civilisation expanding and growing in influence. The church ladies' era of the 1930s prefigures or directly embodies England's decline and fall, and shows a perverse (if understandable) determination to dwell on past miseries in times of present comfort. They miss the atmosphere of imminent crisis, and this longing for the past bears out the theme of mourning, loss and grieving.

The discovery of the deserted medieval village by Miss Vereker successfully unites these two disparate visions of the past. Miss Vereker represents the twentieth century most fully, as constant reference to her as 'the last governess' by Miss Lee and Miss Grundy attests (*FGL*, 106). While wandering in the woods, she accidentally locates the site of the earliest civilisation which Tom imagines, thus causing present and past to meet. To further the anachronism, the novel's ending unites the nineteenth and twentieth centuries, as Dr Gellibrand displays crude medical instruments of the former century at a meeting of the local Historical Society. In this setting, Beatrix Howick determines to interfere in Tom and Emma's lives in the tradition of the Victorian novel, to 'bring [them] together', and it is here that Emma resolves to begin a novel and a love affair (*FGL*, 249).

Another aspect of Pym's social satire is her simultaneous insistence on the fact that times have changed (both in comparison with the 1930s and with the seventeenth century) yet that death remains the great leveller. Dr Gellibrand and Tom Dagnall the rector meet, significantly, in the mausoleum, where they have come individually to meditate on mortality. Here they stand on equal ground and possess equal status – in fact, Tom assumes the ascendant position on the occasion of Miss Lickerish's funeral. The *memento mori* strain in the novel forms a persistent undertone; several characters experience not only minor and vexing physical ailments, but suffer 'spells' akin to prefigured death. Miss Lee sees a ghost and has 'a nasty turn' on the parish outing to a nearby manor house, and Miss Vereker faints in the woods on her journey to the village. Adam Prince suffers severe disquiet from the fact that he suddenly detects a need in himself for other people.

The theme of an elderly person being found in a helpless state dominates Pym's preceding novel, *Quartet in Autumn*. Norman relishes reading out to the others in his office the newspaper article describing an elderly person discovered dead of hypothermia, adding a personal warning: ' "We want to be careful we don't get hypothermia" ', he exults (*QA*, 6). Later in the novel, Letty sees a woman slumped in a subway station, and Marcia is eventually discovered unconscious and malnourished in her own house. This understatement is typical of Pym's approach to important subjects. She looks at death and ageing as it appears from the viewpoint of the elderly person, who seems afraid not so much of dying *per se* as of helplessness, loneliness and, most crucial, the loss of dignity. Marcia's scorn for the interfering social worker Janice Brabner suggests not only that she asserts her own will to die despite others' help and concern, but also that she insists on living life her own way.

Pym's elderly characters are often forceful and authoritative, as if to combat the desire others seem to have to oppress them.[17] One of Pym's unpublished short stories depicts an older woman in hospital drinking sherry in bed, to the dismay of a younger visitor, who seems shocked that a woman so close to death should strive to keep up civilised appearances and to savour life's amenities to the last. Other examples of decisive, if eccentric, behaviour on the part of elderly characters in Pym's novels abound. Mrs Bone in *Excellent Women* does what she can personally to thwart the inevitable Dominion of the Birds (' "I eat as many birds as possible" ', she announces (*EW*, 149)). Miss Grimes in *An Unsuitable Attachment* confides to Ianthe that she buys a bottle of cheap wine every week, to Ianthe's disapproval, who feels that 'Haricot beans and lentils – or chicken breasts in aspic if they could be afforded – were really much more suitable' (*UA*, 77). Mrs Pope in *Quartet in Autumn* becomes the standard-bearer for the elderly in Pym's fictional world. Far from helpless, she uses the excuse of her advanced age to have her own way; in her eightieth year, she declines to do anything she does not want to do. Hypothermia will not be allowed to prevail. When she suspects she will find inadequate heating at her sister's cottage, she refuses to visit her at Christmas, adding a sweeping denunciation: ' "I shall *not* go, neither now or *ever*", Mrs Pope declared . . .' (*QA*, 88).

Pym's three final novels show her concern with the subject of ageing and of reviewing and judging one's life.[18] If one once begins the process of comparing oneself with others, it becomes chronically depressing. Letty in *Quartet in Autumn* begins to avoid Mrs Pope, the woman with whom she shares a house after her retirement, because of the daunting spectacle of others' success: 'Mrs Pope, it seemed, always knew somebody who was doing something wholly admirable . . .' (*QA*, 117). Further, comparing her life with that of her other friends, Letty often wonders 'where in all these years she, Letty, had failed' (*QA*, 125). *The Sweet Dove Died* presents a heroine who judges her life constantly in terms of its aesthetic effect. Leonora disdains the norm, for which Letty searches anxiously. Though it contains a quasi-romantic attachment, its primary subject is ageing. Leonora determines to preserve elegance at all costs, and this goal is significant because with age, the strain and cost of maintaining such perfection increases. Moreover, Leonora illustrates the ultimate danger in isolating oneself from human contact in order to achieve a perfectly arranged life; when she does discover 'something to love' in the figure of James, she is unable to moderate her affection for him because of her overwhelming need.

As an ageing but elegant gentlewoman, Leonora has a counterpart in Miss Foxe, the genteel lady who lives upstairs in Leonora's house when the novel opens, and whom she must 'get rid of' in order to install James in her place. Miss Foxe acts as a double of Leonora; she is a nicer version, in that she values her possessions but does not idolise them. Leonora must exorcise this part of herself in order to acquire James as a possession. Her other corresponding parallels are Liz, the next-door neighbour who keeps Siamese cats, and Meg, Leonora's friend, who dotes on a young homosexual man named Colin. Leonora despises both women for needing 'something to love', and Meg indeed is pitiable. Liz, ironically, achieves better balance; though she fills emotional needs by doting on her cats, they at least are animals and not people, as Colin and James are, to be used.

Still more interesting than Leonora's present efforts to combat loneliness and to shore up waning self-respect is her view of the past. She alludes to a long series of intrigues involving suitors in all the great gardens of Europe, but which, ultimately, had never 'come to' anything. Letty in *Quartet in Autumn* also looks back over her own life in an attempt to analyse it, but comes up still more empty-handed than Leonora, without even the comfort of departed glory; marriage or children have never come her way. In response to this sense of deprivation, she avoids thinking of the past, living 'very much in the present, holding neatly and firmly on to life, coping as

best she could with whatever it had to offer, little though that might
be' (*QA*, 25).

In all three of these later novels Pym is concerned with ageing and
death, with autumn as well as winter. Thus she focuses on what it
feels like to be nearing death and to perceive hope slipping away.
One of the important aspects of this subject is the interest her
characters show in people having led 'distinguished' lives. When
Emma observes the villagers around her at the Gellibrands' sherry
party in *A Few Green Leaves*, she concludes that few of the other
guests seem to have done this.

Not only are the characters in this novel scrutinised in terms of
what they have achieved, but characters from earlier novels die and
are thus evaluated as well. Fabian Driver's obituary appears, and
Emma attends a memorial service for Esther Clovis, a veteran Pym
character from several novels. These cameo appearances offer
private jokes for Pym fans – a reward for herself as an author and for
faithful followers. Only readers of *Jane and Prudence* will recognise
the irony in Fabian's obituary – he has apparently been conquered
by a woman at the last. Appearing almost bigamous, he is summed
up in his obituary as 'devoted husband of Constance and Jessie'.
This insistence on domestic devotion undercuts his conception of
himself as a Don Juan hero. In addition, having been unfaithful to
his first wife, Constance, he has clearly been kept in line by his
second wife, Jessie, who has succeeded in her plans to make a full-
time occupation of keeping him from similar episodes during their
marriage.

Pym's novels often deal with characters who encounter frustration, suffer from unfulfilled hopes and lead dull lives. And this
reflects something of her own experience of life – her high spirits
and great ambitions from early on became subdued; yet they never
entirely died. Thus what she captures in her novels is this
simmering tension. She does not simply infuse a dull life with
interest by insisting, with her character Ianthe in *An Unsuitable
Attachment*, that ' " even the most apparently narrow and uneventful life" ' possesses its own significance (*UA*, 127). Anyone's life
does have drama of a sort.

But Pym captures the poignancy of thwarted effort and energy,
and mourns the loss of the things that never do happen. Unfulfilled
possibilities keep hanging in the air.

If one looks at Pym's own life in this regard, one sees the steady
perseverance she showed against constantly damped hopes. She

seems to have encountered rejection in some form or other from the first, often coping by evasion, or by substituting something else for what she cannot have: the Greater English Poets for Romance, and a career as a novelist for marriage. Her struggle to establish herself as a writer after going down from Oxford is characterised by seriousness of purpose, as the sheer number of unpublished manuscripts written during this period would suggest.

As her diaries and letters from the 1960s reveal, the rejection of the seventh novel was as devastating as it was unexpected. Her initial reaction is terse and full of grief: it is 'a bitter blow on an early Spring evening' (*VPE*, 215). In an elegiac mood, she goes on to list other items conducive to despair, characterising it as 'a year of violence, death and blows'. Pym's subsequent dealing with this disaster becomes more creative in its wry resignation. She mocks herself, writing to Philip Larkin both that she is extremely angry and that she sees herself as a bit of a comic character at the same time, casting herself 'in the role of indignant rejected middle-aged female novelist (a pretty formidable combination, don't you think?)' (*VPE*, 216).

In all of these varying responses, Pym shows a curious combination of openness and reticence. When she did begin to achieve literary notice during the last three years of her life, she displayed some acerbity – the 'rediscovery' which led to reprints of her earlier novels and acceptance of new ones constituted a revenge on Cape: ' "It was . . . very sweet to me" ', she commented in an interview.[19] She refused their inquiry about further manuscripts in no uncertain terms; having forfeited her novels by right of first refusal, they had lost their chance. But always she is generous, wishing that other novelists could have the same luck. Delighting in all the benefits which accompanied her 'rediscovery', she thanked her friends repeatedly and gave them all the credit. ' "It's such a nice thing to happen in my old age" ', Pym told one interviewer, concluding with typical understatement: ' "Of course, if it had happened sooner . . ." But the sentence ends with a shrug and a wry smile.'[20]

In the attendant publicity which followed, Pym retained her power of choice in a manner in which she would have approved, had it been practised by one of her older fictional heroines. She decided quite firmly, after consulting Professor Larkin, that her private papers (solicited by a bookseller) would not under any circumstances go to the States 'to be pored over by earnest Americans' (*VPE*, 315). In preparation for her papers being perused by scholars, she neatly edited those personal portions she wished to destroy. Poetic justice lodged the papers in the Bodleian, scene of so many countless hours of study and day-dreaming. Perhaps time will do even more. Pym recorded the following in her diaries of 1978: 'In Ox. [*sic*] saw a nice Exhibition at the Bodleian of Oxford writers', adding hopefully, '(not me – as yet?)' (MS PYM 79, fol. 9).

On the whole, Pym's novels do not reflect a light heart so much as they do a brave face in the presence of life's frustrations. And it is perhaps striking that Pym's last novel – which she chose to write when remaining time was short and therefore precious – should so closely approximate the seven interlocking novels of a much earlier period. The mild stoicism and amusement revealed in her final novel has its roots in her character of some twenty or thirty years previous to its composition. By contrast, *The Sweet Dove Died* and *Quartet in Autumn* were written during a difficult transition state, and reflect several different tensions; the author was trying at once to get her work published by writing something different (though not to admit too openly to this strategy) and simultaneously not to care about having her work remain unpublished, and thus possibly forestall the pain occasioned by another rejection.[21]

In these two novels, Pym transformed hurtful, difficult experiences – her relationship with Richard Roberts and her retirement from the IAI – in the way that she always had. Still, her resilience in both books wears thin. Her treatment of the unhappy relationship with Roberts which forms the kernel for *Sweet Dove Died* and her surgery and retirement which provided a basis for *Quartet in Autumn* lack the sharpness and brilliance of the 1950s novels. The characters seem thin and angular, and bitterly satirised.

Although it was published after *Quartet in Autumn*, *Sweet Dove Died* was composed before it. It reflects Pym's disappointment regarding the rejection of *An Unsuitable Attachment*, and a determined effort to revise her style according to the lack she perceived in her work; she strove to make it acceptable to a 1960s audience. As a result, the novel deals with more daring themes than her previous work, and contains more consciously suggestive scenes. Sexual nuances are more explicit, as James and Phoebe go to bed together, and as Ned (the evil tempter) is shown capturing James inside a flat decorated with synthetic fur and containing a huge bed.

The novel masquerades as a slightly bizarre love story, but its main subject is ageing, as is the case in *Quartet in Autumn*. *Quartet* reflects the same use of modern and contemporary events and settings, portraying the underside of London in more dramatic situations. Its main theme is the sense of loneliness being held gallantly at bay, and Marcia's growing insanity illustrates the harshest outcome of such isolation. Loneliness, ageing and mortality form the basic subject of these two novels, and stand forth more clearly than they do in Pym's earlier work. Older characters appear consistently throughout her fiction, but these novels are different in that they focus on the horror of the ageing process as other props to the characters' self-esteem correspondingly break down. It seems to me that these two novels are grim because at the time she wrote them, Pym's own worst fears had been confirmed: she was without youth (in her fifties), without a lover (Richard Roberts, the nearest equivalent, having broken with her), without a job (she had retired from work), and without a publisher (several times over).[22] The bleakness of her prospects was reinforced by her desire to persevere in writing and to attempt the difficult task of pleasing editors, without denying her own distinctive literary style.

Aside from personal difficulties Pym was experiencing at the time, with ill-health, death of friends, giving up her job and moving from London to the country, she laboured under the discouragement induced by the strong possibility that her work would never again find a publisher. But *A Few Green Leaves* is unique among all her novels, because it was written from a position of relative confidence and assurance. As the 'rediscovery' of her work in 1977 proved, her 'kind of novel' was acceptable after all, and thus she perhaps felt free to write in her own way. Significantly, in this novel she returned to her earlier style.

In reviewing her writing career as a whole, one of the first things to strike one is the sheer amount of fiction which she wrote. With or without a publisher, she persevered in writing. The early novels, while showing traces of themes which were later to be used – the ambivalent joys of spinsterhood, vicars, literary quotations and so on – tend to overdo the comedy and include simply too much material. But somehow Pym hit her stride in the later 1940s; whatever its source, some helpful combination seems to have been at work: stability, settling down to work, accepting her probable singleness, receiving some satisfaction from a steady, paying job. Philip Larkin has observed that Pym's middle novels from the 1950s show no 'development' as such, and they will remain, I think, the centre part and best of her work.[23] The early fiction anticipates them, and the later novels reflect back on them.

As for *A Few Green Leaves*, it draws her fiction neatly to a close. The death of characters from not only this but from other novels seems to reflect back over the earlier ones and to cast an elegiac mood. The novel provides a picture of England in its contemporary state – saccharine, empty church and all – and of Pym's own life as well. She seems to have projected with accuracy from the beginning of her writing career what it would be like to be old, and eccentricity in her characters combines with half-comic pathos at the inevitable approach of death. The novel serves in part as an *apologia* for Pym's sense of herself and what her achievement in writing has been. It suggests that even in a small village, though it provides modest scope, one can be dignified and distinguished. She has found a deeply satisfying identity: 'Miss Pym the novelist' (MS PYM 77, fol. 7). Further, in returning to her earlier style of writing, she seems to affirm both it and her choice to write rather than to '[follow] an academic career' (*VPE*, 287). *A Few Green Leaves* is a novel about older, single people who live self-consciously and carefully, on occasion bravely. And so, it seems, did Pym.

In closing, I would like to add a note on possible future views of Pym's fiction. Her work has recently gained a large audience and renewed recognition. Although she was not part of an established group of literati, her association with Philip Larkin will doubtless continue to give her eminence as his work gains in recognition. Pym's fiction will probably fall ultimately into the category of 'minor, but elegant' – its old-fashioned, quaint quality does not obscure its value, but her scope is too narrow to exalt her to the category of major novelist. The 'little things in life' are important, but not compelling. In the scramble for literary reputation, she seems to be ascending modestly, partly because of the novelty offered by the recent 'rediscovery' of her fiction, and partly because of her sheer competence as a novelist. It is a delight to read her work.

Barbara Pym's novels have often been compared to those of Jane Austen; Pym's own response to this suggestion when it was first made reveals much about her conception of her art. She would not wish to be seen as a '20th C. Jane Austen', due to her own modesty. She might trail her hand across Austen's little writing desk at Chawton and wish to catch some of her genius, but she would hardly wish to indulge in the presumption of comparing herself directly to her illustrious predecessor. Still, it is characteristic of Pym to define herself by negatives, and I would suggest that she is like Austen in her perception of life; they share a view characterised by irony and occasionally by disappointment. And in this she has much to offer. Regardless of her relation to Austen, Pym seems assured of a lasting place in literary history. 'Her works are miniatures', writes Philip Larkin, 'but will not diminish.'[24]

Notes

INTRODUCTION

1. Special courses have been offered on Pym's work at several universities since, and subsequent literary studies are appearing at a rapid rate. In her checklist of items on Pym's fiction listed in *Bulletin of Bibliography*, published in December 1984, Lorna Peterson offers the following mild reproach to recalcitrant scholars: 'Despite the quality of Barbara Pym's work and the voluminous praise for her witty novels of manners, Barbara Pym has not received the scholarly attention she deserves' (Lorna Peterson, 'Barbara Pym: A Checklist, 1950–1984', *Bulletin of Bibliography*, 41 (December 1984) 201–6). This omission is being repaired with all due haste. An anthology entitled *The Life and Work of Barbara Pym* is forthcoming from Macmillan, edited by Dale Salwak and including essays from such distinguished contributors as Philip Larkin, Robert Liddell, A. N. Wilson, Hazel Holt and John Halperin. Dissertations are not far behind. Kate Browder Heberlein has completed a thesis on Pym's novels at the University of Washington. Studies of Pym's work are forthcoming from the Twayne Series and have appeared in the Ungar Series on modern authors. Most importantly, Hazel Holt, Pym's literary executor, is editing other fiction by Pym for posthumous publication. In addition, she is currently at work on an official biography of Barbara Pym, also to be published by Macmillan.
2. For a more complete description of the contents of the Bodleian collection, see Janice Rossen, 'The Pym Papers', *The Life and Work of Barbara Pym*, ed. Dale Salwak (London: Macmillan, forthcoming).
3. I take this phrase about Henry Harvey from a conversation with Barbara Pym's sister, Hilary Pym.

CHAPTER 1

1. See Elaine Showalter, *A Literature of their Own: British Women Novelists from Brontë to Lessing* (Princeton, New Jersey: Princeton University Press, 1977) for a fuller discussion of this issue.
2. Robert Smith, 'How Pleasant to Know Miss Pym', *Ariel: A Review of International English Literature*, 2 (October 1971) 63.
3. Victorian Glendinning, 'Spontaneous Obsessions, Imposed Restraint', *New York Times Book Review* (8 July 1984) 3.
4. Robert Smith mentions Benson's *Lucia* novels in his essay on Pym's fiction, where he compares the two authors. They both write 'books ...to solace a bad day', he says, adding that 'two characteristics distinguish all such books: they must take the reader into a different, pleasanter world, and they must make his escape easy' (Smith, p. 63).

5. Robert Liddell, *The Novels of Ivy Compton-Burnett* (London: Gollancz, 1955) p. 92.
6. Ibid., p. 93.
7. Ibid., p. 97.
8. Violet Powell, *A Compton-Burnett Compendium* (London: Heinemann, 1973) p. 1.
9. The Larkin tag appears during Marcia's stay inside the hospital, when she is ' "unreachable inside a room" ' (*QA*, 172). Pym was especially conscious of using a quotation from Larkin's poetry in this novel, because at the time she wrote it he was encouraging her in trying to publish it.
10. In keeping with this spare style, the matter of transitions becomes crucial, and constitutes one of Pym's most individual hallmarks. She cuts from scene to scene in the manner of a film editor, breaking directly into the next vignette, avoiding a ponderous explanation of the process of moving characters physically from one place to another: they simply appear – at the train station, the tea-table or the office. She describes journeys when they serve best to show her characters meditating, as in Jane's trip to London in *Jane and Prudence* or her ride on the bus to Prudence's flat. Pym's usual method of transporting characters is to begin a new paragraph or sentence abruptly at the new location.

CHAPTER 2

1. Miles was Rupert's close friend at Oxford, and Pym spent time with both of them together, as she also did with both Henry and Jockie.
2. Hilary Pym Walton entered Lady Margaret Hall to read classical archaeology four years later.
3. Vera Brittain, *The Women at Oxford: A Fragment of History* (New York: The MacMillan Co., 1960) p. 159.
4. Elizabeth Bowen, *The Death of the Heart* (London, 1938; rpt. New York: Knopf, 1963) p. 8.
5. There is a personal connection here as well, as Pym owned a copy of Betjeman's book, inscribed in her own hand with her name followed by 'Christmas 1938'.
6. John Betjeman, *An Oxford University Chest* (London: John Miles, 1938) p. 40.
7. Gleadow received a first at the end of their first year of acquaintance, then returned to Oxford the following autumn to begin graduate studies. The two continued to see each other, but when Pym met Henry Harvey in the middle of her second year he rapidly and almost completely eclipsed her interest in all other men.
8. *Crampton Hodnet* has been edited and published posthumously by Dutton and Macmillan. I continue to quote from the original manuscript here, as there are minor variations in the published text.
9. Another unpublished early novel, *Beatrice Wyatt*, or *The Lumber Room*,

also depicts a romance set in Oxford. The hero is largely based on the figure of Henry Harvey, and the heroine, Beatric, is a don.

10. Miss Birkinshaw tutors Jane, who in turn tutors Prudence, and Jane also sends her daughter Flora to the same Oxford college.

11. It is possible that this character is the Barbara Bird who appears in *Crampton Hodnet*. Jessie Morrow and Miss Doggett, for instance, reappear virtually unaltered in *Jane and Prudence*. Similarly, there are three or four studies of Jane Cleveland in various early manuscripts. It is just as likely, however, that Pym liked the name Bird and simply reused it without intending the two characters to be the same.

12. This description of Bird's novel may be read as a comic inversion of what might be observed about Pym's own work, which is generally composed of relatively 'little incident' yet much wit. A further irony surfaces here, as Pym took the quotation directly from a review of her first novel, *Some Tame Gazelle*.

13. Pym stated in an interview that she and her sister had 'promised each other they would retire to live one day near Oxford, where they both took degrees . . .' Lesley Adamson, *Guardian* (14 September 1977) p. 11.

14. Barbara Pym, 'Across a Crowded Room', *The New Yorker*, 55 (16 July 1979) 39.

CHAPTER 3

1. Robert J. Graham, 'Cumbered with Much Serving: Barbara Pym's "Excellent Women"', *Mosaic*, 27 (Spring 1984) 143.

2. Barbara Pym, *Contemporary Authors – Permanent Series: A Bio-Bibliographical Guide to Current Authors and their Works*, ed. Clare D. Kinsman (Detroit: Gale, 1975) p. 523.

3. Graham, 'Cumbered with Much Serving', p. 146.

4. At one point in her failing relationship with Richard Roberts, Pym notes with sadness in a letter to their mutual friend Robert Smith that perhaps her 'sardonic tongue has sent him away' (*VPE*, 240).

5. Maintaining dignity during solitary meals must be a strong tenet for both Barbara Pym and her sister Hilary (who is an excellent cook). On more than one occasion, when I have had the pleasure of dining with her, she has confessed that she thinks it ridiculous that one would not take trouble over preparing a meal just because one was alone.

6. This story is entitled 'A Sister's Love' (MS PYM 94, fols. 132–48).

7. This story is entitled 'Mothers and Fathers' (MS PYM 94, fols. 1–15).

8. The problem delineated here is that the heroine is betrayed by a double standard in trying to fulfil a Victorian ideal of womanhood. Pym's heroines are often jilted by clergymen, an odd or ironic choice for a cad. But clergymen are to some extent held responsible for limiting women; they ostensibly want an Angel in the House, yet when the heroine adopts this submissive role and suppresses her romantic instincts, he declines to marry her after all. Hence, she is left timid and afraid, with no outlet, feeling resentful.

9.   Wilmet is seen throughout the novel as a distinctly Victorian figure; her name is taken from a Charlotte M. Yonge novel, and she is an elegant, aloof figure in many respects. Professor Root presents his Christmas gift to her with the comment that her beauty is ' "happily not quite of this age" ' (*GB*, 104).

10.   In her letter to critic Helen Philips, Pym describes herself as 'like' Belinda, only, she regrets, 'not as nice' (MS PYM 98, fol. 123).

11.   There is an interesting variation on the figure of Leonora in one of Pym's short stories, entitled 'A Few Days before the Winter'. The elegant heroine, here named Lavinia, goes to a holiday resort town out of nostalgia – she and her husband, now separated, had gone there on their honeymoon some twelve years before. She delights in impressing the other guests with her *savoir faire* (she orders a bottle of wine just for herself for dinner), and in this self-consciousness is similar to Leonora. In the story, however, Lavinia has the felicity of a happy ending: her husband reappears at the conclusion, and they reunite.

12.   Elizabeth Bowen, *To the North* (London 1932; rpt New York: Avon, 1979) p. 23.

13.   Hazel Holt has commented to me on the difficulty Pym had in creating the character of John. She revised the novel several times in an attempt to give him more 'charm', but was never satisfied with the result.

14.   The two figures of Ianthe and Sophia are juxtaposed here, as Sophia has decided to award marriage to her sister Penelope but not to Ianthe. Sophia holds a curious position in the novel; Pym defended her character by writing about Sophia in a letter sent by her to Richard Roberts, who had read the novel at an early stage and offered suggestions. Pym affirmed that Sophia ought to be given freedom to speak in the novel because she needed 'a B Pym [*sic*] woman character to give my angle occasionally' (MS PYM 159/1, fol. 20). In this novel Ianthe represents a woman's need to limit her life in a narrow but pleasant spinsterhood, while Penelope represents a corresponding need to find a husband at whatever cost. Sophia awards these distinctions in a seemingly arbitrary way, thus fragmenting the novel.

CHAPTER 4

1.   Tom Paulin, 'Talkative Transparencies: Recent Fiction', *Encounter* (January 1978) 72.

2.   Karl Miller, 'Ladies in Distress', *New York Review of Books*, 25 (9 November 1978) 24.

3.   Robert Smith, 'How Pleasant to Know Miss Pym', *Ariel: A Review of International English Literature*, 2 (1971) 68.

4.   Philip Larkin, 'The World of Barbara Pym', *Times Literary Supplement* (11 March 1977) 260.

5. At one point in the novel, Sybil makes an arrangement of dried flowers as a centrepiece for the dinner table, but Wilmet (and the maid who throws it out) see it as not only ugly, but 'dead'.

6. Father Thames's statue represents High Church leanings towards aestheticism. Altick points out that the Oxford Movement contributed to ritualism: 'Through its religious associations sensuous beauty eventually gained a place in the scale of Victorian values more or less comparable to that which it had had among the romantics' (Richard Altick, *Victorian People and Ideas* (New York: W.W. Norton & Co., 1973) p. 217).

7. There is a paradox at the root of Tractarianism, which simultaneously sought to establish the church's authority apart from the state by making what Altick calls an 'appeal to history' (p. 213), and by its connection to the Catholic Church. Such an argument, if followed to its conclusion, inevitably leads to a complete conversion to Catholicism, as it did for Newman in 1845.

8. Mildred feels sympathy for Newman ' "as a person" ', she says, while Everard interprets the word sympathy in a spiritual sense; he refers to 'Rome' and ' "its attractions" ' (*EW*, 141).

9. Another example of a character possibly on the brink of 'going over to Rome' is Winifred in *Excellent Women*, who exclaims that the idea of Roman worship is ' "lovely" ', to Mildred's apprehension and dismay (*EW*, 246).

10. Mildred in *Excellent Women* regards her change to a higher church as significant enough to be called a '[rebellion] against [her] upbringing', though she accedes that it is mild and relatively harmless (*EW*, 11).

11. W. H. Carnegie, *Anglicanism: An Introduction to its History and Philosophy* (London: G. P. Putman's Sons, 1925) p. 91.

12. The generalisation about the church 'in Pym's time' may seem an unnecessary distinction, not least because her writing career spanned several decades and ended quite recently. Yet it should be noted that the Anglican/Catholic problem to which Pym refers in her novels has been altered in the present to a surprising degree. Church historian Brian Curnew of St Stephen's, Oxford, has observed to me in conversation that the radical difference between the two churches has been seen to lessen, even in the last decade. There is still a trickle of converts either way, but the process is attended by more cordial good will on both sides, and reflects in general a broader ecumenical feeling.

13. The Oxford Movement influenced hymn-writing also, with its tendency to incorporate poetry and art into worship.

14. Everard Bone hears the archdeacon deliver this sermon at a London church in *Excellent Women*, and confesses to Mildred that he has difficulty in not laughing.

15. In *Jane and Prudence*, Jane shows her total inefficiency as a vicar's wife when she goes alone to look at their new parish church, and sees the well-polished brasses 'without realising the significance' of this (*JP*, 25).

16. Father Lomax in *Jane and Prudence* make a great point of he and Nicholas not competing with each other, or ' "[poaching] on each other's preserves" ', as they were ' "up at Oxford together" ' (*JP*, 23).
17. John Carey has pointed out in his review of *A Very Private Eye* that Pym had a fondness for churchyards – perhaps a specialised taste ('Pym's Little Ironies', *The Sunday Times* (London, 22 July 1984)). He observes that 'tombs comfort her... because they bespeak the sadness of loss, and that chimes with something deep in her nature'.
18. From this description, the church is undoubtedly intended to be seen as part of the gothic revival in the late Victorian period sparked by the Oxford Movement.
19. Anthony Trollope, *The Last Chronicle of Barset* (Oxford University Press, 1980) p. 103.
20. There are, of course, fierce conflicts within the Barsetshire clerical community, particularly in regard to the ritualism of the 'Puseyites' and other matters related to the Oxford Movement. Mrs Proudie herself is sufficient guarantee of turmoil regardless of current theological issues.
21. A similar sort of displacement occurs in the church's role of dispensing the sacraments. The making of a cup of tea on every possible occasion becomes a parody of the church's dispensation of grace and strength through the Eucharist.
22. Trollope, *Last Chronicle*, p. 890.

CHAPTER 5

1. A. H. M. K.-G., 'Barbara Pym 1913–80', Obituary, *Africa*, 50 (1980) 94.
2. Caroline Moorehead, 'How Barbara Pym was Rediscovered After Sixteen Years Out in the Cold', *The Times* (London), 14 September 1977, p. 11.
3. David Cecil, Obituary for Barbara Pym, Royal Society of Literature (1980).
4. Caro's method of 'observing' those around her in the subway is similar to the creative process which Virginia Woolf describes in her essay 'Mr Bennett and Mrs Brown'. She recreates novelist Arnold Bennett's way of describing character through the accumulation of detail, and creates an imaginary 'Mrs Brown', encountered in a railway carriage. Woolf criticises Bennett's approach (as she perceives it). Pym falls somewhere between the two other novelists; she both observes and creates, notes outer details and infers inner states of mind.
5. Harriet and Belinda Bede's struggles with their maid Florrie recall those of the characters in Bennett's *Old Wives*.
6. At the end of the novel, Catherine tells Deirdre that the last time Tom had gone home to visit his family he had wondered if perhaps he had done the right thing, which makes his death all the more ironic.
7. Ned ('the American') does precisely the same thing in *The Sweet Dove*

    Died – when relationships in England become too 'complicated', he leaves the country. James realises this, telling Leonora,' "in the end [Ned] *wanted* to go back. . ."' (*SDD*, 206).

8. Some anthropologists have commented on the increasing trend away from the homespun, outdoorsman image of the anthropologist towards an increasing value for detachment and sociological theory (see Jonathan Lieberson, 'Interpreting the Interpreter', *New York Review of Books* (15 March 1984) 39). Pym echoes this change in several ways, notably in *Excellent Women*, where Rocky remarks to Mildred that ' "it simply isn't done to show a photograph of The Author with his Pygmy Friends" ' (*EW*, 88).

9. She worked on the novel intermittently between 1965 and 1971. Hazel Holt, Pym's literary executor, plans to publish it posthumously under the title *An Academic Question* (Macmillan, forthcoming).

10. Graham, 'Cumbered with Much Serving', p. 144.

11. This discussion of the anthropologist as priest echoes Julian's comments in *Excellent Women* on the clergy having human needs, but being expected to suppress them.

12. The insistence on needing meat suggests obliquely yet forcefully that the men in question need sex; thus the whole issue becomes comically displaced.

13. An interesting side-light on the question of meals out has to do with Pym's social life during the 1950s, her most productive period. Hilary Pym has told me that during the period after the war, people they knew had, in general, less social life, and thus Barbara spent a lot of time writing. At the same time, Hilary Pym writes in a biographical essay in *A Very Private Eye*: 'I never got the feeling that she shut herself away to write, as she always seemed to be available and enjoyed social life and entertaining' (*VPE*, 5).

14. Pym did also travel, but it seems to have left little mark on her imagination, at least in what she wrote about, except for her short stories.

CHAPTER 6

1. Robert Smith, 'How Pleasant to Know Miss Pym', *Ariel*, 2 (October 1971) 63. Pym apparently welcomed this view of her work, referring to the phrase in later discussions of her novels after they became more widely popular.

2. There is a question as to whether Mildred actually writes *Excellent Women* or simply tells or narrates it from her point of view. I think it possible that she does write it, given the equation she makes with *Jane Eyre* early in the novel. She refers to 'plain women who tell their stories in the first person', which seems to indicate that she writes her tale, though she does omit Jane Eyre's famous line: 'Reader, I married him' (*EW*, 7; Charlotte Brontë, *Jane Eyre* (1847; rpt. New York: New American Library, 1960) p. 452).

3. Mildred does undertake research in this distanced way both in her censorship work during the war, in which she read other peoples' letters, and in her job at the agency for 'distressed gentle-women'.

4. Emma Howick of *A Few Green Leaves* is potentially an artist–heroine in Pym's fiction, because she chooses to pursue novel-writing at the end of the book. I shall reserve discussion of her until the next chapter.

5. Wilmet's emotional distance from Rodney is emphasised by the quasi-love affair he begins with Prudence Bates, of the earlier novel *Jane and Prudence*. When he confesses this peccadillo to his wife late in the novel, he adds that Prudence reminded him strongly of Wilmet herself. Both women are similar in their desire for elegant arrangement at the expense of disordering passion. Significantly, Pym regarded both Wilmet and Prudence as her 'own favourites' of the heroines in her fiction (*VPE*, 223).

6. In a letter to Philip Larkin, Pym seconded him in his perception of Keith as an 'incubus' whom Wilmet will never be able to get rid of: 'I think incubus or familiar describes him well', she agreed (*VPE*, 203).

CHAPTER 7

1. One reviewer of the novel points out this correlation: Nicholas Shrimpton, 'Bucolic Bones', *New Statesman*, 100 (15 August 1980) 17. He writes: 'Beneath her inconsequential surface detail, in fact, Barbara Pym is here offering an artistic apologia. Such action as there is has less to do with private emotions than with professional choice. Emma gradually abandons anthropology in order to become a novelist.'

2. The Finstock Church is also of historical interest because it was here that T. S. Eliot was received into the Anglican Church. There is a plaque to honour him on the wall – and now one to honour Barbara Pym as well.

3. Publication of her novels in the United States was Pym's ardent desire since she began publishing in the 1950s. She wrote several times to this effect to her editors, bemoaning the fact that 'the Americans' did not seem to care for her novels. One letter to Cape in 1955 expresses this: 'As you know, I am very anxious to find an American publisher for my books, and I am sure you will go on trying very hard for me . . . I wonder why they don't like them – too English?' (MS PYM 163/2, fol. 283).

4. Constance Malloy, 'The Quest for a Career', *The Life and Work of Barbara Pym*, ed. Dale Salwak (London: Macmillan, forthcoming).

5. Conversation with Hilary Pym.

6. Thus, at least, states the dust jacket on the Dutton edition of the novel, and it seems to me an apt comment.

7. Caroline Moorehead, 'How Barbara Pym was Rediscovered After Sixteen Years Out in the Cold', *The Times* (London), 14 September 1977, p. 11.

8. The ending of *Sweet Dove Died* marks an advance for Leonora – she shows James out of the house just as Humphrey arrives, bearing a large sheaf of peonies. She will not entice James back into his cage, as Meg does with Colin. Yet the presentation of the flowers marks Leonora as typically egotistic; in the novel'a last line, she contemplates the excellence of the flowers, which have 'the added grace of having been presented to oneself' (*SDD*, 208).

9. An uncanny echo of this occurs earlier, in *Jane and Prudence*, with the disposal of Constance Driver's effects ('all those good things of poor Mrs Driver's'), by the eager excellent women Miss Doggett, Miss Morrow and Jane Cleveland (*JP*, 104). Though she dies before the novel opens, the oppressive presence of her things is a constant burden to her widower, Fabian.

10. Pym's mention of Laura Ashley clothes is particularly appropriate in a novel which looks to the past. For the most part, they constitute a reworking of older, Victorian fashions in a contemporary rendition. Their hallmark is nostalgia.

11. An earlier draft of this ending reinforces the emphasis on 'pattern'. In this version, Emma decides roughly the same thing – the novel and the love affair – but it is couched more tentatively: she 'realised that she could perfectly well arrange her life to fit very well into whatever pattern of village life presented itself', in other words a more passive and neutral stance (MS PYM 38, fol. 179).

12. It is interesting to speculate on what sort of novel Emma will write – perhaps *A Few Green Leaves*.

13. Rosemary Dinnage, 'Comic, Sad, Indefinite', *New York Review of Books* (16 August 1984) 16.

14. Philip Larkin, 'Mr Bleaney', *The Whitsun Weddings* (London: Faber & Faber, 1964) p. 10.

15. Philip Larkin, 'Dockery and Son', *The Whitsun Weddings*, p. 37.

16. This sort of tactic is also used by Allegra Gray in *Excellent Women*, when she tells Mildred that ' "things haven't been too easy, you know" ', self-pity which Mildred finds ridiculous (*EW*, 125).

17. Leonora makes several interesting comments on ageing in *Sweet Dove Died*; obviously, she will never be debilitated. She ranges herself with the antagonists, telling James coolly that one must take a firm line with older people: ' "otherwise they *encroach*" ' (*SDD*, 50). As James astutely reflects, 'One day Leonora would be old herself, but obviously it wouldn't be the same' (*SDD*, 50).

18. This is paralleled by the fear which older people in Pym's novels often feel towards younger ones – the vibrant younger people in the office cause the four older ones in *Quartet in Autumn* to feel threatened by their vitality. Pym parodies this in *Jane and Prudence* when the young typists speculate on the ages of others in Dr Grampian's office. ' "I hope I die before I'm thirty" ', says one (*JP*, 97).

19. Moorehead, *The Times* (London), 14 September 1977, p. 11.

20. Lesley Adamson, 'Guardian Women', *Guardian* (14 September 1977) p. 11.
21. Pym wrote a sharp letter reprimanding Cape when the editors refused *An Unsuitable Attachment*, indignant that the press could 'behave like this to one of its authors' (MS PYM 164, fol. 132).
22. Pym did persevere in sending out manuscripts; she wrote to Robert Smith in despair about *The Sweet Dove Died* in 1973: 'Twenty-one publishers is surely enough' (*VPE*, 273).
23. Philip Larkin, 'The World of Barbara Pym', *Times Literary Supplement* (11 March 1977) 260.
24. Philip Larkin, 'Reputations Revisited . . .', *Times Literary Supplement* (21 January 1977) 66.

Index